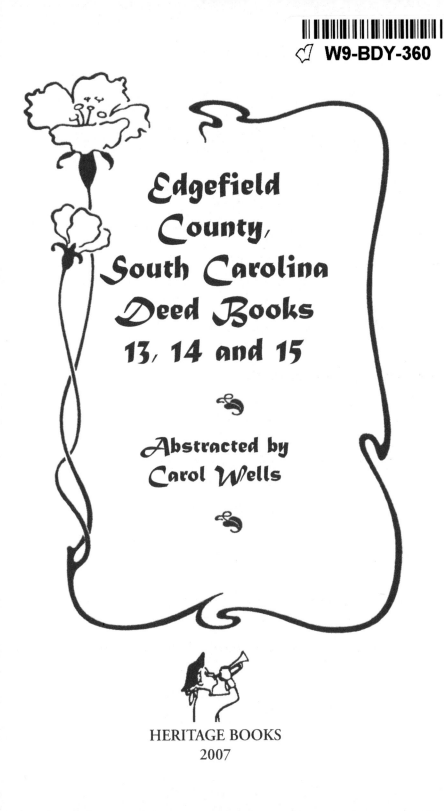

Edgefield County, South Carolina Deed Books 13, 14 and 15

Abstracted by
Carol Wells

HERITAGE BOOKS
2007

HERITAGE BOOKS

AN IMPRINT OF HERITAGE BOOKS, INC.

Books, CDs, and more—Worldwide

For our listing of thousands of titles see our website
at
www.HeritageBooks.com

Published 2007 by
HERITAGE BOOKS, INC.
Publishing Division
65 East Main Street
Westminster, Maryland 21157-5026

International Standard Book Number: 978-0-7884-0600-3

CONTENTS

FOREWORD

At the time these deeds were written, Edgefield contained all or parts of the present counties of Aiken, Greenwood, McCormick, and Saluda. Unless specified otherwise, land and people mentioned were of Edgefield. Deed books contain not only land conveyances, but also powers of attorney, depositions, judicial sales, and sales of household and farm equipment, livestock, and slaves. The deeds in this book were written from the 1770s through the late 1790s, and were recorded between 1796 and 1799.

Names are copied as they seemed to be written in the documents. Certain hand-written letters can be hard to distinguish. Uncrossed t's may look like l's; u & n, r & s, and others may appear alike. This book was abstracted from microfilm; to verify spelling and to obtain additional details, copies of book pages should be obtained.

Every name and all watercourses are indexed. Deeds amplify census material, adding such details as names of wives, children, parents, other kinfolk, previous owners, purchases, inheritances, divisions among heirs, names of witnesses, justices, sheriffs, da' of death, and dates and references to royal and state grants. Names and ages of slaves may be stated, approximate age of minors, and occupations may be given. Other states and counties mentioned may prove family movement at a time in American history when the population was settling into newly opened lands, when the recently-invented cotton gin was changing Southern agriculture, and when seeds of sectional strife were being planted.

ABBREVIATIONS

adj	adjoining
admr	administrator
cr	creek
DS	deputy surveyor
gdn	guardian
JP	justice of the peace
L&R	lease and release
P/A	power of attorney
R	river
rec	recorded
S	south
/s/	signed
wit	witness, witnesses

p.1-2 William Tennent, Sheriff of 96 Dist. to Richard Johnson Junr. Deed of Title for 500 acres. 1 February 1796. At suit of Treasurer against executor of Colonel John Purves, land sold at Cambridge was struck off to sd Richard Johnston for £49 sterling all that tract of land late the property of Lord Charles Gillontague in Ninety Six District on Savannah River bounded east by Bedingfield & Branen, to west and north west by land of heirs of Ezekiel Harlins, south by Bedingfield, north by vacant land. Wit. Josiah Leake, J Hatcher. Proven 16 March 1796 by Jeremiah Hatcher. R Tutt J.P. Recorded 16 March 1796 J Hatcher.

p2-4 Andrew & William Burney to Stephen Garrett. 15 January 1796. Andrew & Wm Burney both of Augusta, Georgia, and Stephen Garrett of Augusta, Georgia. For $728 grant to Stephen Garrett land in Greenville County now Edgefield containing 200 acres bound southeast by Stephens creek, other sides vacant, granted to Ulrich Tobler 13 March 1752 by Governor James Glen. Wit:[blank]. Acknowledged by Stephen Garrett in presence of Saml W Jones, Z Cockraham, Jno Perry. Proved before Richard Tutt J P by Samuel W Jones. Rec. 16 March 1796 Saml W Jones.

p.4-6 Thomas Warren to Arthur H Davis, 13 November 1795 both of Edgefield County, £10 sterling sells 50 acres joining land of John Davis on west, Henry Etheridge on southeast, Thomas Davis on north east. Wit. Thomas Deen, John (x) Williams, Martha (x) Williams. Signed Thomas (M his mark) Warren. 16 March 1796 before Russell Wilson J P proven by Thos Deen. Rec. 16 March 1796 Thomas Deen.

p.6-9 Thomas Man to Elizabeth Man. Lease & Release. 1 March 1793. Thomas Man to Widow Elizabeth Man for 10 shillings current money of the State sells 100 acres on branch of Little Saluda River on the waggon road from Gramby to Augusta where Elizabeth Man now lives, bounded on all sides by vacant lands, granted to Peter Cree 27 August 1764 and from him conveyed to John Wates Man and sd Thomas Man being heir at law of sd John Wats Man to Elizabeth Man, yearly rent of one pepper corn if demanded. Wit: William Norris, Nathan Norris, Ned (x) Brooks. Signed Thomas (x) Man. 2 March 1793 Thomas Mann to Elizabeth Man, for £50 current money of State paid by Elizabeth Man, confirms sale to her made for one whole year by indenture of date next before date of these presents, 100 acres on branch of Little Saluda River on road by Gramby to Augusta where sd Elizabeth Man now lives bounded by vacant land at time of original survey, granted 27 Aug 1764 unto Peter Cree, from Peter Cree to John Wats Man; sd Thomas Man being eldest son and heir of John Wats Man conveys to Elizabeth Mann. Wit. William Norris, Nathan Norris, Ned (x) p.9 Brooks. Signed Thomas (x) Man. Proven before John Thos Fairchild J P by William Norris 15 June 1793. Rec. 17 March 1796.

p.9-11 John Berwick, Thomas Wearing & John Ewing Colhoun commissioners of T J to John Garrett of Augusta, Georgia. 9 July 1783. Berwick, Wearing and Colhoun were commissioned by SC in pursuance of an Act for disposing of certain estates and banishing certain persons therein mentioned, to expose to sale at Public auction the lands hereinafter mentioned being part of the real estates in sd Act mentioned. John Garrett was highest bidder for 5 shillings lawful money of State, three adjoining plantations late the property of the Cherekesau Indians situate in Ninety Six district, 517 acres, bound by Savanna River, north by lands of Ralph Phillips, rent one peppercorn. Wit: Richd Gough, Andrew Pickens. /S/ Thos Warring Senr, Jno Ewing Colhoun. Proved 16 March 1796 by Andrew Pickens Esqr before Joseph

1

Hightower J P.   Rec 17 March 1796.

p.11-12 Ambrose Ripley to Eugene Brenan guardian for Sarah Dolby. Release. 5 shillings. Negroe Wench called Leah and her two children Ben and Beck, also Negro boy George late the estate of Spencer Dolby. Wit Samps Butler. Signed Ambrose Ripley. Proved by Sampson Butler 19 March 1796 before R Tutt J P.   Rec 19 Mar 1796.

p.12-14 James Butler Sr, planter, to James Butler Jr planter. 21 March 1796. £25 sterling money of the state. 77 acres on Chavers Creek waters of Stephens Creek & Savannah R. Wit Charles Banks, David Shaw. /S/ James Butler. Plat: tract 77 acres part of two tracts originally granted to sd James Butler Sr. Adj Drewry Murfey. 22 Mar 1796 proved by David Shaw before R Tutt J P. Rec 22 Mar 1796

p.14-17 James Butler Sr, planter, to David Shaw, planter, 21 March 1796, £25.4 money of the State. 102 acres being part of two surveys granted to sd Jas Butler, on Chavers Creek. Wit Charles Banks, James (B) Butler. /s/ James Butler. Plat by Chas Banks DS. Proved by James Butler Jr before R Tutt. Rec 22 Mar 1796.

p.17-18 Eugene Brenan gdn for Sarah Dolby to Ambrose Ripley. Release. For 5 shillings Negro boy Soloman late property of Spencer Dolby, exonerate sd Ambrose or his wife Nancy from all claims which sd Sarah may have in law or equity for moneys due by sd Nancy to estate of Spencer Dolby. Wit Samp Butler. /s/ Eugene Brenan gdn for S Dolby. Proved by Sampson Butler before Richard Tutt 24 Mar 1796. Rec 24 Mar 1796.

p.18-20 Jeremiah Hatcher Shff to George Ker mercht. 7 Feb 1795. Judgment against Lewis Collins for £10.13.8 writ by Richard Tutt clerk of Court 14 Jan 1795 executed 7 Feb 1795 on 125 acres adj John Purvis Esqr, James Coursey, Cage Garner, Absolom Williams on south branches of Turkey cr waters of Savannah R sold unto Geo Ker for £9.10 sterling money he being highest bidder. Wit Geo H Perrin, W Simkins. Proved by George H Perrin before R Tutt 24 Mar 1796.   Rec 24 Mar 1796.

p.20-21 Robert Birton to Samuel Jenkins. 6 Feb 1796 £30 Sterling money of state, 200 acres, part of 2 tracts granted to sd Robert Burton on Turkey cr & Savannah R adj Hill, Samuel Jenkins, Puckets branch on Little Turkey cr to Squire Simkins line to Chandlers. Wit Edward Burt, James Coate. /s/ Robert Birton. Proved by James Coats before John Blocker J P, 2 April 1796.   Rec 2 April 1796

p.21-25 Jno Olliphant to Jesse Frazier. L&R. 1 Oct 1788, John Oliphant and Nancy his wife to Jesse Frazier, planter. 10 shillings sterling, 100 acres on a little branch S side Beaverdam Cr waters of Stephens Cr. Wit Thos Hagens, John Frazier, Elizabeth (x) Frazier. /s/ John Oliphant, Nancy (x) Oliphant. 2 Oct 1788 John Oliphant & wife Nancy to Jesse Frazier, grant dated 25 April 1774 from Gov Wm Bull to John Oliphant 100 acres on Beaverdam Cr rec in Book M p 532 2 Aug 1774, also Memorial in Book 32 p 84. Sd John Oliphant & wife Nancy for £100 sterling to Jesse Frazier. Wit Thos Hagens, John Frazier, Elizabeth (x) Frazier. /s/ John Oliphant, Nancy (x) Oliphant. Proved 6 Apr 1796 by John Frazier before Richard Tutt. Rec 6 April 1796 John Frazier.

p.26-27 John Gormon Senr to John Gormon Junr. £150 sterling, to son John Spragins Gormon 300 acres on Great Saluda R part whereof originally granted to Michael Abney

& conveyed to John Gormon Sr, near the spring John Gormon Sr uses, by Thos Berrys spring, the remainder is part of 300 acres originally granted to sd John Gormon Sr joining above mentioned land adj land John Gormon Sr sold to Joseph Trotter. 6 Apr 1796. Wit John Abney, Thos Carson, Cullen Lark. /s/ John Gormon. Proven 6 April 1796 by John Abney before Nathl Abney J P.   Rec 9 Apr 1796, John Abney.

p.27-29 Howell Sellers to Mary Fike for £65 sterling, 123 acres NW side of land granted to Thomas Sellers of 193 acres on Log Cr of Turkey Cr adj on NE by Thomas McGinnes, SE by Mexoal(?)'s land, SW by John Youngblood, & 9 acres adj above land, part of grant to Thos McGinnes. Wit Isaac Grubbs, John (x) Youngblood. /s/ Howel Sellers. Arthur Simkins, J P, certifies that Sarah Sellers wife of Howel Sellers signed deed freely. Arthur Simkins. Sarah (x) Sellers.   Proven by John Youngblood 5 Apr 1796 before Arthur Simkins.   Rec 9 Apr 1796.

p.29-32 John Hammond & wife Elizabeth to Peter Carns of Augusta, Georgia. L&R. 10 May 1796. 10 shillings sterling Lott 16 in Falmouth bounded by Union Street, Teasdale Street, Rutledge Street. Wit Joshua Hammond, A Stewart. /s/ John Hammond, Eliz Hammond. 21 May 1791 John Hammond & wife Elizabeth to Peter Carns of Augusta, GA, £5 sterling of SC, lot 16 in Falmouth. Wit Sarah Hammond, Joshua Hammond, A Stewart. /s/ John Hammond, Eliz Hammond. Proven 2 Apr 1796 by Joshua Hammond before Joseph Hightower.   Rec 10 Apr 1796 Joshua Hammond.

p.32-34 Abraham Richardson & wife Winnifred to David Sandidge of Richmond County, Georgia, 2 Apr 1796. £275 State money, lot in Campbellton whereon is Campbells tobacco warehouse. Wit William (M) Moseley, Nathan Napper, Charles (x) Randall. /s/ A Richardson, Winnifred (x) Richardson.   Proven 4 Apr 1796 by Wm Moseley before Joseph Hightower JP.   Rec 10 April 1796.

p.35-36 Stephen Bettis admr to his brother Mathew Bettis. 11 April 1796 P/A to negotiate in Green County, GA, suit against George Dawson for recovery of Negro boy Toney belonging to estate of John Bettis decd. Wit Saml Marsh, Rd Tutt. /s/Stephen Bettis admr. Proved by Saml Marsh 11 Apr 1796; R Tutt. Rec 11 Apr 1796.

p.36-38 Eliza. Calliham to Samuel Scott. 2 Nov 1795 $30, 75 acres on Stephens Cr granted to sd Elizabeth Calliham 3 Apr 1786 in grant bk HHHH p 509 by Gov Wm Moultrie bound SE by Patrick Smith. Wit David Thomas, Saml Scott, James Scott. /s/ Elizabeth (x) Calliham.   Proved 5 Apr 1796 by Samuel C Scott before S Mays J P. Rec 19 April 1796.

p.37-39 Sheriff Samuel Mays to Willis Anderson. 10 September 1793; Thomas Moseley judgment agt Daniel Johnson for £4.6; execution by Richard Tutt 9 March 1793 to sell Daniel Johnson's land to satisfy debt; 103 acres on Edisto R bound SW by Aron Kirkland, NW by Robert Stark, NE by Jacob Read, SE on Horse Cr, 103 acres to Willis Anderson for £7.7 sterling. Wit Samp Butler, Ezekiel Perry. /s/ S Mays.   Proven 16 Apr 1796 Sampson Butler before Richd Tutt.   Rec 16 Apr 1796, S Butler.

p.40-41 Reuben Pyles to Simon Totevine. Laurence County, Ninety Six Dist, SC. 7 Jan 1795 Reuben Pyles of Laurence County to Simon Totevine of Edgefield, £80 sterling 816 acres in Edgefield surveyed for Thomas Lamar 17 March 1786, elapsed, granted to Ayers Gorely by Gov Wm Moultrie 1 Jan 1787 and conveyed to Reuben Pyles.

Wit Elisha Hunt, Isaac (x) Filpot. /s/ Reuben Pyles. Proven 6 Jan 1796(?) by Elisha
Hunt before Charles Saxon J P. Rec. 16 April 1796.

p.41-43 Elizabeth Hammond to Richard Thorp Keating. 27 Feb 1794 Deed of Renuncia-
tion, town lot Beaufort, SC. Hugh Middleton, Aquila Miles & Joseph Hightower to
examine Right of dower of Elizabeth Hammond wife of John Hammond Senr in Lot 141 in
Beaufort SC conveyed by sd John Hammond to Richard Thorp Keating. 7 Nov 1794 sd
Elizabeth says she signed renunciation freely. /s/ Eliz Hammond, Hugh Middleton,
Aquila Miles. Rec. 21 April 1796.

p.43-44 Andrew Mock to Eli Thorndon. 20 Decr 1794 Andrew Mook of Warren county,
GA to Eli Thorndon of Edgefield, £200 Sterling of SC 100 acres originally granted
to sd Andw Mook 5 Sep 1769. Wit George B Moore, Timothy Kelly, Elisha Brook. /s/
Andrew Mock. Plat 5 Sep 1769 by Patk Cunningham Vol XI p 240. Danl Jas Ravenel
Survr Genl. Proven 2 May 1796 Elisha Brooks; Wm Anderson. Rec 2 May 1796.

p.45-46 Elisha Brooks of Newberry SC to John Perry of Edgefield, 2 April 1796 £100,
100 acres Hardlabor Cr, original grant to Mary Wilson. Wit Wm Allen, Eli Thornton.
/s/ Elisha Brooks. Judge William Anderson certifies that Nancy Brooks wife of
Elisha Brooks, examined separately, signed freely. Proven by Eli Thornton 2 May
1796; W Anderson. Rec 2 May 1796.

p.46-48 Sheriff Jeremiah Hatcher to Thomas Swearengen. 2 January 1796. At suit of
Stephen Bettis against William Robinson, sheriff sold to the highest bidder Thomas
Swearengen for £10 sterling 314 acres on Shaws Creek of South Edistoe River bounded
by Abraham Odom, Thomas Swearengen, Wm Martin. Wit Eugene Brenan, Step Norris. /s/
J Hatcher. Proven by Stephen Norris 7 May 1796 before Van Swearengen J P.
Recorded 7 May 1796.

p.48-50 Sheriff Jeremiah Hatcher to Thomas Swearengen. 2 Jan 1796. At suit of
Stephen Bettis agt William Robinson, sheriff sold to highest bidder Thomas Swear-
engen for £5 50 acres on Shaws Cr of South Edistoe R. Wit Eugene Brenan, Stn
Norris. /s/ J Hatcher. Proven 7 May 1796 by Stephen Norris before Van Swearengen
J P. /s/ Stn Norris. Recorded 7 May 1796.

p.50-52 Alexander Wilson and wife of Edgefield to Thomas Elliott of Laurens County
SC, 9 December 1795, £40 sterling 123 acres on Pen Creek of Little Saluda River
orignally granted by Gov Charles Pinckney unto John Mobley 5 Nov 1792 bounded NW by
Write Nicholson, W by Wm Hart, SE by Robert Starks Jr, conveyed by John Mobley to
Alexander Wilson. Wit Mumford Perryman, George Elliott, Elisabeth Perryman. /s/
Alexr Wilson, Martha Wilson. Proven 5 May 1796 by George Elliott before Wm Daniel
J P. /s/ Geo Elliott. Rec 9 May 1796.

p.52-53 Thomas Plunkett to Amasa Baugh. Bill of Sale for £12 sterling bed, sheets,
coverlids, bolsters, pillows, [& much household equipment]. Wit W Jeter Junr.
/s/ Thomas Plunket. Proven by W Jeter Junr 4 May 1796 before Aquila Miles J P.
Recorded 11 May 1796.

p.54-58 Wormley Bland to Anne Bland. L&R. 25 Feb 1796 for 10 shillings sterling
money, 120 acres on Main Road from Ninety Six to Charleston, separated out of two

surveys by a new line, adj old grant line, a small part of land conveyed by George Mason to sd Anne Bland, originally granted unto William Little 1 Jan 1787 and by sd Wm Little unto Anne Bland 8 June 1787, & by Anne Bland to Wormley Bland 1 Nov 1792. Wit Presley Bland, Moses Hadox. /s/ Wormley Bland. 26 Feb 1796 Wormly Bland to Anne Bland, for £20 sterling money 120 acres on main Road from Ninety Six p.56 to Charleston, part of two surveys, adj land conveyed by George Mason to Anne Bland, also tract originally granted to William Little 1 Jan 1767 and conveyed by Wm Little to Anne Bland 8 June 1787 and by Anne Bland part of sd two tracts to sd Wormly Bland 2 Nov 1792. Wit Presley Bland, Moses (x) Hadox. /s/ Wormley 8 Bland. Proven 16 May 1796 by Presley Bland before Wm Daniel, who saw Wormley Bland sign deed to Nancy Bland, and saw Moses Haddocks signed his name as other witness thereto. /s/ P Bland, Wm Daniel J P.   Recorded 18 May 1796.

p.58-59 Nancy Bland to Presley Bland, 16 May 1796, £20 sterling money to Presley Bland 105 acres, north side Road from the Ridge to Ninety Six being layed off by Shadrack Stokes a Deputy Surveyor to Presley Bland on Red Bank Cr waters of Little Saluda R adj Wormley Bland, James Bland, Mumford Perryman, Joseph Nunn, William Humphreys, William Daniel. Wit William (x) Brown, Sally Bland. /s/ Nancy (A) Bland Proven 16 May 1796 by William Brown before Wm Daniel.   Rec 18 May 1796.

p.60-61 Nancy Bland to grandson Jacob Brown. 16 May 1796, for love, 50 acres being plantation whereon William Brown now lives joining Wm Daniel's land, part of a tract of 350 acres granted to William Brown by Gov William Moultrie 1 Jan 1787, conveyed by Brown to Nancy Bland. Nancy Bland put Mary Brown in possession to have use of sd 50 acres during her natural life, then to Jacob Brown. Wit P Bland, Salley Bland. /s/ Nancy (A) Bland.   Proven 16 May 1796 by P Bland before Wm Daniel J P.   Rec 18 May 1796.

p.61-65 Robert Stark late sheriff to William Anderson. 3 Feb 1789. Whereas Henry Pendleton Esqr in 17-- obtained judgment agt John Dooley for £439.17.5 current money of province, sold to highest bidder Francis Sinquefield for £250 current money of province, unto William Anderson executor of the estate of Francis Sinquefield now deceased to be conveyed by sd William Anderson as is directed by will of Francis Sinquefield, 300 acres south side of Saludy R bounded by Wm Low, Morris Gwin, James Chappell, original grant to Catharine Youngblood 7 March p.65[there is no page 64] 1770. Wit Sophia Stark Edward Couch. /s/ Robert Stark. Proven 5 Sept 1789 by Edward Couch before Russell Wilson JP.   Rec 23 May 1796.

p.66-67 W Anderson exr to Rachael & Jane Sinquefield & alias Maxwell. Francis Sinquefield by last will & testament 4 Dec 1780 bequeathed to dau Rachell and Jane 200 acres head of Chaves Creek originally granted to Jason Ryan, also 50 acres originally granted to Wm Anderson on Saluday R also 150 acres being half of a 300 acre tract granted to Catharine Youngblood on sd river to be equally divided between them share & share alike, and whereas sd Francis Sinquefield by will apptd Wm Anderson, Arthur Simkins and Thos Anderson extrs, and whereas sd Arthur Simkins and Thomas Anderson decline acting as exrs, sd trust devolved upon sd Wm Anderson. To fulfill intentions of testator the three parcells of land are divided, 9 Dec 1788. Wit Zac Sinquefield, Wm Smith. /s/ William Anderson. Rachel Sinquefield. Jane (x) Maxwell. Proven 12 May 1796 by Zachariah Sinquefield; Wm Robinson J P. Recorded 23 May 1796.

p.67-68 Thomas Chappel of Newberry county, SC, to Zachariah Sinquefield. 28 March 1794 Two Negroes Randol & Frank for £60 lawfull money of SC. Wit: Morris Gwyn, William (x) Jones. /s/ Thos Chappell. Proven 10 May 1796 by Morris Gwin before William Anderson. Rec 23 May 1796.

p.68-69 Daniel Rodgers to Shemuel Nicholson. 11 May 1796, for £116 lawful current money 210 acres on N side Beaver Dam Cr in two tracts, one of 60 acres part of land granted to James Robinson 9 Sept 1774 and conveyed by James Robinson to sd Daniel Rodgers 12 & 12 May 1775; the other tract of 150 acres granted to William Gunnels on 9 Sept 1774 butting on afsd tract was conveyed by sd Wm Gunnels to sd Daniel Rodgers in May 1775. Wit Mathew Sullivan, William Osbourn. /s/ Daniel (O) Rodgers. 11 May 1796 Judge William Anderson certifies that Mary Rodgers wife of Daniel Rodgers examined privately says she freely executed deed. /s/ Mary (W) Rodgers. Proven 11 May 1796 by Mathew Sullivan before Wm Anderson. Rec 23 May 1796.

p.70-71 Jesse Frazier to Shemuel Nicholson. 23 May 1796 for £20 sterling, 40 acres N side Beaverdam Cr a branch of Turkey Creek waters of Savannah River. Wit Eugene Brenan, John Simkins, Stn Norris. /s/ Jesse (M) Frazier. Proven 23 May 1796 by Stephen Norris before Richard Tutt J P. Rec 23 May 1796.

p.71-73 Shemuel Nicholson to John Simkins. £116 sterling, 210 acres N side Beaverdam Cr in two tracts, one of 60 acres part of 200 acres granted to James Robinson 9 Sept 1774 and conveyed by Jas Robinson to Daniel Rodgers 12 & 13 May 1775, the other of 150 acres granted to William Gunnells 9 Sept 1774 conveyed by Wm Gunnels to Daniel Rodgers May 1775, also all that other parcell of land containing 40 acres on Beaverdam Cr. Wit Richard Gantt, John Robertson, J Hatcher. /s/ Shemuel Nicholson. Proven by J Hatcher 24 May 1796 before Richard Tutt J P. /s/ Rd Tutt J P. J Hatcher. Recorded 24 May 1796.

p.73-79 Elias Gibson of Abbeville County, SC, to Thomas Radcliffe, surviving executor of will of Andrew Williamson [also Williams] deceased. L&R. 4 May 1795. 5 May 1795, 100 acres on Stephens Creek originally granted to [blank] Hutchinson and called the English mans tract in Abbeville County, bounding on sd Elias Gibson, John Thompson, & [blank] Crone. Bond £26.13.4 with condition for payment of £13.6.8 with interest thereon./s/ Elias Gibson. Charleston District, SC, proven by Josiah Leeke before J Nichols J P. /s/ Josiah Leake. Recorded 24 May 1796.

p.79-83 Leroy Hammond to John Hammond. L&R. 12 Nov 1795, 5 shillings sterling money, 683 acres on Boggy Branch, the plat certified by Charles Banks 12 June 1794, Wit Asaph Waterman, Giles Y Raines. /s/ LRoy Hammond. 13 Nov 1795, Leroy Hammond to John Hammond, £100 lawful sterling money paid by John Hammond, 683 acres on Boggy branch, plat certified by Charles Banks 12 June 1794. Wit Asaph Waterman, Giles Y Raines. /s/ Leroy Hammond. Proven 3 June 1796 by Giles Y Rains before Richard Tutt. Plat shows 683 acres laid off to Robert Cochran which contains 32 acres, it being a resurvey to shew what land was taken by the intersection of older surveys from a survey granted to LRoy Hammond, certified 12 June 1794 by Charles Banks. [An included plat shows the Chickeesaw line, five knoch road, Philips line, old road to Augusta.]

p.84-86 Sheriff Jeremiah Hatcher to John Flick. 7 May 1796. Official sale of land at suit of Arthur and Mary Watson against James Perry administrator of Willis Watson deceased, to highest bidder for £42.10, 195 acres on Clouds Creek a branch of Little Saluda, part of two tracts containing 235 acres originally granted to John Carlin and Arthur Watson. Wit Eugene Brenan, Samp Butler. /s/ J Hatcher. Proven 4 June 1796 by Eugene Brenan before Richd Tutt JP. Rec 4 June 1796.

p.86-92 Samuel Crafton to Simeon Theus and John G Guignard commissioners of the Treasury of SC, 7 March 1796/8 March 1796, L&R by mortgage,£100, 364 acres formerly property of Moses Kirkland. Wit Hugh Middleton, Daniel Barksdale. /s/ Saml Crafton. Proved by Danl Barksdale 13 May 1796; Hugh Middleton J P. Rec 18 June 1796.

p.92-96 Treasurer Benjamin Warring at Columbia to Thomas Bacon Esqr of Edgefield. L&R. 21 December 1793/22 Decr 1793, £100 sterling, lands as follows: 250 acres granted 8 July 1774 to Isaac Mitchell bounded at time of survey by John Stewart & Robt Wallace, Bryant & vacant land, situate on Cuffeetown Creek, also 100 acres on Cuffeetown Creek granted to John Swilling 23 January 1773 and then bound by Robert Mitchell & vacant land, also 150 acres at Cuffee town granted to John Williams 27 August 1764 then bounded by heirs of Humphreys Barrott. Wit: J G Guignard, S Lunsford. /s/ B Waring, Treas. Proved 6 June 1794 by John G Guignard before Martyn Alken, J P, Richland County. Rec 21 June 1796

p.96-98 William Clark of Georgia to Agness Cunningham admx estate of John Cunningham decd, 12 January 1795, £35 lawful money of SC to him paid by decedent and wife Agness Cunningham now admx/estate, 154.5 acres on Stephens Creek being part of 350 acres granted to John Clark, adj B Jones & Palmer, John Garrett. Wit James Clark, John Prince. /s/ William Clark. Proved by 26 February 1795 by James Clark before Aquila Miles J P. Rec 23 June 1796.

p.98-103   Daniel Parker to Sarah Gunnels. L&R. 1 Jan 1796/2 Jan 1796, £10 sterling, 29 acres on branches of Log Creek of Savannah R, bounded by land granted to Thomas Cotton, being part of a tract granted to John Vernon for 150 acres by Lieut Gov William Bull; transferred by John Vernon to Thomas Cotton, and by L&R by Thos Cotton to Danl Parker 6 & 7 July 1795, plat by R\Wm Prichard DS. Wit Geo H Perrin, Presley Bland. /s/ Daniel Parker. [sketch shows land of Daniel Gunnels] Proven 24 June 1796 by George Henry Perrin; Richard Tutt J P. Rec 24 June 1796.

p.103-109   Samuel Saxon Sheriff of Ninety Six District to Charles Goodwin Esqr attorney at law; Leroy Hammond Esqr died seized of three parcels of land, one of 450 acres originally granted to Elizabeth Miller at time of original grant bounded by Savannah River & Daniel Pepper, George Sommers; tract of 58 acres, and another tract of 38 acres both part of 250 acres originally granted to Benjamin Allen. Creditors John Blakes, Henry Poole, Wm Dawson, John Yarnston, Wm Hornby obtained judgment against estate of Leroy Hammond Esqr decd for £14,308 interest & costs by John Rutledge chief justice of State at Cambridge 8 April 1792. Sheriff levied against goods in hands of Mary Ann Hammond LRoy Hammond Charles Goodwin and George Whitefield, sold 13 April 1794 at Campbellton in 96 District to highest bidder Charles Goodwin for £135 lawfull sterling money. /s/ Samuel Saxon Sheriff 96 Dist. Wit Whitf Wilson, Jonan Moore. Proven 16 June 1796 by Jonathan Moore; Jno Trotter JP. Plat: certified by Charles Banks D S 9 April 1794, surveyed for Elizabeth Miller 1785[shows Savannah R, Waggon Path] Plat: Land granted to

Benjamin Allen inersected by other surveys which were older, shows 38 acres and 58 acres, surveyed 11 April 1794 by Charles Banks D S, [shows Sarah Bakers land now held by James McQueen, McQueens mill, Campbellton road, Leroy Hammond, Eliz Miller, George Sommers land]

p.109-115   Charles Goodwin Esqr to LeRoy Hammond & George Whitefield exrs of will of Leroy Hammond decd, L&R and mortgage, 12 April 1794/13 April 1794, 5 shillings lawful sterling money, 3 tracts, one of 450 acres original grant to Elizabeth Miller [land described as above]. Wit Whitf Wilson, Jona Moore. /s/ Charles Goodwin. Proven 16 June 1796 by Jonathan Moore; Jno Trotter.   Rec 27 June 1796.

p.115-118   Samuel Saxon late Sheriff of Ninety Six district to LeRoy Hammond of New Richmond in sd District, planter, late of Snow Hill in sd district. 4 January 1796. Plantation of LeRoy Hammond, deceased, 800 acres on Savannah R bounded E on Elizabeth Millers tract now belonging to Charles Goodwin, SW on Savannah R, NW on land granted to William Drake called now Richmond now belonging to sd LeRoy Hammond, and on other side partly on land granted to Benjamin Allen and John Bynan which tract is known as Thompsons hill and was granted to George Summers; suit of Eyre, Athemeon & Walter of City of London, merchants, who obtained judgment agt Leroy Hammond for sd sum, costs and charges by them paid in obtaining sd judgment; writ of John Rutledge dated at Cambridge 18 April 1792 to levy on estate of LeRoy Hammond decd to recover agt sd sums at public auction; sold to highest bidder LeRoy Hammond for £100 sterling. Wit Whitf Wilson, Jonan Moore. /s/ S Saxon, Shff 96 Dist. Proven 16 June 1796 by Jonathan Moore; Jno Trotter. Rec 27 June 1796.

p.119-122   Samuel W Goode of Georgia to Edmund Pursell[Pursley], L&R, 27 December 1785/18(sic) Decr 1795, £125 sterling, 150 acres on Horns Cr water of Stephens Cr willed to Samuel Goode by his father bounded by Andrew Burney, Mackerness Goode, Saml Gardner, John Swillivan. Wit George Farrar, John C Garrett. /s/ Saml W Goode. Proven 8 June 1796 by Geo Farrar; Aquila Miles JP. Rec 28 June 1796.

p.123   Rice Swearengen to Jacob Wise, Bill of Sale, 19 March 1796, £40 sterling, a Negro girl Betty about age nine. Wit Absalom Napper, Benja Hatcher. /s/ Rice Swearengen. Proven 1 June 1796 by Absalom Napper; Joseph Hightower JP. Rec 29 June 1796.

p.124-127   James Hargrove and wife Mary to Edward Mitchell. L&R, 30 October 1795/14 Octr 1795, £10 sterling, 83.5 acres bound by Jeters Lang, Welches, Doolittle, Matthews. Wit Hinchey Mitchell, Wm Hargrove. /s/ Jas Hargrove, Mary (x) Hargrove. Proven 2 July 1796 by Hinchey Mitchell; Richard Tutt. Rec 2 July 1796

p.127-129   John Still and wife Jeane Still to Benjamin Eddins late of Abbeville County SC, £200, 555 acres, resurvey by William Coursey, part of 500 acres granted to Richard Buckelew decd & descended by heirship to George Buckelew and conveyed by same to Jas Buckelew and from James Buckelew to John Still and part of 1500 acres granted to Hugh Rose lying on Little Steavens Creek. Wit James Eddins, James Blocker. John (I) Still, Jean (I) Still. Proven 1 July 1796 by James Eddins; John Blocker J P.   Rec 2nd July 1796.

p.129-132   Daniel Stevens of City of Charleston to James Coursey of 96

District, L&R. 8 March 1796/9 March 1796, £60 current money of SC, 300 acres on Beaver Dam branch of Turkey Creek bounded by Hezekiah Williams, Robert Melvelle, William Goode. Wit James Prichard, Caul Collins. /s/ Danl Stevens. Proven 6 April 1796 by Caul Collins; John Blocker J P. Rec 4 July 1796.

p.132-135   Shiles Marsh and wife Mary to Ezekiel McClendon. L&R. 9 August 1795/10 Aug 1795, £50 sterling, 205 acres being the upper and east part where sd Shiles now lives, part of 410 acres granted unto Samuel Marsh decd by Gov Wm Moultrie in 1786, bound by Wm Marsh, Wm Frazure. Wit Ezekiel Robuck, William Marsh. /s/ Shiles Marsh. Proven 14 March 1796 by Ezekiel Robuck; Van Swearengen J P. Rec 4 July 1796.

p.136-139   Valentine Brazeel to James Herring. L&R. 19 August 1794/20 Aug 1794, 10 shillings sterling of SC, 126 acres on branches of Edisto River south of Saluda below Anchent boundary line near the Jester Ponds, beginning on land of Thomas Adams, incl improvement that Breton Brazeel now lives on, adj Benjamin McKinney, being part of 226 acres granted to Valentine Breazeel by Gov Charles Pinckney 4 April 1791. Wit Edward Couch, Elisha Baronton, Bibby Bush. /s/ Valentine (V) Breazeel. Proven 4 July 1796 by Bibby Bush; John Blocker J P. Rec 4 July 1796.

p.139-141   Bartlett Bledsoe to William Humphreys. Release. 20 June 1795, £20 sterling 200 acres on Red Bank Cr of Little Saluda R, original grant to Larkin Brown 1786 by Gov Wm Moultrie, and conveyed from Larkin Brown to Bartlett Bledsoe. Wit Henry King, Demcy Wever. /s/ Bartlett Bledsoe. Proven 5 March 1796 by Henry King; Wm Daniel J P. Rec 4th July 1796.

p.141-143   Thomas Reed Senr to John Blalock of Newberry County SC. Deed 8 January 1795, £65 sterling, 100 akers part of 300 akers granted to Ann Dean by Gov Wm Bull on 8 July 1774 on Persimmon Cr of Little Saluda, conveyed by George Dean unto Saml More[Mare?] then from Saml Mare unto Thomas Reed Senr. Wit Jas Rutherford, Sammuel (x) Crow, Jno Blalock Junr. /s/ Thomas Reed. Proven 4 July 1796 by Saml Crow; Richard Tutt. Rec. 4th July 1796.

p.143-145   David Bell of Charleston SC to Charles Yancey of Amherst County, Province of Virginia. Deed. 26 December 1772, grant made 24 December 1772 by Gov Charles Granville Montague grant 200 acres in Granville County both sides Stevens Creek, sd David Bell for 10 shillings lawfull money of SC sold to Chas Yancey for one year 200 acres. Wit John Clark, John Mason, William Fitzpatrick. /s/ David Bell. 27 Dec 1772 recd £22.10 current money of SC. /s/ David Bell. Proven 4 August 1775 by John Clark; Arthur Jenkins J P. Rec 4th July 1796.

p.145-149   John Swearengen to John Wimberley. L&R. 13 November 1792/12 Nov 1792, £10 sterling, part of 530 acres granted 7 August 1786 to John Swearengen on Shaws Creek, adj Peter Hilliard, and now 450 acres where John Swearengen now lives conveyed by sd John Swearengen to sd John Wimberly. Wit Henry Swearengen, Joseph Jones. /s/ Jno Swearengen. Proven 3 Dec 1795 by Joseph Jones; Van Swearengen. Rec. 4th July 1796.

p.149-150   John Lucas Senr to John Lucas Junr. Deed. 119 acres adj Laurence Rambo, Capt John Ryan, John Lucas Sr, & surveyed by Bennett Crafton DS, part of land late property of Moses Kirkland being conveyed unto John Ryan by Jno Berwick, Thos Warring, John Ewing Colhoun commrs of forfeited estates on 9 July 1783 and by sd Ryan to John Lucas Senr on 5 August 1786. Wit George H Perrin, Stephen Norris. /s/ John (IL) Lucas Senr. Certification by Arthur Simkins J P on 5 July 1796 that Mary Lucas wife of within John Lucas Senr appeared and declares she freely signed deed. /s/ Mary (x) Lucas. Proven 3 July 1796 by Stephen Norris; Richard Tutt J P. Rec 5 July 1796.

p.150-152   Elizabeth Carns executrix of Peter Carnes Esqr deceased of Richmond County, Georgia, to Reuben Cooper. Deed, 16 February 1796, £50 sterling, 100 acres in Edgefield County lying between Dry Creek and Buckhalters Cr, bounding on John Tolson, Matthew Devore, Willis Whartley, Richard Johnson, originally granted to Eveleigh and others. Wit Seaborn Jones, Richd Johnson, Wm Dobey. /s/ Eliza. Carns. Proven 5 July 1790 by Wm Dobey; Rd Tutt. Rec 5th July 1796.

p.152-156   Eliza Carns Exx of estate of Peter Carns Esqr decd of Richmond Co, Georgia, to William Dobey of Edgefield, L&R, 15 February 1796/16 Feb 1796, £200, 200 acres part of Independant Hill tract including where sd Wm Dobey now resides, adj land formerly Thomas Lamar. Wit. Richd Johnson, Reuben Cooper, Seaborn Jones. /s/ Eliza. Carns. Proven 5 July 1796 by Reuben Cooper; Rd Tutt. Rec 5 July 1796.

p.156-160   John Berwick, Thomas Waring and John Ewing Colhoun Commissioners of forfeited estates to Benjamin Waller Isbell of Charleston, auctioneer, highest bidder for 8 tracts of land, 8 July 1783/9 July 1783, £460.17 sterling money of Great Britain, land late property of Charles Atkins known in General Plat by numbers 1, 2, 3, 4, 5, & 8, 9, 10 containing 2304 acres on Little Saluda River at Walnut Neck and including Prospect Hill, bounded on Thomas West, Nathan Melton, Peter Whitton, Jacob Pope, Prescot Bush, John Warren, Lott Ethridge, Cornelius Rowe and on #7 purchased by John Wyld Esqr, and John Chesnut. Wit Archd Carson, Chs H Simmons. /s/ Jno Ewing Colhoun, Thomas Waring Senr. Proven 2 April 1796 by Charles H Simmons; Jas Nicholson. Recorded 18 July 1796.

p.161-164   Benjamin Waller Isbell to John Ewing Colhoun. L&R. 12 July 1783/ 13 July 1783, 2304 acres, £460.17 sterling money of SC. 8 plantations late property of Charles Atkins, in General Plat #1, 2, 3, 4, 5, 8, 9, 10 containing 2304 acres on Little Saluda River at Walnut Neck including Prospect Hill, bounded by Thos West, Nathan Melton, Peter Whitton, Jacob Pope, Cornelius Rowe, John Chesnut, John Wyld, Prescot Bush, John Warren, Lot Etheredge. Wit Peter Brimar, Benjamin Elfe. /s/ Ben Waller Isbell. Proven 4 April 1786 by Benjamin Elfe; Jas Nicholson. Rec 18th July 1796.

p.164-165   Archibald McKay for love and affection to son Hugh McKay. 17 March 1796, Deed/Gift, cows, calves, mare, bed, crop, tools, and names friend Samuel Dagnell as guardian untill Hugh McKay comes to age. Wit Joseph Covington, Burril (x) Johnson. /s/ Archibald McKay. Proven 23 July 1796 by Joseph Covington; John Blocker J P. Rec 25 July 1796.

p.165-166   James Harrison and wife Suckey of 96 District to Peter Jones. 21 December 1795, £30 sterling of SC 364 acres excepting such part of sd land as was originally granted to Peter Manigold and convaid to Col Gilyard now in possession of Joseph Dawson, on branch of Mountain Creek of Turkey Creek, granted to sd James Harrison 3 April 1786, adj land granted to Cathrin White. Wit Andrew Jones, Edward Harrison, Patsey Pardue. /s/ Jas Harrison, Suckey Harrison. Proven 25 July 1796 by Andrew Jones; Wm Robinson J P. Rec 26th July 1796.

p.166-168   Thomas Bacon and wife Martha Bacon to William White. Deed. 14 November 1795, 300 acres on Hardlabor creek, part of tract granted to Benjamin Tutt of 2638 acres, sd 300 acres adj Major Benjamin Tutt, Logan, Yelding, Thomas Bacon. Wit Ellexander (x) White, Henry (x) Cook, James Yeldell. /s/ Thos Bacon /s/ Martha Bacon. Proven 4 April 1796 by James Yelden; Jas Harrison J P. /s/ James Yeldell. Rec. 5th July 1796.

p.168-169   William Todd to Andrew Jones, 6 August 1796, £30, 184 acres on Mountain Creek of Turkey Creek adj William Todd, Thomas Gray. Wit W C Hamilton, John (x) Arledge. /s/ William Todd. Proven 6 August 1796 by William Hamilton; John Blocker J P. Rec 6th Aug 1796.

p.169-170   Samuel Gardner Senr to beloved friend Nancey Quarles, Deed, 19 March 1791, Negro girl Murreah. Wit John Slater, William Akins Blanton, John Gardner. /s/ Samuel (x) Gardner. Proven 10 March 1792 by William Akins Blanton; Joseph Hightower J P. Rec 6th August 1796.

p.170-171   Samuel Gardner to Nancy Quarles, Deed, 4 April 1796, Negro woman Silevery; sd woman is now in possession of sd Nancy Quarles. Wit John Gardner, Mark Goode. /s/ Saml (+) Gardner. Proven 5 August 1796 by John Garner; Aquila Miles J P. Rec 6th August 1796.

p.171-172   Richard Johnson Senr of Turkey Creek, planter, to Robert Willis. Deed, 13 April 1796, £50 sterling money of SC, 100 acres part of two surveys on Turkey Creek, one granted by governor containing 250 acres to Richard Johnson Junr and conveyed to me by Richd Johnson Jr, and a plantation containing 448 acres granted to me by governor, sd 200 acres, 78 acres out of the 250 acre survey, sd 200 acres bounded by heirs of James Hall, by Joseph Williams and myself. Wit Moore Johnson, Jas Scott. /s/ Richard (R) Johnson. Proven 6 Aug 1796 by Moore Johnson; Richard Tutt, J P. [Plat shows 78 acres of old survey; 122 acres of new survey; land of James Hall, Augusta Road, Richard Jones] Plat date 11 April 1795, Robert Lang DS. Recorded 6 August 1796.

p.172-173   Richard Quarles Senr to William Quarles, Deed, 11 March 1796, for £108.10 sterling money, 155¼ acres on Turkey Cr, Thomas Burnett, James Quarles, Joseph Hightower. Wit James Quarles, Wm Watson Senr. /s/ Richard Quarles. Proven 5 August 1796 by James Quarles; Aquila Miles J P. Rec 6th August 1796.

p.173-174   William Covington of Campbellton SC to Mackerness Goode, Bill of 10 March 1796, £90, one wench named Suck and her child Betty. Wit: David Boswell. /s/ Wm Covington. Proven 6 Aug 1796 by David Boswell; Aquila Miles J P. Rec 6th August 1796.

p.174-175   Andrew Burney of Augusta, Richmond County, Georgia, planter, to George B Moore & Co, Augusta, GA. Bill of Sale. 10 August 1796, $1285.71, fourteen negroes Mary, Ned, Sutter, Sam, Peter, French, Peter, Bull, Peter, Butcher, Morris, John, Alexander, Dolly, Peter, John, Anthony. Wit Jno Gray Junr, Morgan Merrah. /s/ A Burney. Proven 12 August 1796 by John Gray Jr; Isaac Herbert J P. Rec Nathl Cocke Dep Clk. Proven 15 August 1796 by Morgan Murrah; Joseph Hightower. Recorded 16th August 1796.

p.175-177   James Baker to Joel Grizzel, Bond Mortg & Agreement, 2 April 1796, Jas Baker bound unto Joel Grizzel sum $378 SC money, to pay unto Joel Grizzel $189 on or before 5 Decr with lawful interest thereon. Wit Benjamin Hightower, Joseph Cunningham. /s/ Jas Baker. Indenture made 2 April 1796 between James Baker and Joel Grizzel $189 and interest, mortgages Negro man Dick. Wit Benja Hightower, Joseph Cunningham. /s/ Jas Baker. Proven 13 August 1796 by Benjamin Hightower; Joseph Hightower. Rec 17th August 1796.

p.177-180   Richard Withengton to John Stringer. L&R. 5 February 1788/6 Feb 1788, £15 sterling, 100 acres on south side of Stephens Cr adj Wm Stringer, granted to sd Richd Withinton by Gov Wm Moultrie 6 Nov 1786. Wit Absolam (A) Roberts, Wm Watson, Thomas Key. /s/ Richard (C) Witherton. Proven 15 Aug 1796 by Wm Watson; Aquila Miles J P. Rec 17th Augst 1796.

p.180-181   James Coursey & wife Betsey Coursey to Jemima Garner, £20 sterling, 96 acres below Turkey Cr where road from Long Kane to Charleston crosses road from Cambridge to Campbellton & Augusta on the Dreans of Turkey Creek adj Charles Williams, and land granted by Gov Chas Pinckney unto James Coursey 3 Octr 1791. Wit: W M Dawson, Ben Harry. /s/ James Coursey /s/ Elizabeth (X) Coursey. Proven 24 August 1796 by Benjamin Harry; John Blocker J P. Rec 24th August 1796.

p.181-184   Thomas Golphin one of executors/will of George Golphin Esqr decd to John Hammond of Mount Airey, land formerly property of Edward Barnard Esqr late of Augusta, Ga, decd, several tracts in Edgefield adjoining property of Macartan Campbell Esq of Charleston whereon is a little village known as Campbellton, also bound northward on land of John Hammond, also NE on Col John Purvis, SW on land originally granted to James Parsons late of Charlestown SC decd and known by the name of Phillipses Land which several tracts was mortgaged by afsd Edward Barnard before his death to afsd George Golphen Esqr decd for money due and given by sd Barnard to sd George Golphin, land to be sold together with one other tract joining afsd mortgaged tracts which belong to estate of sd George Golphin decd. Sd John Hammond hath agreed with sd Thomas Golphin to pay sd Thos Golphin £200 current money to be discharged in crop tobacco inspected and lying in any publick inspections at Augusta, Georgia, in Campbelltown & Falmouth in SC at current market price not to exceed 16 shillings 4 pence /pr hundred, subject to discount of 14 shillings/pr hogshead for freight to Savannah. Sd John Hammond farther agrees to pay Thomas Golphin £300 at end of nine months after Thomas Golphin doth make good title to John Hammond, to be discharged in crop tobacco in same manner. Wit Daniel McMurphey, Walter Taylor. /s/ Thos Galphin /s/ John Hammond. 10 Septr 1795 received of John Hammond £192.1 sterling in full of first payment of £200 for purchase of within mentioned lands. Proven 12 August 1796 by Walter Taylor; John Clarke J P. Rec 25th August 1796

p.184-185   William Deen to William Moore, Bill/sale, £89.17 sterling of SC,

12

negro man Mal age 29 or 30; boy named Lewis age 12, 25 hogs [livestock and household furniture]. Wit Thos Heron, David Cureton. /s/ W (M) Deen. Receipt for sd sum. Proven 22 Aug 1796 by Thomas Heron; W Anderson. Rec 25 August 1796.

p.186-187   Joel Pardue to William Moore, Bill/sale, £12.13.7 SC money, negro girl Rachel and a rifle. Wit Thomas Heron, Samuel Savage. /s/ Joel Pardue. Proven 22 August 1796 by Thomas Heron; W Anderson. Rec 25 August 1796.

p.187-188   Ambrose Ripley, planter, to Eugene Brenan, Deed,21 March 1796, 206 acres on Cyder Branch of Stevensons Creek adj lands of John Olliphant, Mrs Sarah Marsh, John Frazier Senr. /s/ Ambrose Ripley. Proven 3 August 1796 by Stephen Norris; Richard Tutt. Rec 23 August 1796.

p.189-190   James Baker, planter, to Kevan & Tayloe. Mortgage. 7 July 1796, owes payment of £35 by 1 March 1797, mortgage Negro John about 20 years of age, girl about 5 yrs named Dinah. Wit B Howerth, Charles Old. /s/ Jas Baker. Proven 13 July 1796 by Benjamin Howerth; Aquila Miles J P. Rec 25th August 1796.

p.190-192   Samuel Clayton of Wilks County, GA, to William Cox of Edgefield, L&R, 28 March 1796/29 March 1796, £35 sterling, 100 acres on Stephens Cr. Wit Thos (T) Ownby, Joseph Tucker. /s/ Samuel Clayton. Proven 30 July 1796 by Thomas Ownby; Henry Key. /s/ Thomas (T) Ownby. Rec 29 August 1796.

p.193-194   Robert Brooks and wife Anne Brooks to Elisabeth Holmes. 17 August 1796, $60, 37 acres on Beaverdam Cr of Turkey Cr adj Fk Holmes, Danl Brunson, Obediah Killcrease being part of land purchased from Wm Coursey which was part of 1000 acres originally granted unto Edwd Kann(?) and by him conveyed to Coursey. Wit H Coursey, Mary (x) Coursey, Anney (x) Holmes. /s/ Robert (x) Brooks, Anne (x) Brooks. Proven 30 Aug 1796 by William Coursey; John Blocker JP. Rec 30 Aug 1796.

p.194-195   Laurance Rambo of Orangeburg District to James Hargrove. 13 August 1796, £60 sterling 265 acres on Horns and Dry Cr adj John Cogbourn, Lewis Noble, James Cobb Junr, Fielding Reonolds, Littleberry Adams, Reedy Branch, William Wash. Wit William Wash, Wm Hargrove. /s/ Larrance Rambo. Relinquishment of dower by Mary Rambo wife of Larrence Rambo 30 Aug 1796; Arthur Simkins. Proven 30 Aug 1796 by William Hargrove; Rd Tutt. Rec 30th August 1796.

p.195-196   Thomas Warring(Warren) to Lot Etheredge. Deed 9 January 1796, £30 sterling 300 acres adj John Davis, Hester Kysell, Lot Etheredge, granted to Aron Harkins. Wit Henry Etheredge, Christopher (H) Cobborn. /s/ Thomas (M) Warring /s/ Bethther (x) Warring. Proven 4 Aug 1796 by Henry Etheredge; Russell Wilson JP. Rec 31 August 1796.

p.196-197   Peter Jones to Moses Jones. Deed, 2 September 1796, $100 200 acres on Mountain Cr of Turkey Cr, part of 364 acres originally granted to James Harrison and by sd Harrison transferred to sd Peter Jones and now by Peter Jones to Moses Jones; crossing Augusta Road. Wit Stephen Norris, Wm Burt. /s/ Peter Jones. Proved 2 Sept 1796 by Stephen Norris; R Tutt. Rec 2 Sept 1796.

p.197-198   James Monday to George Hagwood. Deed, 25 February 1796, £25 sterling, 100 acres surveyed by William Tolbert 8 November 1786 out of a survey of 800 granted unto Henry Ware Esqr of Wilks County, Georgia, 16 April 1773, by deed conveyed from Ware to sd Monday, on branches of Rocky Cr of Savannah R, by Campbellton Rd, adj Jeberts land. Wit William Burt, Stn Worres, Paul Williams. /s/ James Monday. Proven 5 March 1796 by Paul Williams; R Tutt. Rec 3d Sept 1796.

p.198-200   George Hagood to William Ogal. Deed, 7 March 1796, £40 sterling, 100 acres on Rockey Cr of Savannah R taken out of 800 acres held by James Monday. Wit Joab Blackwell, James Hagood, Ransom Banks. /s/ George Hagood, /s/ Elizabeth (x) Hagood. Proven 4 Aug 1796 by Joab Blackwell; Henry Key JP. Rec 3d Sept 1796.

p.200-202   Abraham Herndon to James May. L&R. 15 September 1794/16 Sept 1794, £200 sterling, 350 acres known as Hatchers Ponds, originally granted to Solomon Wood. Wit Reuben (x) Monday, Danl Ritchey. /s/ Abraham Herndon. Proved 14 October 1794 by Daniel Ritchey; Aquila Miles J P. Rec 12 Sept 1796.

p.203   James Richards to Walter Taylor. Bill/sale, 27 June 1796, $400, two Negroes Giney and Will. Wit Samuel Devall, Reed Dupree. /s/ Jas Richards. Proved same day by Reed Dupree; John Clarke J P. Rec 21 September 1796.

p.203-206   John Hammond to Daniel Masycke & Elias Smerdon. Mortgage 1 July 1790. Daniel Mazycke late Captain of the Second Redgment of South Carolina and Elias Smerdon of the City of Charleston, merchants, were securities of John Hammond in a bond to William Hasell Gibbes master/Court of chancery £1600 current money. Elizabeth Hammond wife of John Hammond was entitled as a legatee under will of Lancelot Bland to two equal thirds parts of Negroes and personal estate, Lewis Bond executor; John & Eliz Hammond instituted suit in Chancery to obtain account of proceeds of sd estate and his wife's share thereof; John Hammond and Lucy Bond agreed sd Negroes and other property of sd estate should in December next be divided by judges indifferently [certain other provisions omitted]; sell to Daniel Mazycke and Elias Smerdon all those two thirds parts of estate of Lancelot Bland, & following slaves Sylvia the Elder, Joe, Fortune, Amy, Sarah, Venus. Wit Stephen Ravenel. /s/ John Hammond. Proven 3 March 1796 by Stephen Ravenel Deputy Secretary/State of SC; Stephen Ravenel. Bremar J P. Rec in Mortgage Book HHH p 365-367 8 March 1792. Stephen Ravenel. Rec 24 sept 1796.

p.206-209   John Mock and wife Mary to Samuel Doolittle. L&R. 14 December 1792, £50 sterling, 171 acres where John and Mary now live, 115 of sd land being part of 300 acres taken up by John Stringer and conveyed from him to John Scott and from him to George Mock deceased and willed by George to his son John Mock; and 50 acres of sd land being part of 300 acres taken up by George Mock decd and willed to his son John Mock being so divided by Robert Lanq. Wit Drury Adams, Amasa Baugh, Thomas Miles. /s/ John Mock, /s/ Mary (x) Mock. Proven 25 Decr 1792 by Drury Adams; Aquila Miles J P. Rec 30 September 1796.

p.209-210   Zacharius Tharp, preacher, and Catharine his wife to Eleazar Tharp Senr, schoolmaster, Deed, 12 January 1796, 25 acres originally granted to Ward Taylor by Gov William Bull 9 Sept 1774. Wit Moses Taylor, William Prichard. /s/ Zacharias Tharp./s/ Catharine (x) Tharp. Proven 13 January 1796 by Moses Taylor; John Blocker. Rec 1 October 1796.

p.210-211   Daniel Rogers Senr to Frederick Williams, Deed, 3 October 1796, £150 sterling 200 acres on Big Saluda River adj David Kelly decd, Thomas Chappel surveyed 3 Febnruary 1769 and granted 25 Aug 1769 memorial entered Book 9 p 397. Wit Peter (+) Johnson, Sion Mitchell. Daniel (P) Rogers. Proven 3 October 1796 by Peter Johnson & Sion Mitchell; Russell Wilson J P. Rec 7th October 1796.

p.211-212   Daniel Rogers Senr to Frederick Williams, Bill/sale, 7 April 1796 £278 sterling of SC, negro man Tomb, negro woman Dinah, negro woman Bess, negro girl Dise, negro boy George [also livestock]. Wit Sion Mitchell, Peter (x) Johnson. Daniel (P) Rogers. Proven 3 October 1796 by Peter Johnson and Sion Mitchell; Russell Wilson J P. Rec 7th October 1796.

p.212-213   Daniel Rogers Senr to Frederick Williams, Bill/sale. £48 sterling, negro man Dick, [also household equipment]. Wit Sion Mitchell, Peter (x) Johnson. Daniel (P) Rogers. Proven 3 Oct 1796 by Sion Mitchell & Peter Johnson; Russell Wilson J P. Rec 7th October 1796.

p.213-214   Elizabeth Cheatam to her Children. Deed/gift for love, 16 June 1796, husband Peter Cheatam deceased, all my estate real and personal, likewise a part of a legacy I am to receive of my Father John Thurmond, deceased, estate hereafter, only reserving my right of dower as long as I may live. Wit Thos Jones, Chas Jones. /s/ Elizabeth (x) Cheatam. 7 June 1796 William Mealer agrees on marriage with Elizabeth Cheatam to deliver up within mentioned estate at any time that she thinks proper, /s/ William Mealer. Mealer agrees that of her next years crop he will give Elizabeth's son Gutrage Cheatam a good suit of cloaths. Wit Thos Jones, Charles Jones. /s/ William Mealer. Proven 5 October 1796 by Thomas Jones that he saw Elizabeth Cheatam and William Mealer sign before their marriage; Rd Tutt J P. Rec 7th Oct 1796.

p.214-215   Jesse Youngblood to William Youngblood, Deed, 31 July 1791, £60 sterling, 200 acres called Rocky Spring. Wit John Anderson, Robt Seagrove. /s/ Jesse (+) Youngblood. St Marys: sworn before me this 1st day of August 1791. Robt Seagrove J P. Title assigned unto James McMillan, 4 Dec 1792. Wit William Walker, John (F) Walker. /s/ William (x) Youngblood. Rec 10th Octr 1796.

p.215-217   William Youngblood of Camden County, Georgia, to James McMillan, Deed, 22 December 1792, £60 current SC money, 200 acres joining Peter Youngblood, Henry Youngblood, Samuel Holladay originally granted to John McIntosh by grant 13 May 1768 on the kings bounty. Wit B McMillan, James Walker. /s/ Willliam (x) Youngblood.   Proven 10 Octr 1796 by Bennett McMillan; Richard Tutt J P. Rec 10th Octr 1796.

p.218   Susanna Ray, widow, to Sally, James, & Mathew Ray. Deed/gift to her children, for love, 14 January 1796, two negroes Sue and Nepton. Wit James McMillan, Arthe(?), Mathew (m) McMillan. /s/ Susannah (x) Ray. Proven 10 Octr 1796 by James McMillan; Richard Tutt.   Rec 10 Oct 1796.

p.219   Elizabeth Tamer to Mathew Devore. Deed of gift, for love, 8 October 1796, two negroes Grace and Joe and all household goods. Wit John Devore, Jonathan Devore. /s/ Elizabeth (+) Tamer. Proven 10 Oct 1796 before Rd Tutt. Rec

15

10 Oct 1796.

p.219-220   Peter Morgan to William Key, planter, Bill/sale, 18 September 1792, £20 sterling of SC, one negro boy Ames. Wit Edmund Cox, Wm Brooks. /s/ Peter (+) Morgan. Proven 1 November 1792 by Edmond Cox; Thos Bacon J P. Rec 17 Dec 1792.

p.220-223   William Melton to John Hester, L&R, 6 February 1792/7 February 1792, £10 current money, 100 acres on Rockey Creek of South Edisto River where John Hester now lives, original grant 1 March 1790 by Gov Chas Pinckney to sd Wm Melton. Wit Edward Couch, James (J) Whitehead, Eleazr Tharp. /s/ William Melton, /s/ Hanah (x) Melton. Proved 3 May 1792 by Edwd Couch; Henry King J P.   Rec 14 Oct 1795.

p.223-224   Shadrack Henderson and Ellener his wife to James Sandefur, Deed, 23 February 1796, £50 current money, 200 acres where he now lives, part of two tracts; one of 200 acres granted to sd Shadrack Henderson 4 January 1785; the other is of 517 acres originally granted to sd Shadrack Henderson by grant 4 July 1785, sd lands of 200 acres situate on Jacks Branch waters of Cuffeetown & Beaver Dam creeks adj Robert Spence in the Long branch, on William Ramsey to James Hollowday, Nathaniel Henderson, Abraham Thornton, Spencers line. Wit Nathaniel Henderson Junr, James Holladay. /s/ Shadrack Henderson, /s/ Ellenor (x) Henderson.   Proven 3 April 1796 by James Holladay; Wm Robinson J P.   Rec 10 October 1796.

p.225-226   Abner Watson to Arthur Watson, Deed, 29 February 1796, £2, 200 acres on Ingin Creek on road from ridge to Ninety Six, original grant to Abner Watson adj Arthur Watson, James Edson, Benjamin Arrinton, James Daniel. Wit John Eidson, John Heron[Hearn], Brittain Partain. /s/ Abner Watson. Proven 16 August 1796 by John Hearn; Russell Wilson J P.   Rec 10 October 1796.

p.226-230   Catherine Shaw of New Windsor Town Ship, SC, to Mary Benson wife of William Benson, L&R, 21 January 1776/22 January 1776, £20 sterling money of Great Britain, 50 acres whereon sd Catharine Shaw now liveth, Originally granted unto sd Catherine Shaw. Wit Casper Nail, Leonard Meyer. /s/ Catherine (+) Shaw. Proven 25 November 1776 by Casper Nail; David Zubly J P.   Rec 10 October 1796.

p.230-233   Jessee Pitts to Charles Fooeshee, L&R, 8 April 1794/9 April 1794, £20 sterling, 100 acres on Saluda River part of 650 acres granted to sd Jesse Pitts 4 June 1792 by Gov Chas Pinckney, divided from Charles Fooeshee by a line. Wit Robt Newport, William Wheeler. /s/ Jesse Pitts. Proven 26 April 1794 by William Wheeler; Henry King J P.   Rec 10th October 1796.

p.233-235   Thomas Dalton to Benjamin May, Deed, 11 June 1793, £100 sterling, 150 acres on Savannah River being part of a grant to Richard Kennedy 1 December 1772. Wit Peggey (R) Reynold, Joseph Tucker. /s/ Thomas (D) Dalton.   Proven 1 September 1796 by Joseph Tucker; Henry Key J P.   Rec 10 October 1796.

p.235-236   Thomas Dalton to Benjamin May. Deed, 11 June 1793, £50 sterling, 100 acres on Savannah River, adj Christopher Cox, Charles Ashley, Kennedy, originally granted to William Brooks 3 July 1786. Wit Peggey Reynold, Joseph Tucker. /s/ Thomas (D) Dalton. Proven 1 Septr 1796 by Joseph Tucker; Henry Key J P. Rec 10th October 1796.

p.236-239   William Pardue to Richard Kirkland, L&R, 23 February 1795/24 Feby 1795, £30, 170 acres part of a tract of 420 acres originally granted to Arthur Watson, the NW end of land on Beach Creek and Dry Creek of Mine Creek of Little Saluda River on the road from the Ridge to Augusta adj Willis Murphey Watson and Jacob Watson, and Rolan Williams. Wit Willis Fredrick, Jane (x) Fredrick. /s/ William Pardue. Proven 10 October 1796 by Willis Fredrick; Van Swearingen J P. Rec 10th Octr 1796.

p.240-242   James Minge Burton of North Carolina to Jacob Pope, L&R, 5 January 1791/5 January 1791, £100, land granted to Peter Whitten 1200 acres except a part granted to him before this date, and a part to Hezekiah Gentry joining Nathan Melton, Robert Christie, Jacob Pope, part of 1200 acres granted to Peter Whitten, from him to William Cobb from him to James Minge Burton, original grant is in hands of James Hunt of Columbia SC. Wit Elijah Pope, Nancy (x) Dockins. /s/ James M Burton. Proven 9 April 1791 by Elijah Pope; James Spann J P.   Rec 10th October 1796.

p.242-246   Jessee Jernegan, yeoman, to Asa Jernegan. L&R. 14 May 1791/13 May 1791, £10 sterling, 75 acres on Red bank Creek of Saluda River part of 400 acres originally granted to Thomas Deloach Senr by Lt Gov Wm Bull 31 Aug 1774, 200 acres thereof conveyed to sd Jesse Jernegan by sd Thos Deloach 7 & 8 March 1777, adj Jesse Jernegan, Josiah Thomas. Wit Henry King, Paul C Abney. /s/ Jesse (H) Jernegan. Proven 16 Novr 1793 by Paul C Abney; Henry King J P.   Rec 10 Oct 1796.

p.247-249   Anjelicha Jernegan, widow of Jessee Jernegan, and James Hart Elizabeth his wife, Esau Parnell and Anjelicha his wife, Kezia Jernegen heirs & Heiress at law of sd deceased of the one part to William Burditt.   Deed 8 April 1795, £6.12 sterling, 75 acres on Red Bank Cr of Little Saluda River, part of 400 acres originally granted to Thomas Deloach 31 August 1774 by Lt Gov Wm Bull and 200 acres of sd tract conveyed to Jesse Jernegan by Thos Deloach 7 & 8 March 1777. Adj Jesse Hart, John Smedley, mouth/Harts branch, old waggon ford to Asa Jernegan. Wit Henry King, Joel Brown, Averellah (A) King. /s/ Anjelicha (x) Jernegen, James J Hart, Elizabeth (x) Hart, Esau (E) Parnell, Anjelicha (x) Parnell, Kezia (x) Jernegen. Proved 5 March 1796 by Henry King; Wm Daniel J P.   Rec 10th Octr 1796.

p.249-250   John McDaniel[MacDaniel] & Simon Beck to John Spann late of North Carolina. Bond £100 SC money, obligation if John MacDaniel or Simon Beck on 1 Jan next deliver unto John Spann a conveyance in fee simple to 100 acres pattented by Moses Powell joining land where sd Spann now lives known as Patridges old field and was taken up by Snider, then the above obligation to be void. Wit William McDaniel, Henry Spann. /s/ John McDaniel, Simon (X) Beck.   Proven 10 Octr 1796 by Henry Spann; Rd Tutt.   Rec 10 Octr 1796.

p.250-252   Daniel Gill and wife Susannah Gill of Abbeville County to Charles Old. Deed, for $200, 200 acres near the mouth of Stephens Creek adjoining lands of Reuben Frazier, Joseph Ferguson, William Covington, Robert Gardner and vacant land. Wit Robert Green, William Baskin. /s/ Daniel Gill, /s/ Susannah (x) Gill. Relinquishment of Dower by Susannah Gill wife of within named Daniel Gill, 3 Octr 1796; Andrew Hamilton J P.   Proven 6 April 1796 by Robert Green; Sam Linton J P. Recorded 10th Octr 1796.

p.252-253   William Purselly to Luke Gardner, Deed, 8 September 1796, £25 sterling, 45 acres on branch of Dry Creek adj George Horns, David Besswell, John Purselly, Henry Ellenberger. Witness Wm Watson Senr, Menoah (W) Withrington. /s/ William (M) Pursley. Relinquishment of Mary (x) Pursley wife of William Pursley; 10 October 1796; Joseph Hightower J P. Proven 10 Octr 1796 by William Watson; Aquila Miles J P. Rec 10th October 1796.

p.253-257   Thomas Deloach, planter, to Jesse Jernegin[Janachan], planter, L&R. 7 March 1777/8 March 1777, £200 money/province, 200 acres on Red bank creek, adj James Dison, Saml Everedges. Original grant 31 August 1774 by Lt Gov Wm Bull to Thomas Deloach 400 acres on Red bank Creek adj Saml Everedge. Wit John Collen [Cotten?] Thomas (x) Deloach Junr, Charity Collen[Cotten?]. /s/ Thos Deloach. Proved 2 Sept 1765 by Thos Deloach Jr; Solomon Pope JP. Rec 10 Oct 1796.

p.257-260   John Herndon to John Pursley. L&R, 9 January 1790/9 Jany 1790 £100 sterling, 174 acres late property of Moses Kirkland on Chavers Creek north side of Dry Creek adj Richard Jones, Mathew Devour, Christian Limbacker when plantation was sold at publick auction by John Berwick, Thomas Warring and John Ewing Colhoun commissioner of forfeited estates to sd John Herndon 8 & 9 July 1783. Wit Danl Ritchey, Jacob Clackler. /s/ John Herndon. Receipt for £100 sterling. Wit Danl Ritchy, John Hancock. Relinquishment of dower by Ruth (x) Herndon wife of John Herndon, 10 October 1796; Joseph Hightower JP. Proved 4 Oct 1790 by Daniel Ritchey; Aquila Miles J P. Rec 10th October 1796.

p.261-164   John Clackler[Glickler] to John Pursell. L&R, 2 October 1791/3 October 1791, £100 sterling my full part of my Fathers estate 20 acres Dry Creek by virtue of my being a son & heir at law to estate of late John Glickler decd and by virtue of an agreement made between sd John Glackler and sd John Pursley 7 April 1790 recorded Bk F p 152-153 & examined by Richard Tutt clerk of Edgefield County. Wit Wm Fudge, Wm Watson Senr. /s/ John (C) Clackler Junr. Proven 10 October 1796 by William Watson; Aquila Miles J P. Rec 10th Octr 1790.

p.264-267   John Herndon to John Clackler Senr, L&R, 14 January 1788/15 Jany 1788, £75 sterling, 150 acres on Dry Creek of Savannah River adj John Herndons land adj Mathew Devon, Limbacker. Wit Wm Watson, Anthony Butler. /s/ John Herndon. Relinquishment of dower by Ruth (I) Herndon, 10 October 1796; Joseph Hightower JP. Proven 10 October 1796 by William Watson; Rd Tutt J P. Rec 10 Oct 1796.

p.267-269   Edward Couch to John Spann. Deed, 16 April 1796, £50 150 acres part of grant to sd Couch 5 August 1793, Horse Creek, Loseway Branch, plantation where Tomerlin formerly lived on west side of Caraway Branch. Wit John Permenter, Jacob (D) Dove, John Kent. /s/ Edward Couch. Relinquishment of dower by Absela Couch widow of within named Edward Couch decd, 10 October 1796; Joseph Hightower. Proven 10 Octr 1796 by John Kent; Rd Tutt. Rec 10 Oct 1796.

p.269-270   William Mayson & Charles Colcock to William Wimberley. Deed 14 March 1796, $100 for 100 acres on Peters Creek of Saludy River adj Bartley Martin. Wit: Wm Butler, E Ramsay. /s/ Chas J Colcock. Proven 13th March 1796 by Genl Wm Butler; John Hunter J P. Rec 10th October 1796.

p.270   John Lewis to Robert & John Boyd. Bond 1000 guineas.   17 March
1791, condition John Lewis pay sd Boyds 500 acres adj Samuel Scott, Hugh Middleton
Esqr, Savannah River, payment to be made on or before 25 Decr next. Wit Richard
White, Edward Prince, John Paulett. /s/ Jno Lewis. Proven 10 Oct 1796 by Edward
Prince; Henry Key J P.   Rec 10th Act 1796.

p.271-273   Arthur Watson & Robert Stark Exrs of Michael Watson decd to Jacob
Odum[Odam]. L&R. 1 February 1788/2 Feb 1788. £41, 125 acres being the lower half
of 250 acres originally granted to William Lamar, conveyed by Wm Lamar to William
Watson decd father to afsd Michael Watson, adj Moses Kirkland, John Anderson, Wm
Watson. Wit Saml Sotcher, Henry King. /s/ Arthur (A) Watson, /s/ Robt Stark.
Proven 5 March 1792 by Samuel Sotcher; William Anderson.   Rec 10 Octr 1796.

p.274-276   David Johnson to Elisha Brooks guardian to Allen Cox's heirs.
Mortgage. Newberry County, 2 January 1796, £40 sterling 150 acres on Saluda River
formerly granted to Martha Ramsay and by heirship to Samuel Ramsey, by him conveyed
to sd David Johnson the same land whereon sd David Johnson now lives. Wit James
Dyson, Wm Allen. /s/ David Johnson. Proven 2 May 1796 by William Allen; William
Anderson. Rec 10th Actr 1796.

p.276-279   Abraham Kraker & Maria Kraker of the Congarees in Orangeburgh
District, planter, to Darling Glover. L&R. 24 January 1796/25 January 1796, £50
sterling current money of SC, 100 acres near Cuffee Town certified 25 March 1765 by
John Fairchild D S, new plat made 17 Nov 1792 by David Cunningham D S. Wit Mickel
Kagler, William (x) Glover, William Glover. /s/ Abraham Kraker /s/ Maria Kraker.
Proven 30 July 1796 by William Glover; Jas Hanson J P.   Rec 10th October 1796.

p.279-280   Sarah Lott to William Holston, Bill/sale, 25 April 1796, £80 sterling, negroe girl named Peg. Wit Rolan Williams, John Fedrick, Moses Holstun. /s/
Sarah (x) Lott. Proven 14 May 1796 by Moses Holstun; Wm Daniel JP. Rec 10 Oct 1796.

p.280-283   William Moseley of Winton County to Daniel Devore. L&R. 7 April
1796/8 April 1796, £50 sterling, 69 acres between two Dry Creeks part of 667 acres
originally granted to William Mosley 11 May 1785 adj Wm Glover, Henry Allenburgh,
George Mosley, John Akridge, Robert Glover. Wit Wm Watson Senr, Absalom Mosley.
/s/ William (M) Mosley Senr. Proven 10 October 1790 by William Watson; Aquila
Miles J P. Recorded 10th Octr 1796.

p.283-284   Darling Glover and wife Mary to Alexander Burnett. Deed, £50
sterling, 90 acres originally granted to Abraham Kraker 3 Decr 1794, convaid from
sd Kraker to Darling Glover 5 January 1796 lying on Little Horse Pen Creek water of
Cuffeytown Cr of Savaner River adj Henry Audulph, David Rush. Wit James Harrison,
William Glover. /s/ Darlin (x) Glover, /s/ Mary (x) Glover. Proven 7 Oct 1796 by
William Glover; Jas Harrison J P.   Rec 10th October 1796.

p.285-286   Caul Collins and wife Elizabeth Collins to William Walch. Deed, 20
September 1796, $100, 185 acres on Crooked Run of Turkey Creek, originally granted
to Caul Collins by Gov Wm Moultrie 21 May [no year]. /s/ Caul Collins, /s/ Elizabeth (I) Collins. Receipt witnessed by William Prichard, James Coursey. Proven 10
October 1796 by James Coursey; Van Swearingen J P.   Rec 10th Octr 1796.

p.286-287   Cornelius Ravity to Wiatt Morris. Deed, 2 June 1796, £16, 182 acres adj John Wideman, William Rowan, Moses Braford, Rockey Creek, surveyed for Cornelius Ravity 25 August 1793 by Robert Carson. Wit Archd Thomson, James Abel. /s/ Cornelius (x) Ravity. Proven 7 October 1796 by James Abel; Jas Harrison J P. Rec 10 Octr 1796.

p.287-288   Cornelius Ravity to James Abel. Deed, 2 June 1796, £20, 120 acres adj Rocky Creek, Moses Brawford surveyed for Cornelius Ravity by Robert Carson 26 August 1793. Wit Archd Thomson, Wiatt (x) Morris. Cornelius (V) Ravity. Proven 7 Oct 1796 by Wiatt Morris; Jas Harrison J P.   Rec 10th October 1796.

p.289-292   Uriah Wicker of Newberry County to Henry Glover. L&R, 15 February 1793/15 Feb 1793, £46.15 current money, adjoining plantations on a small branch of Cuffeytown Creek, grants from Gov Wm Bull, one of 100 acres on branch of Cuffey town Creek dated 14 August 1770 to John Murphey, the other 25 May 1774 to Ursula Myre 100 acres on the kings bounty. Wit Jas McMillan, Wm Glover. /s/ Uriah Wicker. Proved 7 Oct 1796 by William Glover; Jas Harrison J P.   Rec 10th Octr 1796.

p.292-293   Edward Couch to John Kent. Deed, 10 October 1796, £50, 150 acres being part of a grant to sd Couch 5 August 1793, on Horse Creek. Wit J Spann, Asceila (X) Permenter. /s/ Edward Couch. Renunciation of dower by Asselia Couch widow of within named Edward Couch 10 Oct 1796; Joseph Hightower, /s/ Asselia Couch.   Proven 10 Oct 1796 by John Spann; Richard Tutt.   Rec 10 Octr 1796.

p.294-295   William Pursell to Henry Allenburger. Deed, 10 October 1796, £50 sterling 82 acres Dry Creek, Little Dry Creek. Wit Wm Watson Senr, Luke (x) Gardner. /s/ William (M) Pursley. Renunciation of dower 10 Oct 1796 by Mary Pursley wife of within named William Pursell; Joseph Hightower; /s/ Mary (x) Pursley. Proven 10 Oct 1796 by Wm Watson; Aquila Miles J P. Rec 10 Oct 1796.

p.295-300   John Gray of New Windsor Township in Granville County SC, school master, to Henry Jones of Parish of Saint George, province of Georgia. L&R, 4 April 1774/5 April 1774, £100 sterling of Georgia, grant dated 12 August 1737 by Lt Gov Thomas Broughton unto Martha McGillvary 400 acress in New Windsor Twp at Savannah Town about two miles from his Majesties Garrison fort Moore, bounding on Savannah River, transferred to John Baxter 10 March 1760; sd John Baxter with Ann his wife of Saint Andrews Parish transferred same unto Peter Turkeynetz 19 March 1763, sd Peter Turkeynetz and wife Christian transferred 390 acres of sd tract unto Fredrick Hartley 10 July 1766 sd Fredrick Hartley and wife Elizabeth transferred sd 390 acres unto Hieronymus Zinn by name Cronimus Zinn; sd Hieronymus to John Gray. Wit Robert Phillips, Jacob Wise, Daniel Jones. /s/ Jno Gray. Personally appeared James McManny, sworn, says he was well acquainted with within named John Gray in his life time and of his knowledge it is the handwriting of sd John Gray that is subscribed to within deed, sworn 21 Novr 1795; John Clarke.   Rec 10 Octr 1796.

p.300-301   Henry Jones Senr to daughters Sarah & Mary Jones. Deed of gift for love & affection, 7 December 1795, 390 acres in Edgefield butting on Savannah River originally granted Martha McGillvry 12 Aug 1737. Witness Henry Jones Junr, Joseph Booth, Thomas Jones. /s/ Henry Jones Senr. On 21 March 1796 appeared Henry Jones Junr who swears he did see Henry Jones Senr sign within deed, and also saw Joseph

Booth and Thomas Jones subscribe their names as witnesses thereto; John Clarke J P. Rec 10th October 1796.

p.301-302   Batte Jones & James Jones of Georgia to Jonathan Meyer. Deed, 12 December 1795, £200 current money of So Carolina, 390 acres on Savannah River originally granted to Martha McGillvery. Wit Thos Jones, Henry Jones J. /s/ Batt Jones, James Jones. On 21 March 1796 Henry Jones Junr of Georgia swears he did see within named Batt Jones and James Jones sign within deed of conveyance with Thomas Jones as witnesses thereto sworn; John Clarke J P.   Rec 10 Oct 1796.

p.302-303   William Mayson of Abbeville County to Barrot Travis of Edgefield county. Deed, 6 October 1796, £14.18, 149 acres unto sd Barrot Traverse. Wit M Perryman, Patk Kays. /s/ W Mayson.   [plat: 149 acres Barrot Traverse land, Ogdon Cockrith, John Mobley. Surveyed 6 Oct 1796 by W Mayson D.S.] Proven 10th Oct 1796 by Mumford Perryman; Richard Tutt J P.   Rec 10th Octr 1796.

p.303-304   John Currie and wife Kezia to John Hardy. Deed, 22 Sept 1795, £14 sterling, 504 acres between Shaws Creek and South Edisto adj land surveyed for John Hardy, other sides vacant. Wit Cader Currie, George Storup[?]. /s/ John (x) Currie. Proven 2 January 1796 by George Storup; Joseph Hightower J P.   Rec 10 Oct 1796.

p.304-305   William Wimberley to James Smith. Deed, 21 March 1796, £100, 100 acres on Peters Creek of Saluda River that I bought of Chas J Colcock adj Bartley Martin. Wit J Spann, Henry Spann, Turner Smith. /s/ William Wimberley. Renunciation of dower by Elizabeth Wimberley wife of William Wimberley, 1 August 1796; Arthur Simkins J P. /s/ Elizabeth (x) Wimberley. Proven 10th Oct 1796 by John Spann; Richard Tutt J P.   Recorded 10th Octr 1796.

p.305-307   Daniel Nail decd Estate Divided. Daniel Nail of Bush Island in New Windsor, deceased, by will directed his estate be divided between sons John, Gasper and Daniel and daughters Ann and Elizabeth. John being also dead, his estate was administered by George Miller who married Keziah his widow; his daughter Ann married and is now wife of Nathaniel Howell; Elizabeth is now wife of John Savage. Amicable division was made 20 March 1796. Wit Jona Meyer, Geo Bender, Jacob Zinn, William Tobler. /s/ Geo Miller admr Jno Nail. /s/ Casper Nail. /s/ Daniel Nail. /s/ Nathl Howell for self & wife. /s/ John Savage for self & wife. Schedule: Negroes Delia, Betty, Billy to estate of John Nail. Cola, Cloe, Cull to Gasper Nail. Sabonn, Peter, York to Daniel Nail. Tom, Rachel to Nathl Howell. Cassander, Harry, Isaac, Agg to John Savage. The rest of the personal estate was at same time satisfactorily divided. Proven by Jona Meyer swears he saw George Miller, Casper Nail, Daniel Nail, Nathaniel Howell for self & wife, & John Savage for self and wife sign within instrument, 10 October 1796.   Rec 10 Octr 1796.

p.307-308   Arthur Watson to Richmond Watson. Deed 8 October 1796, £3, 30 acres on Clouds Creek, part of 500 acres formerly granted unto Robert Pringle Esqr and by heirship fell to Julius Pringle and conveyed from him to Arthur Watson and now by sd Arthur Watson to Richman Watson, land adj Arthur Rice Watson. Wit Arthur Rice Watson, John Edson, John Hearn. /s/ Arthur (A) Watson. Proven by John Edson, 10 October 1796; Rd Tutt.   Rec 10 Octr 1796.

p.308-313   Moses Kirkland Esqr, planter, to Richard Williams.   L&R, 21 March
1775/22 March 1775, £600 lawful current money of SC, 600 acres part of tract of 802
acres in Granville County granted 19 November 1772 by Gov Chas Grevill Montague unto William Mazyck bounded on James Thompson, Wm Clark, Benjamin Bell, Moses Clark,
Nilus Stephens, Benjamin Garrett, Joel Threwits, Moses Kirkland Esqr, Benjn Mazyck,
James Miller, Jacob Messer Smith; Wm Mazyck sold unto Moses Kirkland 802 acres on
Rockey Creek branch of Stephens Creek. Wit Will Martin, John (O) Nibblett, Jeffer-
son Williams. /s/ Moses Kirkland. Proven 30 December 1775 by Jefferson Williams;
Arthur Simkins J P.   Certification dated 21 March 1775 by Moses Kirkland D S of
survey laid out to Richard Williams of 600 acres originally granted to William
Mazyck on forks of roads from Ridge to Longcane, other from Augusta to Saluda.
[Plat shows 600 acres adj land of James Scott, Moses Kirkland, William Clark, Ben-
jamin Bell, John Thomas and crossroads]. Proven 30 December 1775 by Jefferson
Williams; Arthur Simkins J P.   Rec 18 Octr 1796.

p.313-216   Arthur Watson & Robert Stark exors of will of Michael Watson decd
to Richmond Watson. L&R, 1 February 1788/2 February 1788, £17 lawful money, 150
acres in Colleton County near Clouds Creek adj William Watson, Edward Couch, John
Watson. Wit: Samuel Sotcher, Henry King. /s/ Arthur (A) Watson. /s/ Robert Stark.
Proven 10 Oct 1796 by Henry King; Rd Tutt.   Rec 10 Octr 1796.

p.316-317   Arthur Watson to John Edson. Deed 8 October 1796, £11.3.6 paid by
John Eidson for 100 acres part of 500 acres granted to Robert Pringle and conveyed
by John Julius Pringle to Arthur Watson, joining lands of James Perry, Arthur Rice
Watson, Richmond Watson, and John Edson. Wit Arthur Rice Watson, Richmond Watson,
John Hearn. /s/ Arthur (A) Watson. Proven 10 Oct 1796 by Richmond Watson; Rd Tutt.
Rec 10th Octr 1796.

p.317-319   Joseph Robertson and wife Martha to George Bussey. Deed, 20
October 1795, £25 sterling land originally granted to Sammuel Scott and part of a
tract granted to Joseph Robertson including 180 acres on Stevens Creek adj Francis
Meh[?] Hills[?], James Scott, Sammuel Scott, road by Capt Paces. Wit Demcy Bussey,
George Bussey Senr. /s/ Joseph Robertson. Proven 10 Oct 1796 by Demcy Bussey;
Aquila Miles J P.   Rec 10th October 1796.

p.319-320   George Bussey and wife to his son Joshua Bussey. Deed, 4 October
1796, for love and affection as also five shillings paid by Joshua Bussey, gives
163 acres part of tract originally granted to James Russell on Stevens and Gunels
Creeks, adj Mr Shadowick. Wit George Bussey Jr, Demcy Bussey. /s/ George Bussey,
Sebba (x) Bussey. Proven 6 Oct 1796 by George Bussey who saw George Bussey Senr
and Febsy Bussey his wife sign within instrument to Joshua Bussey; Hugh Middleton
J P.   Rec 10th Octr 1796.

p.320-322   Simon Beck to John Spann. Deed, 27 February 1796, £20 for 76
acres south of Saluda River on head branches of Horse Creek waters of South Edisto
River adj James Gunnels, Robert Stark, Prescot Bush at time of original survey date
2 September 1793, Simon Becks corner to James Tomlins corner. Wit Turner Smith,
Ezekiel Wimberley. /s/ Simon (X) Beck. Renunciation of dower 10 Oct 1796 by
Elender Beck wife of Simon Beck before Judge Joseph Hightower /s/ Elender (C)
Beck. Proved 10 Oct 1796 by Turner Smith; Richard Tutt.   Rec 10 Oct 1796.

p.322-323   John Gormon Senr to Claborn Gormon. 18 December 1795, Bond, £200 sterling to be paid to Claborn Gormon, condition to make title to 200 acres granted to sd John Gormon by Gov Wm Moultrie 5 Sept 1785. Wit Wm Spragins, Andrew Brown. /s/ John (I) Gormon. Proven 10 Oct 1796 by William Spragins; Nathl Abney. Rec 10 Oct 1796.

p.323-324   Jesse Pitts to Reps Osborn, Deed, 5 April 1796, $214, 120 acres on Little Saludy River granted to Robert Laws and adjoining Henry Kings land, also eighty adjoining acres adj Benjamin Wages part of 650 acres granted to sd Jesse Pitts. Wit Henry King, Thomas Pitts, David Osborn. /s/ Jesse Pitts. Proven 7 Oct 1796 by Henry King; Wm Daniel J P. Rec 10th Octr 1796.

p.324-325   Jesse Pitts and wife Sarah and Francis Posey and wife Amelia to Benj Wages. Deed, 16 Feb 1796. £40 sterling, 100 acres on Little Saludy R, part of 250 acres originally granted to sd Jesse Pitts 4 June 1792 by Gov Chas Pinckney, adj Brown. Wit Henry King, Joel Brown. /s/ Jesse Pitts. /s/ Sarah (+) Pitts. /s/ Francis (x) Posey, /s/ Amelia (x) Posey. Proven 8th Octr 1796 by Henry King; Wm Daniel J P. Rec 10th Octr 1796.

p.325-329   Andrew Robertson to Sir Patk Houston, Bart. Deed. 3 April 1780/4 April 1780, £10,000 current money of SC, 300 acres in Ninety Six district on the Savannah River originally granted 3 March 1775 by Lt gov William Bull unto Andrew Robertson, adj James Jackson and John Jennings. Wit James Gordon, Achilles Tandy. /s/ Andw Robertson. Proven 4 April 1780 by James Gordon; Malcom Brown JP. Rec 10 Oct 1796.

p.329-330   John Rustin[Ruston] & wife to James Hitson. Deed, 26 May 1796, £60 sterling, 350 acres adj John Gillon and Dry Creek. Wit Samuel Humphreys, Phillip Ikner. /s/ John (+) Rustin. /s/ Levicy (x) Rustin. Proven 22 July 1796 by Phillip Ikner; Russell Wilson J P. Rec 10th Octr 1796.

p.330-332   Richmond Watson to John Edson[Eidson]. L&R, 4 February 1790/3 Feby 1790, £8.10 lawful money of SC, 75 acres part of 150 acres originally granted to Michael Watson on a branch of Clouds Creek of Saludy River adj Mary Watson, sd Richmond Watson, Pringle, Couche, and Jacob Odam. Wit John Vardell, Abner Watson, Samuel Sotcher. /s/ Richmond Watson. Proven 10 Oct 1796 by John Vardell; Rd Tutt. Rec 10 Oct 1796.

p.333-334   Jeremiah Hatcher to Lacon and John Elder Ryan. Sheriffs titles. 7 February 1795. At suit of Garret & Holleman against Benjamin Ryan Junr, execution issued for Sheriff to sell land at public auction. Struck off to Lacon Ryan and John Elder Ryan, 603 acres on Horns Creek of Savannah River: 200 acres granted Lacon Ryan Decd except 125 acres conveyed to Benjamin Ryan Sr, 123 acres purchased by sd Lacon Ryan decd from Commrs of Forfeited Estates except 45 acres conveyed by L&R to Benjamin Darby and 250 acres originally granted to David Lockhart and John Vernon making 603 acres. Wit David Glover, Samp Butler. /s/ J Hatcher S E C. Proven 11 Octr 1796 by Sampson Butler; Richard Tutt. Rec 11th Octr 1796.

p.334-338   Lucy Pardue et al to Joseph Hightower. Deed of Settlement, 23 July 1796 between Lucy Perdue relict & widow of decd Fielder Perdue of Edgefield, Benja-

23

min Exum, planter, Joseph Hightower, whereas there is a marriage by Gods permission intended shortly to be had between sd Lucy Perdue and sd Benjamin Exum, and whereas Lucy is possessed of a Freehold estate being her right of Dower as widow and a male slave Caesar, bay more & colt, three beds and household furniture, Lucy grants her land known as Liberty Hill 350 acres and also 250 acres near Cuffee Town, also land in Campbellton at present occupied by Thomas Dalton; in consideration of $5 paid to sd Lucy Perdue by Joseph Hightower, all made over in trust to sd Joseph Hightower for the benefit and use of sd Lucy Perdue, after marriage sd Benjamin Exum and Lucy his wife to receive the rents and profitsr. Wit Gidn Pardue, Leroy Pardue, Martha Pardue. /s/ Lucy Pardue. /s/ B Exum. /s/ Joseph Hightower. Proven 11 October 1796 by Gideon Pardue; Henry Key J P. Rec 11 Oct 1796.

p.338-340   Mary Fike to John Landrum. Deed, 8 September 1796, £40 sterling, 123 acres that Howel Sellers now liveth on being part of two surveys, 9 acres part of land granted to Thomas McGinnes and conveyed by McGinnes to Thomas Sellers which is the tract sd Sellers now liveth on, both sides of Log Creek, conveyed by Thomas Sellers to his son Howel Sellers, and 114 of above mentioned 123 acres is part of a tract containing 193 acres granted to above mentioned Thomas Sellers lying south of Log Creek, the 114 acres is all of the last mentioned survey that lyeth on NW side of Horse Pen Branch. Wit James Brown, Lewis Youngblood. /s/ Mary (x) Fike. Proven 11 Oct 1796 by Lewis Youngblood; John Blocker J P.   Rec 11 Octr 1796.

p.340   Joseph Hightower attorney in fact for Andrew Pickens & Co to Lucy Pardue. B/Sale, $300, one negro man Cezar. Wit Gidn Pardue, LeRoye Pardue. /s/ Joseph Hightower attorney in fact for Andrew Pickens & Co. Proven 11 October 1796 by Gideon Pardue; Henry Key J P.   Rec 11 Octr 1796.

p.341   Lucy Pardue to Joseph Hightower. Bill/sale, 23 July 1796, $400, negro man Cezar, bay mare & her colt, 3 beds as trustee to a marriage settlement entered into by myself and Benjamin Exum. Gidn Pardue, LeRoye Pardue. /s/ Lucy Pardue. Proven 11 Octr 1796 by Gideon Pardue; Henry Key J P.   Rec 11 Oct 1796.

p.342-343   Rowlan Williams Senr to Bowling[Bowlen] Dees Senr. Deed.   23 November 1795, £100 starling money of SC, 300 acres granted 1 January 1787 by Gov Wm Moultrie, being part of 762 acres on Dry fork of Mine Creek and Edisto on both sides of Old Ridge Road adj Smith, Gamilion, Bobby Bush, Landrom, James Harring including the plantation where Joel Dees lives. Wit Edward Couch, Joel (+) Dees, Asceilea Couch. /s/ Rolan Williams. Proven 7 October 1796 by Asceliea Couch; Van Swearingen J P.   Rec 11 Oct 1796.

p.343-345   Ezekiel Walker to Joseph Walker. Deed, 1 January 1796, £50 Starling, 150 acres N side Edistoe River granted to Ezekiel Walker by Gov Wm Moultrie 1793 adj James Jonakin, Shadrick Dees, Benjamin Clark confiscated land. Wit Nathan Godwin, Francis Walker. /s/ Ezekiel (x) Walker. Proven 11 Octr 1796 by Francis Walker; Rd Tutt J P. Rec 11 Octr 1796.

p.345-346   Alex Edmunds to Aquila Miles Esqr. Deed, 11 October 1796, £50, 100 acres on Horns Creek adj Robert Lang, John Martin, Penny Howlet, mouth of Dry Creek. Wit John Rainsford, John (x) Cockborn. /s/ Alexander Edmunds. Proven 11 Octr 1796 by John Rainsford; John Blocker J P. Rec 11th Octr 1796.

p.341-342   Abraham Herndon to William Reed. Deed, 13 Sept 1796. £100 money of SC 100 acres on main road from Augusta to the Ridge known by as ohowills[?] granted to Fielding Reonolds 3 April 1786; also 147 acres on the waggon road from the pine woods house to Augusta granted unto John Ryan 1 January 1787. Wit Daniel Ritchy, William Mallite. /s/ A Herndon. Relinquishment of dower by Nancy Herndon wife of Abraham Herndon. /s/ Nancy (x) Herndon. /s/ Joseph Hightower J P. Proven 11 Oct 1796 by Daniel Ritchy; John Blocker J P. Rec. 11 October 1796.

p.342   Mary Stott wife of Abdel Stott to Jno Landrum. Renunciation of dower, 11 October 1796, deed dated 5 & 6 May 1795, 988 acres. /s/ Mary (x) Stott. /s/ Joseph Hightower J P. Rec 11 Octr 1796.

p.342-350   James Wallace[Wallis], blacksmith, to Tolaver[Tolliver] Cox, planter. Deed, 4 November 1795, £20 starling, 50 acres, plat by Ephraim Mitchell Dep Suvr, part of 100 acres granted unto Andrew Ross by Gov Wm Moultrie at Charleston 3 April 1786. Wit William Cox. /s/ James (x) Wallas. Receipt witnessed by James Pickett./s/ James (x) Wallas. Proven 7 May 1796 by James Picket, that he was present and saw James Wallas subscribe his mark; Henry Key J P. Rec 11 Oct 1796.

p.350-351   James Baker, planter, to William Whitlock, planter. Mortgage, 13 September 1796, £18 sterling with legal interest thereon before 1 Decr 1797, on negro Abba. /s/ Robert Robinson, Saml Crafton. /s/ Jas Baker. Receipt. Proven 11 Oct 1796 by Saml Crafton; Rd Tutt J P. Rec 11th Octr 1796.

p.352-353   Samuel Messer to William Fowler. Deed 13 June 1794, £35 starling, 232 acres originally granted by Gov Chas Pinckney 7 Feb 1791 to Samuel Messer on Mores Creek of Saludy River on prong of Clouds Creek adj Jessey Harbin, Thomas Warren, Richard Howard, examined by Peter Bremar pro secretary. Wit Adam Efurt, Enoch Fowler, Lewis Dashazo. /s/ Saml Messer. Proven 5 July 1794 by Adam Efurt; Russell Wilson J P. Rec 11th Octr 1796.

p.354   Thomas Mann to James Fowler. Deed, 7 Oct 1796, $150, 150 acres on Clouds Creek adjoining Jno Watts Mann, Crees pond, granted to Jno Watts Mann 13 August 1774. Wit Enoch Fowler, Adam Efert. /s/ Thomas Mann. Proven 7 Oct 1796 by Enoch Fowler; Elkanah Sawyer J P. Rec 11 Octr 1796.

p.355   Thomas Warren to Thomas Mann. Deed, 4 October 1796, $150, 150 acres on Clouds Creek adj Jno Watts Mann, Crees pond, originally granted to John Watts Mann 13 August 1774. Wit Enoch Fowler, William (F) Fowler. /s/ Thomas (x) Warren. Proven 7 Oct 1796 by Enoch Fowler; Elkanah Sawyer. Rec 11 Octr 1796.

p.356-358   Daniel Laremon and wife Mary to Adam Elfert of Fairfield County. Agreement, 14 January 1793, £80 SC money, 50 acres Frazers Creek of Little Saludy; also 50 acres SW of the first 50 acres; also 50 acres S of sd 50 acres, adj John Watts Man, James McCartney, Simeon Tolevine, William Warren; wit Jno P Bond, Elisha Buzbee, Elijah Martin. /s/ Daniel Laremon. /s/ Mary (x) Laremon. Receipt. Proven 10 August 1793 by Elijah Martin Juner; Thos Fairchild J P. Rec 11th Octr 1796.

p.358-359   Thos Mann to Henry Evans. Deed, 6 April 1796, $100, 100 acres taken off 250 acres granted to John Watts Mann 1 March 1775, Saludy River adj Wm

25

Johnston, John Watts Mann at original survey; now adj Widow Johnston; Thos Mann eldest son and heir of John Wats Man. Wit Abigail (A) Bond, Watts Mann. /s/ Thomas (T) Mann. Proven 6 April 1796 by Watts Mann; Jno P Bond, J P. Rec 11 Oct 1796.

p.359-360   Thomas Phillips to Micajah Phillips. 26 September 1796. Be it remembered that some time in 1789 or 1790 I received a deed of gift from my father Micajah Phillips for 3 negroes, 150 acres and sundry articles which stands recorded in Clerks office; I now relinquish my right to sd deed/gift unto my father Micajah Phillips for value recd of him. Wit Jno Martin, E D Martin. /s/ Thos Phillips. Proven 11 Octr 1796 by Thomas Phillips; Richard Tutt.   Rec 11th Octr 1796.

p.360   Simeon & Judith Cushmon. Dep. We testify we were acquainted with Catharine Shaw deceased and often heard her declare her will in regard to her land, that it should be equally divided between her three daughters Mary, Nancy, & Anner and all the household furniture and the Negroes to her son Daniel Shaw. Sworn 7 March 1796. /s/ Simeon Cushmon. /s/ Judith (C) Cushman.   Rec 11th Octr 1796.

p.360-361   Micke McKie to Wilson Conner. Deed, 11 Octr 1796, £10, 570 acres head of Beaver dam Cr of Big Horse Cr surveyed for McKie 27 July 1792, adj Daniel Mazikes. Wit Ezekiel McClendon, Stephen (+) Medlock, /s/ Mike McKie. Proven 11 Oct 1796 by Ezekiel McClendon; Van Swearingen J P. Rec 11 Oct 1796.

p.362-363   William Deen to Gideon Christian & Sarah Christian his wife. Deed, 1 April 1795, £100 sterling, 220 acres on Big Creek of Little Saluda, part of 390 acres originally granted to John Chenea by Gov Moultrie 20 March 1785, adj James Chenea, John Chenea, land laid out from Wm Deen to Saml Mays, Wrolley Doggin, James Chenea, Joel Pardue. Wit John Mosely, James Lane, Jane(+) Mosley. /s/ William (M) Deen. /s/ Ruth Deen. Proven 27 Feb 1796 by John Mosley; Nathl Abney J P. Recorded 11th Octr 1796.

p.363-366   Simon Beck & wife Eleanor to Abraham Powell. L&R, 10 March 1795/11 March 1795, £80 sterling, 200 acres on Boggy branch granted unto sd Simon Beck 7 Sept 1789, adj Wm Kirkland, Arthur Middleton, Robt Lang at time of original survey. Wit Samuel Sotcher, Henry Noble. /s/ Simon (x) Beck. /s/ Eleanor (C) Beck. Proven 11 Oct 1796 by Samuel Sotcher; Richard Tutt. Rec 11 Oct 1796.

p.366-367   James Jones to John Jones. Deed, 20 May 1796, £14 sterling, 45.5 acres originally granted to Phillip Lamar on Horse Creek. Wit Robert Lamar, Philip Lamar. /s/ James Jones. Proven 20 May 1796 by Philip Lamar; Joseph Hightower J P. Rec 11th Octr 1796.

p.367-368   Thomas Lamar to Bertond Briton[Britton] Jones. 7 May 1796, £5 SC sterling, 50 acres adj Thos Lamar. Wit Jas Exum, Phillip Lamar. /s/ Thos Lamar. Proven 31 May 1796 by Philip Lamar; Joseph Hightower, J P.   Rec 11 Octr 1798.

p.369-370   Charles Banks to LeRoy Hammond. Mortgage, 12 May 1796, $100 paid by Leroy Hammond, negro Ben about age 35. In default of payment of $100 with lawful interest Banks agrees Hammond may hold Ben as his property. Wit Wm Matthews, John Meridith. /s/ Charles Banks. Proven 11 Oct 1796 by John Meridith; Joseph Hightower, J P. Rec 11 Oct 1796.

p.370-371   William Bailey & wife Elizabeth to John Terry. Deed, 10 October 1796, £20 sterling, 133 acres on Rockey Creek of Turkey Creek of Savannah River, adj John Terry, land granted to Alexander Wilson, plat made by Wm Coursey D.S. being part of 437 acres granted to Joseph Jinkins by Gov Wm Moultrie December 1786, by sd Joseph Jinkins conveyed to sd Wm Bayley. Wit Obah Clement, Simon Clement. /s/ William Baley. /s/ Elizabeth (x) Baley. Proven 11 Octr 1796 by Obediah Clement; John Blocker J P.   Rec 11 Octr 1796.

p.371-373   Asa Hix to Alexander Hannah. Deed, 24 December 1792, £50 sterling, 900 acres on Town Creek, part of 1000 acres granted to sd Asa Hix on 4 June 1792 by Gov Chas Pinckney, surveyed by William Evans D S. Wit Wm Evans, Daniel Hannah. /s/ Asa Hix. Proven 3 Oct 1796 by Daniel Hannah; John Clarke J P.   Rec 11 Oct 1796.

p.373-375   Joshua Deen, planter, to William Moore, merchant. Bond, 11 October 1796, Deen's debt is £60 sterling with legal interest to be paid before 25 November 1797, mortgages Negro woman Nell with her future increase. Wit Eugene Brenan, Edward Burt. /s/ Joshua (HH) Deen. At time of executing these presents a delivery of a Penknife in name of all goods & chattles mentioned in this mortgage was made by sd Joshua Deen to sd William Moore. Wit Eugene Brenan. Proved by Eugene Brenan 23 Octr 1796. Rec 12th Octr 1796; Rd Tutt J P.

p.376-377   Van Swearengen to Sarah Pine[Poins]. Deed, 30 April 1796, £100 current money, 84 acres on Big Horse Creek, sd acres originally granted to Henery Adolph, from him conveyed to Thomas Franklin from thence to Vann Swearengen by L&R; also 20 acres joining sd 84 acres adj Robuck. Wit Absalom Napper, Sanders (S) Day, Silas (H) Green. /s/ Van Swearingen. Proven 10 Octr 1796 by Silas Green; Van Swearingen J P.   Rec 12th Octr 1796.

p.377-378   Nicholas H Bugg to Ephraim Ramsay. Mortgage, 22 October 1796. Nicholas H Bugg in consideration of five shillings paid by Ephraim Ramsay, grant mulatto boy Stephney about 11 pr 12 years old, condition Ephm Ramsay on 24 March in present year became together with Nicholas H Bugg jointly bound by note of hand to pay unto Julius Nichols of Cambridge £20 sterling, sd Ephraim Ramsay joined in sd note only as security for payment thereof and without having received any value therefor, now sd Ramsay covenants with N H Bugg to pay sd sum to Julius Nichols together with interest, null & void should N H Bugg pay. Wit William Williamson, Wm Garrett. /s/ N H Bugg. Proven 11 Nov 1796 by William Garrett; S Mays J P. Rec 12th Octr 1796.

p.378-380   Burrel Johnson and wife Disey Johnson to John Tillery. Deed, 1796, £34 sterling, 175 acres on branches of Horse Creek of Savannah River adj John Purves heirs, John Swillivan, Reuben Hatcher, Boyd, Fredk Tillman. Plat by Wm Coursey D S, part of 192 acres granted unto sd Burrel Johnson by Gov Arnoldos Vanderhorst 2 November 1795 and on resurvey of Tillmans land 17 acres of sd grant fell into Tillmans land. Wit David Tillman, Serane Parkman. /s/ Burrel (+) Johnson, /s/ Disey (+) Johnson. Proven 11 Octr 1796 by Sarana Parkman; Aquila Miles J P. Rec 12th Octr 1796.

p.380-381   Sheriff Jeremiah Hatcher to Mackerness Goode. Shff Title, 6 August 1796; suit of John Beckum against Reuben Beckum; Sheriff to sell to highest bidder

135 acres Horns Creek adj Swallow, John Williams, George Cowan, Mordecai Mattock; struck off to Mackerness Goode for £6. Wit Eugene Brenan, Elias Blackbourn. /s/ J Hatcher, S E C. Proven 1796 by Eugene Brenan; Rd Tutt J P. Rec 14 Octr 1796.

p.381-382   James Hart to Jesse Hart. £150 sterling, 150 acres whereon sd James Hart now lives, 3 horses, 13 cattle, 20 hogs, household furniture. Wit Saml D Loach, Vincen White. /s/ James Hart. Proven 17 Octr 1796 by Vincen White; Rd Tutt J P. Rec 17th Octr 1796.

p.382-383   Tilly Merrick of Pendleton County SC to Joshua Jackson, tailor. 29 November 1791, £30 sterling of SC, condition whereas Joshua Jackson by obligation is bound to sd Tilly Merrick for full payment £7.10 sterling money with interest on or before 1 December 1791, further sum of £7.10 sterling money on or before 1 Decr 1793, now if full payment sd Tilly to give L&R in fee simple tract of 150 acres on Beaver Dam Creek waters of Turkey Creek granted to Augustus Merrick by Gov Wm Moultrie 15 Jan 1787, less land of Daniel Mayzyck Esqr of Charleston. Wit Chs Tourtellot, Elias Blackbourn. /s/ Tilly Merrick. Proved 21 June 1796 by Elias Blackbourn; Rd Tutt J P. Rec 2nd October 1796.

p.383-384   Joshua Jackson to Richard Gantt Esqr. July 15, 1794, Joshua Jackson assigns to Richard Gantt all his right & title to within bond; Joshua Jackson authorises Tilly Merrick to convey within expressed land to Richard Gantt. Wit Eugene Brenan, Rd Tutt. /s/ Joshua Jackson. Proved by Eugene Brenan 2d Novr 1796; Rd Tutt J P. Rec 2nd November 1796.

p.384-385   Joshua Jackson, tailor, to Tilly Merrick of Pendleton County. Bond, 29 November 1791, £7.10 sterling money with interest, also £7.10 sterling money with interest on or before 1 Decr 1793. Wit Chas Tourtellot, Elias Blackbourn. /s/ Joshua Jackson. Recd 16th Septr 1795 of Joshua Jackson by hands of Richd Gantt £18.9 the same being principle & interest on within bond also one pound in full of costs. Wm Tennent. Assigned over to Messrs W & Turpen; wit. Samuel Maverick. /s/ Tilly Merrick. Proven 21 June 1796 by Elias Blackbourn; Rd Tutt J P. Recorded 2nd Novr 1796.

p.385-386   George Miller of Augusta, Georgia, to Richd Gantt Esqr atty at law. Deed 29 October 1796, $500, 200 acres on Buckhalters mill Creek and Stephens Creek adj John Ryan originally granted to Lawrence Rambo by Gov C Montague, surveyed 27th March 1771. Wit John Channing, Orsamus Allen. /s/ Geo Miller. Proven 2d Novr 1796 by Orsamus Allen; Richard Tutt J P. Rec 2nd Novr 1796.

p.387-388   John Logan of Colleton County, Charleston District, to Thomas Jones. Deed, 28 May 1796, £100 sterling, 1000 acres granted to Thomas Lynch Esqr 5 Sept 1774 except 63 acres out of the 1000 which was given by John Logan Senr to Ezekias Williams, adj Purvis, Williams, Turkey Creek, Melville, Allen, Stewart. Wit James L Richards, Chas Jones. /s/ Jno Logan. Proven 10 Nov 1796 by Charles Jones; Richard Tutt, J P. Rec 10 Nov 1796.

p.388   James Coursey, planter, and wife Elizabeth to John McFatrick. Deed, 16 April 1796, £20 current money, 55 acres on branches of Beaverdam Creek of Turkey Creek of Savannah River granted unto James Coursey and Robt Melvil decd adj

land held for Goodes orphans, plat by Wm Coursey D S, being part of 300 acres
granted by Gov Chas Montague at Charleston 13 Novr 1772 unto Danl Stephens, transferred by L&R 8 & 9 March 1796 unto James Coursey whereof above 55 acres is part.
Wit H Coursey, Mary (S) Coursey. /s/ James Coursey /s/ Elizabeth (x) Coursey.
Proven 4 May 1796 by H Coursey; John Blocker J P.   Rec 10th Novr 1796.

p.390-391   Alexander Downer to Lemuel Young admr/estate of William Evans.
Deed, 29 October 1796, $10; 50 acres, part of tract granted to sd Alexr Downer 5
June 1786 adj Henry Jones, Lud Williams, Henry Jones.   Wit Seaborn Jones, John
Savage. /s/ Alexr Downer. Proven 10th Novr 1796 by John Savage; Richard Tutt.
Recorded 10th Novr 1796.

p.391-392   Josiah Kirk to James Quarles. Bill/sale, 3 June 1796, $400 negroe
boy Tom sixteen years old, condition that if sd Kirk shall pay $212 by 1 Decr 1796
this shall be null & void. Should sd negro die previous to time, Kirk to pay within
mentioned sum. Wit George Farrar. /s/ Jsa Kirk.   Proven 10th Novr 1796 by George
Farrar; Rd Tutt J P.   Recorded the 10th Novr 1796.

p.392-393   Jesse Griffin to Edmund[Edmond] Riggs[Rigs].   Deed, 10 April 1795,
£100 sterling, 267 acres on Big Creek of Little Saluda, part of tract originally
granted to(sic) Wm Moultrie in 1772 adj sd Jesse Griffin, a tract originally
granted to Tobias Myers, line John Abney ran for sd Griffin. Wit Zachariah Prator,
James McKnight. /s/ Jesse Griffin.   Proven 31 Octr 1796 by Zachariah Prayter;
Nathaniel Abney J P.   Recorded 16th Novr 1796.

p.393-394   R Hampton to Abner Corley.   Deed, 29 December 1791, part of tract
originally granted to Charles Atkins; conveyed to Abner Corley by Commrs of
Confiscated Estates, adj main road from Mrs Wests Ford on Little Saluda to
Charleston except a small part of the upper end of sd tract supposed to contain 40
acres sold to Catlet Corley. Wit Catlet Corley, William Hame. /s/ R Hampton.
Proven 18 Novr 1796 by Catlet Corley; Rd Tutt.   Rec 18th Novr 1796.

p.394-395   Joseph Fuller to Abraham Ardis.   Deed, 12 March 1796, £40
sterling, 129.5 acres in New Windsor Twp, Edgefield County, on road from Fort Moore
Bluff, Savannah River, to Charleston adj Jasper Nogle, Henry Zinn, Cronimus Zinn,
Thomas Rogers. Wit Cradk Burnell, David Ardis. /s/ Joseph Fuller.   Proven 22 Novr
1796 by Cradk Burnell; John Clarke J P.   Rec 24 Novr 1796.

p.395-396   Bowling Dees & wife Anne Dees to Henry McClendon.   Power/attorney,
31 Oct 1796, to sue, recover, receive from persons whatsoever in Wayne County,
North Carolina, especially William Readfurd, such debts arising from dowery; Anne
Dees is lawfull daughter of afsd William Readfurd now decd, by and from executor of
afsd deceased. Wit George H Perrin, Rd Tutt. /s/ Bowling (+) Dees. Anne (x) Dees.
Proven 21 Novr 1796 by George H Perrin; Rd Tutt J P.   Rec 21st Nov 1796.

p.396-398   Thomas Adams to John Walker Senr. Deed, 11 January 1796, £50 money
of SC, 150 acres being part of 700 acres on Rockey & Beach Creek branches granted
to Elvington Squires by Gov Wm Moultrie 5 August 1793, sd 150 acres on South side
Beach Cr adj line of John Walker Senr & Thos Adams, William Donoho. Wit Elvington
Squires, Ezekiel (+) Walker, Willm Beads. /s/ Thomas (x) Adams. Mary (M) Adams.

Proven 14 March 1796 by Ezekiel Walker; Van Swearingen J P.   Rec 21 Nov 1796.

p.398-400   John Norwood to Benjamin Glover & Co. Mortgage, 9 December 1796,
£109.14.5.5 sterling, condition for payment of £54.17.2.3 with lawful interest from
above date, negroe girl eighteen months old the daughter of Patt and named Cupey,
[and named livestock]. /s/ John Norwood. A penknife being also delivered at same
time by sd John Norwood to afsd Benjn Glover by way of Livery & vesting the
property afsd in afsd Benjn Glover. Wit: Wm Nibb, John McKellar. Proven 17 Decr
1796 by John McKellar; J Nichols J P.   Rec 23d December 1796.

p.400-402   William Anderson executor estate of Francis Sinquefield Esqr decd
to Anderson Crawford. Deed, 12 May 1796. £5 current money paid by Anderson Crawford
of State/Georgia, granted to sd Anderson Crawford, husband of Rachael Sinquefield,
150 acres on Saluda River, part of 300 acres originally granted to Catharine Youngblood and was sold by Robert Stark Esqr sheriff of Ninety Six as property of John
Dooly, purchased by Francis and Samuel Sinquefield jointly; no titles ever being
made to same, to sd Francis Sinquefield by sd sheriff on 3d February 1789, same to
William Anderson executor of sd Francis Sinquefield, for purpose that sd William
Anderson should convey same as directed in will of sd Francis Sinquefield; whereas
sd William Anderson and Rachael Sinquefield & Jane Sinquefield then Jane Maxwell
the legatees of sd Francis, being of full age met together 9 Decr 1788 to execute
deed/partition for sd land, whereby above described 150 acres with other land fell
to Rachel Sinquefield now Rachel Crawford. Wit Mathew Sullivan, William Osbourn,
Zac Sinquefield. /s/ W Anderson exr of Francis Sinquefield. [Plat shows Zachariah
Sinquefields land, Morriss Givins land, Thomas Chappels land]. Whereas by will of
Francis Sinquefield Esqr decd date 4 Decr 1780 among other lands did devise 400
acres to be equally divided between his two daughters Rachel and Jane Sinquefield
on separate tracts, sd Rachel and Jane being of full age did agree to divide same:
Rachel to have 50 acres on Saluda River, 150 joining Morriss Givin; Jane to have
200 acres on Chavises Creek but the 150 acres to Rachel Sinquefield as a part of
300 acres granted to Catharine Youngblood which sd Francis purchased with his
brother Samuel Sinquefield at Sheriffs sale and never had any title to same, there-
fore sheriff made letters to me as his executor for purpose of conveying same to
legatees of sd Francis; 10 May 1796; W Anderson exr.   Proven 13 May 1796 by Zach
Sinquefield; Wm Robinson J P.   Rec 24 Jan 1796.

p.402-404   John Norwood to Isham Norwood & Nancy Norwood. Deed/Gift, 6 Decr
1796, for love, affection & 5 shillings sterling, to son Isham Norwood & daughter
Nancy Norwood, Negroes Tom age about 20; Little Jem about 8 yrs old; should Isham
or Nancy die before they have lawful issue, their share or shares to be divided
among survivors or survivor of my children by my first wife Mourning Norwood and
their issue lawfully begotten; sd John Norwood retains possession of sd slaves
during his natural life. Wit Nathaniel Norwood. /s/ John Norwood. Receipt for 5
shillings from Isham and Nancy Norwood /s/ John Norwood. Proven 4 Decr 1796 by
Nathaniel Norwood; Wm Robinson J P.   Rec 10th Decr 1796.

p.404-407   John Norwood to Nathaniel, Williamson, Polly & Eliza Norwood. Deed
of Gift, 14 November 1796, to provide for support and livelihood of dear & dutiful
children, for love, affection and five shillings sterling paid by Allen Glover and
Isham Norwood, grant to Allen Glover and Isham Norwood Negroes Hall about age 14 in

trust for benefit of beloved child Nathaniel Norwood; boy Jem about 10 for benefit of beloved child Williamson Norwood; wench Patt about 18 yrs to benefit of beloved daughter Polly Norwood, wench Amy about 30 and girl Lotty about 4 yrs old to benefit of daughter Elizabeth Norwood; also boy Mack son of afsd Amy about 2 months old to two daughters Polly and Elizabeth when they attain age 21 years. Wit William Burton. /s/ John Norwood. Receipt, from Allen Glover and Isham Norwood 5 shillings; wit Wm Burton, /s/ John Norwood. Proven 9 Decr 1796 by Wm Burton; Wm Robinson J P. Recorded 10th Decr 1796.

p.408-411   James Goudy to Allen Glover. Release, 3 October 1796. £100 sterling, 150 acres adj at time of original survey on Daniel Micklen (now in possession of Joseph Burton), Robert Goudy (now in possession of William Shaw Esqr) other sides vacant but now in possession of James Goudy, Fredrick Glover and Allen Glover. Wit J Bullock, N Cooper, John Moore Junr. /s/ James Gouedy. Proven 3 Oct 1796 by John Moore Junr; Julius Nichols J P. Relinquishment of dower by Elizabeth Gouedy wife of within named James Gouedy, 3 Oct 1796, /s/ Betsey Gouedy; W Anderson J C E. Recorded 10th Decr 1796.

p.411-412   Sheriff William Tennent to William Anderson. Sheriff Title, 6 June 1796. Suit of Eliza Ann Purvis now Eliza A Anderson widow of John Purvis deceased against Estate of sd Col John Purvis for her dower, Shff directed to sell to highest bidder for ready money at Cambridge, was struck off to William Anderson for £6.15, 400 acres on a branch of Turkey Creek called Stony Run adj Robert Melvill, Hezekiah Williams. Wit Thos Anderson, John Purvis. /s/ Wm Tennent Shff 96 Dist. Proven 19 Decr 1796 by Thomas Anderson; Julius Nichols. Rec 21 Decr 1796.

p.412-413   Sheriff William Tennent to William Anderson. Sheriff Title, 6 June 1796. At suit of Eliza Ann Purvis (now Eliza A Anderson) widow of Col John Purvis decd agt estate of sd John Purvis for her dower, Sheriff to sell to highest bidder for ready money at Cambridge; land struck off to William Anderson for £12 sterling he being highest & last bidder, 640 acres on Savannah River adj land surveyed for Patrick McCutchin, land of Mitchells heirs, same granted to John Rivers 15 October 1784. Wit Thos Anderson, John Purvis. /s/ Wm Tennent Shff 96 Dist. Proven 19 Decr 1796 by Thos Anderson; Julius Nichols J P. Recorded 21st day of December 1796.

p.414-420   Sheriff William Tennent to William Anderson. Release, 30 May 1796. At suit of Eliza Ann Purvis widow of John Purvis but now Eliza Ann Anderson against James McQueen and others for £578.3.4 which sum was assessed by John Hammond, John Ryan and Barkley Martin three of the commissioners named in a Writ of Dower in her late husbands real estate, directed sheriff sell ten tracts containing 3056 acres, sold 1 Feb 1796 to highest bidder on 12 mos credit at Cambridge, struck off to Wm Anderson for £141 current money, 1300 acres part of land original grant to Francis Brimar for 1500 acres 5 May 1775 adj LeRoy Hammond, Sarah Baker, McMullin, Martin Campbell, Edward Barnard, George Galphin, Ralph Phillips, also another tract of 240 acres near Savannah river adj survey of Pat McCutchin, John Purvis and originally granted to Elizabeth Calleham 5 Sept 1785, also tract of 150 acres on Stevens Creek adj Henry Ware, Stringer, originally granted to John Rutledge 5 Sept 1785, also 216 acres on Bedingfields Cr of Savannah River adj John Day Esqr, Beddingfields land, heirs of Fredrick Winters originally granted to William Brooks 1 May 1786; also 150 acres on Turkey Creek of Savannah River adj Thomas Williams, originally surveyed

for John Purvis 24 May 1770; also 500 acres on Pike Creek of Turkey Creek adj John
Purvis originally granted to William Coursey 25 June 1771; also 100 acres on Turkey
Creek surveyed for John Purvis, original grant to Thomas Williams; also 100 acres
on Turkey Cr adj John Allen, John Gordon, Hezekiah Williams, John Purvis, Turkey Cr
originally granted to John Purvis 7 May 1787; also 150 acres originally granted to
Barkly Jones; also 150 acres original grant to John Purvis. Wit Patrk McDonall,
Thos Anderson. /s/ Wm Tennent Shff 96 Dt. Proven 30 May 1796 by Thomas Anderson;
John Trotter J P. [followed by 7 small plats]

p.421-422   Thomas Sellers to John Wall. 27 September 1796. £100 for 175 acres
being part of three surveys, 92 acres where sd Sellers now liveth except 8 or 9
acres, the survey contains 100 acres granted to Thomas McGinnes and conveyed by
McGinnes to sd Sellers and lyeth both sides Log Cr & Horsepen branch, afsd excepted
9 acres is that part of sd survey that lyeth on S side Log Cr & W side afsd branch,
77 acres being part of a survey containing 100 acres and 93 acres granted to sd
Thomas Sellers lying S side Log Creek & both sides Horsepen branch and the above
mentioned 77 acres being formerly held by Wescoat now by Arthur Simkins, 5 acres of
above mentioned 170 & 5 acres conveyed by Arthur Simkins to sd Thomas Sellers adj
above survey granted to McGinnes, the three pieces containing 175 acres. Proven 2
January 1797 by George H Perrin; John Blocker J P. Recorded 2d July 1797.

p.422-425   Jeremiah Thomas, of Georgia, to John Jones. L&R, 28 October
1795/29 October 1795. £20 sterling, 100 acres being part of 300 acres on Rockey
Creek of Little Stevens Creek of Savanna River adj Messersmith, Elisha Stephens,
Neales Stevens, Charles Partin, John Jones, granted to sd Jeremiah Thomas 6 October
1794 by Gov Wm Moultrie, laid off next to sd John Jones's older granted land by a
line from a pine on sd Jones's former line, crosses great road to oak on Charles
Partins land, dividing line between sd Jones and Moses Clarke. Wit James Coate,
Jesse Clark, Jas Scott. /s/ Jeremiah (x) Thomas. Proven 31 December 1796 by James
Scott; John Blocker J P. Recorded 2 Jany 1797.

p.425-428   Moses Brown to John Dugless. L&R, 22 May 1792/23 May 1792, £50
sterling, 50 acres on Pen Creek of Little Saludy River as directed by L&R date 31
January 1789, part of 400 acres granted to Thos Deloach 31 August 1774 by Lt Gov Wm
Bull; also a tract of 45 acres adj sd 50 acres, being part of 90 acres granted to
sd Moses Brown by Gov Chas Pinckney 4 July 1791, divided from the remainder by line
near Saml Deloach. Wit Averillah (A) King. Elizabeth (x) Smedley. /s/ Moses (+)
Brown. Proven 23 May 1792 by Averellah (A) King; Henry King JP. Rec 7 Jan 1797.

p.428-429   Jacob Fudge to William Mallet. £25 94 acres on Chavers Creek adj
at time of original survey John Ryans, Wm Haregrove, granted afsd Jacob Fudge 5
December 1785. Wit William Griffin, Mathew Hamilton. /s/ Jacob Fudge. Proven 2
Jany 1797 by William Griffin; Rd Tutt J P. Rec. 2 Jany 1797.

p.429-430   Thomas Rogers to John Carter. Deed, 1 October 1796, £10 sterling
of SC, 635 acres on Big Horse Creek granted unto sd Thomas Rogers 5 Decr 1785. Wit
Alexander Ogden, Joseph Hightower. /s/ Thomas Rogers. Proven 4 October 1796 by
Alexander Ogden; Joseph Hightower JPEC. Recorded 2nd Jany 1797.

p.430-432   Samuel Mays to Thomas Anderson Senr. Deed, 1 December 1796. $10, for 32 acres on Saludy River adj Thomas Anderson, John Lewis Jarey and sd Samuel May, part of tract granted sd Samuel May 5 Decr 1796 for 60 acres. Wit W Anderson, John (+) Thomson, James (+) Camble. /s/ S Mays. Certification 5 Decr 1796 for Thomas Anderson Senr of 32 acres on Saluda River, part of tract granted 5 Decr 1796; S Mays. Relinquishment of dower by Nancy Mays wife of Samuel Mays, 31 Decr 1796; Judge William Anderson. /s/ Nancy Mays. Proven 2 January 1797 by by William Anderson; Arthur Simkins J E C. Recorded 2nd January 1797.

p.432-436   James Minge Burton, North Carolina, to Hezekiah Gentry of Edge-field. L&R, 10 October 1793/11 October 1793 for £100 sterling, 250 acres part of 1200 originally granted to Peter Whitten 21 April 1775 by Lt Gov Wm Bull, on Indian Creek of Saludy River adj Wm Waddell, Thos Green, Jas Petty, Micajah Corley, Nathan Melton, Thos West; from Whitten conveyed to Wm Cobb and from him to sd James M Burton, adj Robt Christy crossing Indian Creek and Little Saludy River. Wit Jesse Samford, Zacheus (+) Corley, Mary (x) Samford. /s/ James Minge Burton. Proven 12 April 1794 by Jesse Samford; Henry King.   Rec 2d Jany 1797.

p.436-437   John Cheney[Chenea] to William Dean[Deen]. Deed, 30 March 1795. £100 sterling, 390 acres on Big Creek of Little Saludy originally granted to sd John Chanea by Gov Wm Moultrie 20 March 1785 adj land of sd John Chenea. Wit Rd Tutt, George H Perrin, Joshua (I) Deen. /s/ John Cheney. Proven 2 January 1797 by George Henry Perrin; Rd Tutt J P.   Recorded 2 Jany 1797.

p.437-441   Joseph Drew of Kingston, Kings County, New Brunswick by his attorney William Anderson Esqr, to John Thomson. L&R, 29 July 1793/30 July 1793, by ltr/atty dated 14 Oct 1790 for £40 SC money, 100 acres originally granted to sd Joseph Drew on Halfway Swamp adj Paul Frasier, John Edwards, Joseph Thomas, and by 50 acres formerly sold by sd Joseph Drew. Wit Lewis Mathews, Thomas Anders, Rebecca Anderson. /s/ Joseph Drew by his Attorney Wm Anderson. Plat 10 May 1773 by John Bremar D S. Deed proven 30 Dec 1796 by Thomas Anderson Junr; S Mays J P. Recorded 3d January 1797.

p.441-445   John Edwards to Stockley Towles. L&R, 21 September 1779/21 Sept 1779 for £2000 current SC money, 100 acres on Halfway Swamp originally granted unto Edward Edwards 13 Aug 1756, sd John Edwards a son & heir of sd Edward Edwards decd. Wit Richd Allison, Thomas Norrell, Samuel Thomas. /s/ John Edwards. Proven 26 July 1796 by Thomas Norrell; S Mays J P.   Recorded 3d January 1797.

p.445-446   Robert Marsh to Dionysius Oliver Junr. Deed 6 January 1797, £10 sterling, 10 acres near Edgefield Court house, adj new road from Edgefield Court house to Augusta, Richard Tutt, by Dionysius Oliver Jr; Wit William Marsh, Eliza-beth Marsh. Proven 6 January 1797 by Richard Tutt; Rd Tutt J P. Rec 6 Jany 1797.

p.446   Elizabeth Mealer to Gutteridge Cheatam. Deed of Gift, 6 January 1797, for love & good will to son Gutteridge Cheatam had by husband Peter Cheatam decd, all that Elizabeth possesses or will possess, after her death to be equally divided among the legatees. Wit John Terry, William (x) Williams. /s/ Elizabeth (x) Mealer. Proven 7 Jan 1797 by John Terry; Rd Tutt J P.   Rec 7 Jan 1797.

p.446-447   Gutteridge Cheatam to his mother Elizabeth Mealer, 6 January 1797;

binds Gutteridge Cheatham to lend his mother whatever she wants to support the Family. Wit John Terry, William (x) Williams. /s/ Gutteridge Cheatham. Proven 7th January 1797 by John Terry; Rd Tutt J P. Recorded 7th January 1797.

p.447-448   James Nelson of Abbeville County, John Gibson, and Mary Nelson to Henry Zimmerman. Deed, 23 August 1796, $200, 100 acres in Edgefield on Hardlabour Crk adj George Perkins, Phillip Zimmerman, Conrad Mark, Stephen Mantz. Wit Isaac Nelson, Robert Perrin. /s/ James Nelson, John Gibson, Mary Nelson. Relinquishment of dower 21 December 1796 by Mary Nelson wife of James Nelson; Judge Andrew Hamilton. Proven 3 January 1797 by Robert Perrin; Jas Harrison J P. Recorded 11 January 1797.

p.448-449   Lemuel Young and wife Mary Young of Richmond County, Georgia, to Melines C Leavensworth. Deed, 17 July 1796, £60 sterling, the one undivided moiety of tract of land on Town Creek 5700 acres within lines of Thomas Lamar, Widow Zinn, Robert Lamar, James Jones, Joseph Hays, Isaac Parker. Wit Philip Lamar, Thomas Young. /s/ Lemuel (L) Young. /s/ Mary Young. Proven 13 January 1797 by Philip Lamar; John Clarke J P. Recorded 16th January 1797.

p.450-451   Melines Conkling Leavensworth to John Fox, merchant of Richmond County, Georgia. Deed, 4 July 1796; £60; 550 acres on Jonakins branch and on the road from old wells to Cherokee ponds adj Jacob Fudge, John Herndon, Lucy Sinjohn, Robert Samuel; Wit Philip Lamar, John Randal. /s/ Melines C Leavensworth. Proven 13th January 1797 by Philip Lamar; John Clarke J P. Rec 16th January 1797.

p.451-453   John Norwood, planter, to Littleberry Bluford Norwood and Lovevina Floid Norwood. Deed of Gift, John Norwood being aged and uncertain of death when his dear children Littleberry Bluford Norwood, Lovevina Floid Norwood will be deprived and destitute of parents and be exposed to misfortunes of this world, to provide for maintenance of dear children afsd, deed of gift of following slaves and chattels: girl Kesiah about 18 months old; Mack about 3 months old to Littleberry Bluford Norwood; man named Doctor about 20 years old and girl Patience to Lovevina Floid Norwood together with future issue; covenant with Toliver Bostick. Should either chid die without heirs before age 21, his or her share to survivor of child by last wife Nancy Norwood. Wit William Smith, Jacob Norrell. /s/ John Norwood. Receipt for five shillings from Toliver Bostick. South Carolina, Abbeville County, 4 January 1797, John Norwood subscriber to within conveyance being sworn sayeth conveyance of Negro boy Mack in conveyance of October 1796 is an error and not an intention of his but that he shall be conveyed to his son Littleberry Bluford Norwood as specifyed in the within conveyance; John Trotter JP. /s/ John Norwood. Proven 20 January 1797 by William Smith; Jno Trotter J P. Rec 21 Jany 1797.

p.453-454   John Norwood to Toliver Bostick. Deed, 15 December 1796; 5 shillings and in consideration of natural love which sd John Norrell(sic) doth bear for Toliver Bostick, sell to Toliver Bostick certain Negroes: wench Ada about 28 years old, girl Nol about 13 and the increase of the females; it is expressly intended that before mentioned Negroes shall be and remain free except from Liberty of being sold by sd Toliver Bostick on account of any debts which he may heretofore or here-after contract, but shall hold sd Negroes for use of Nancy Norwood the last wife of sd John Norwood. Wit William Smith, Jacob Norrell. /s/ John Norwood. Proven, Abbeville SC, 20 January 1797 by William Smith; John Trotter J P. Recorded 21st January 1797.

p.454-456   James Coursey and wife Elizabeth to Benjamin Harry, preacher. Deed, 3 August 1796, $300, 382 acres Beaverdam of Turkey creek of Savannah river adj Goodes orphans, John McPatrick being part of 462 acres granted for 300 acres unto Daniel Stephens by Gov Chs Montagu 19 Novr 1772, and by Stephens transferred 8 & 9 March 1796 unto sd James Coursey, plat by Wm Coursey DS. Wit W Coursey, John Harry. /s/ James Coursey, Elizabeth (x) Coursey. Proven 24 August 1796 by John Harry; John Blocker J P. Judge Arthur Simkins certifies relinquishment of dower by Elizabeth Coursey 4 January 1797. Rec 21st January 1797.

p.456-457   Robert H Waring of town of Columbia, SC, to Zachariah Lunday. Deed, 13 December 1796, $200, 200 acres in Colleton County at time of survey now Edgefield on waters of Stephens Creek adj George Buffey, George Lunday, was surveyed 27 February 1773 for my father Robert Waring now deceased, granted to him 27 August 1774 by Lt Gov Wm Bull. Wit Jno Martin, Wm Key. /s/ R H Waring. Judge Arthur Simkins certifies relinquishment of dower by Mary H Waring wife of within R H Waring 15 December 1796. Proven 26 January 1797 by William Key; Rd Tutt J P. Recorded 26th January 1797.

p.457-459   Sheriff William Tennent to William Mollett. Deed, 5 October 1795, whereas Thomas Lamar was seized of 115 acres in Ninety Six District when originally granted adj Richard Kirkland per plat late the property of Moses Kirkland. Thomas Lamar & Richard Johnson by joint bond indebted to William Parker and Edward Blake Commissioners of the Treasury in sum £34.10 together with interest thereon; to recover sd debt and costs, John Rutledge Chief Justice of SC by writ 16 Nov 1794 at Cambridge, directs Sheriff to sell sd land to highest bidder. Sold to sd William Mollett for £6 sterling. Wit James Leslie, Thomas Key. /s/ Wm Tennent Shff 96 Dist. Proven 7 January 1797 by James Leslie; Chas Old J P. Rec 27 Jan 1797.

p.460   Nathan Tally to Lewis Tillman, Edmund Boyd, & Charles Broadwaters, commrs of Religious Society, Talleys Meeting House. Deed, 26 Jany 1797, 5 shillings, land with privilege of taking water from my spring in the time of public worship whereon the Meeting House now stands containing 1.5 acres on waters of Beaverdam Creek near the five nochd road. Wit William Tillory, Daniel Tillman, Phillip Thurmond. /s/ Nathan Tally. Proven 26 Jany 1797 by Phillip Thurmond; Rd Tutt J P. Recorded 26th Jany 1797.

p.461   William Little records the mark of his cattle & hogs, 6 February 1797; Rd Tutt J P. Recorded 6 February 1797.

p.461-462   Charles Fooshee and wife Rachel to William Little. Deed 17 March 1796. £20 sterling, 130 acres on Little Saluda River, part of a tract of 200 acres granted to sd Charles Fooshee 7 May 1792 by Chas Pinkney adj Simkins line. Witness Henry King, Wm (+) Burdett, Ben (B) Wages. /s/ Charles (x) Fooshee /s/ Rachel (+) Fooshee. Proven 2 Feb 1797 by Henry King; Wm Daniel J P. Rec 6 Feby 1797.

p.462-463   Alexander Oden & wife Felicia to Charles Blackwell. Deed, 10 Feby 1795, £35 sterling, 100 acres on Stevens Creek adj Scotts Branch, Mathew Cass, John

Garret, part of a tract of 371 acres granted to sd Alexander Oden 1 Feb 1790. Wit Barnebe Caps, Joseph Prince. /s/ Alexander Oden /s/ Felicia (x) Oden. Proven 1 April 1795 by Joseph Prince; Hugh Middleton J P. Rec 6 Feby 1797.

p.463-466   George Swilling & wife Martha to Mary Gibson. Deed, 2 December 1782, £162.10, 100 acres on Hardlabour Creek adj Phillip Zimmerman originally granted to John Swilling by Gov Chas Granville 6 Feby 1773, and willed to his son George. Wit John James Stussel, Amos Anderson. /s/ George (E) Swilling. /s/ Martha Swilling. Proven 2 January 1797 Amos Anderson; Jas Harrison J P. Rec 7th Feb 1797.

p.467   Samuel Landrum to Reuben Landrum. Deed, 20 September 1796, £300, Negroes, fellow Sunn aged 19, lad Jacob age 17, boy Jack age 14, wench Hannah and her male child Tom, boy Preston age 10, also livestock, and two stills. Wit James Brown. Proven by James Brown 2 January 1797; John Blocker J P. Rec 9 Feby 1797.

p.468   Mathew Wells[Wills] to Jones Wills. Bond, 8 January 1790. £500 to be paid to Jones Wells. Condition Mathew Wills makes unto Jones Wills lawfull titles to 134 acres, the land whereon sd Jones Wills now lives & composed of three tracts: 76 acres survey Richd Coleman lives upon, 52 acres granted to Matw Wells, 6 acres granted to Sarah McQueen, all of which having been laid off by John Abney D S, adj Richd Tate and Wm Stewarts lands and sd Mathw Wills lands & Saluda River. Wit William Spragins, Thomas Berry. /s/ Mathew Wills. Proven 27 January 1797 by William Spragins; Nathl Abney J P; Rec 11th February 1797.

p.469-470   Thomas Carson & Thomas Williams to John Jolley. Deed, 1 June 1796. £50. 50 acres the western part of tract granted to Thomas Carson and Thos Williams by Gov Wm Moultrie, containing 1000 acres on branches of Little Stevens and Sleepy Creeks, adj William Adams, Buckelew, Dutch County Land, Gualleburns, Kirksey, Augusta road, Wm Morris, Wm Odoms, the road being dividing line between Thos Williams and John Jolley. Wit John (x) Jolly Junr, Joseph Newton, Thomas Bond. /s/ Thos Carson, /s/ Thos Williams. Proven 7 September 1796 by John Jolley Junr; John Blocker J P. Recorded 11 Feby 1797.

p.470-471   Wm Humphreys to Phillip Ikner. Deed 29 December 1792, £20, 25 acres, part of 100 acres on Mine Creek waters of Little Saluda originally granted to Drury Fort 1765 by Gov Wm Bull, adj Edward Holmes. Wit Samuel Humphreys, Wm Parkerson. /s/ W Humphreys. Peaceable sezion of land made 29 December 1792 by Wm Humphreys unto Phillip Ikner. Wit Samuel Humphreys, Wm Parkerson. /s/ W Humphreys. Proven 6 Feby 1793 by Samuel Humphreys; Henry King J P. Rec 11th Feby 1797.

p.472-473   William Humphreys to Philip Ikner. Deed, 11 October 1793, £3, 250 acres on Dry Creek branch of Mine Creek, part of a tract of 922 acres granted to William Humphreys by Gov Charles Pinckney 1792, 250 acres adj John Gillon, John Rushton, Charles Partin[Partain], sd Ikner near Homes Branch, Cove. Wit Nathaniel Bolton, Solomon Eikner. /s/ W Humphreys. Peaceable sezion made 11 Ocober 1793. Proven 14 November 1793 by Solomon Eikner; Henry King, J P. Rec 11 Feb 1797.

p.473-475   Edward Holmes, planter, to Philip Ikner[Eikner], blacksmith. Deed, 15 February 1794. £20, 20 acres on Mine Creek of Little Saluda, part of 100 acres originally granted to Drury Fort by Gov Wm Bull 1765, conveyed by Fort to

Henry Bolton, from Bolton to Brittain Brasswell, and Braswell to sd Edward Holmes, 20 acres bounded by Mine Cr, sd Homes, heirs of Frederick Sisson, sd Eikner. Wit Solomon Eikner, Jonah Howell. /s/ Edward Homes. Suzion 15 Feb 1794. Proven 17 May 1794 by Solomon Eikner; Henry King, J P. Recorded 11th February 1797.

p.475-477   Edward Holmes to Philip Ikner. 15 December 1791, £20, fifty acres, part of 100 acres on branch of little Saludah granted to Drury Fort by Gov Wm Bull 1769, conveyed by L&R to Edward Homes, 50 acres adj Wm Humphreys, Charles Partain, sd Homes. Wit Solomon Eikner, William Sisson. /s/ Edward Homes. Sizon 15 Decr 1791. Proven 6 February 1793 by Solomon Eikner; Henry King J P.   Rec 11 Feby 1797.

p.477-478   Absolam Williams to John Taylor Senr. Deed 31 May 1794, £40 sterling, 100 acres on Savanah River adj Westcoats Creek, Robert Russell, D Francis; 150 acres granted unto John Watkins 31 Aug 1774, sd 100 acres begins on Lick branch emptying in Wescoat Cr, conveyed by John Watkins unto Charles Williams 26 Jan 1779 & unto sd Absolom Williams by lawful heirship. Wit Jesse Copeland, John (x) Taylor Junr, Ezekiel Hudnall. /s/ Absolam Williams. Proven 20 Sept 1794 by John (x) Taylor Junr; J Harrison J P.   Recorded 14th Feby 1797.

p.479-480   Absolam Williams to John Taylor Jr. Deed, 21 May 1794, £20 sterling, 50 acres part of 150 acres granted John Watkins 31 Aug 1774 on Savannah R on Westcoats Cr adj Robert Russell, D Francis; this 50 acres conveyed by John Watkins unto Charles Williams 26 Jan 1779, unto Absolam Williams by heirship. Wit Jesse Copeland, Jno (+) Taylor Senr, Ezekiel Hudnall. /s/ Absolam Williams. Proven 20 Sept 1794; James Harrison J P.   Recorded 14 Feby 1797.

p.480-484   James Jackson Esqr of City of London, Great Britain, merchant, to Sir Patrick Houston, Baronet, in South Carolina. Deed of Feoffmt, 2 November 1778. £1000 lawful money of S C, 100 acres in Granville County adj Savannah River granted to sd James Jackson 20 August 1767. James Jackson by indenture deed 13 August 1773 sold unto Andrew McLean of Augusta, Georgia, merchant, land held jointly with LeRoy Hammond & Company among which was the afsd plantation of 100 acres; James Jackson and his lawful attorney Andrew McLean grant to Sir Patrick Houston sd premises. Jas Jackson and Andrew McLean appoint Donald Cameron and James Grierson of Augusta, Georgia, Esqrs, their lawful attorneys. Wit J Grierson J P, Donald Cameron. /s/ James Jackson, /s/ And McLean. Possession 29 December 1778; J Grierson, Donald Cameron. Proven 17 Feby 1797 by John Willson [Wilson] Esqr of Augusta; Rd Tutt J P. Recorded 17th Feby 1797.

p.484-485   Mary Johnson, sole heiress to her father John Savage, to Samuel Savage, planter. Deed, £100 sterling, 150 acres on Ninety Six Creek originally granted to Samuel Thomas, also 100 acres adj above tract, bounded by Samuel Thomas, Thomas Bell, Robert Dillon, William Davis, Benjamin Durburon originally granted to William Panton, also adjoining 52 acres originally granted to Robert Mills and conveyed by Wm Anderson to John Savage. Wit Thomas Anderson, John Purves, William Prichard. /s/ Mary Johnston. Proven 29 September 1796 by William Prichard; Wm Anderson. Recorded 20th Feby 1797.

p.485-488   Elisha Banks and Elijah Banks to Sherwood Corley. L&R. 14 February 1791/15 February 1791, £60 starling, 100 acres on Clouds Creek, part of grant to

Charles Bank, adj William West, Holletree. Wit Francis Davis, William (x) Etheridge, Catlett Corley. /s/ Elisha Banks, /s/ Sarah (+) Banks, /s/ Elijah Banks. Proven 16 December 1796 by Francis Davis; Elkanah Sawyer J P. Rec 23d Feby 1797.

p.488-489   Edward Kirksey and wife Winney to Jeremiah Allen, planter. Deed, 5 December 1796, £50 sterling, 154 acres on Horse Pen Creek of Savanna R, part of land James Morris bought of sd Kirksey. Wit James Morris, Joseph (x) Jolley. /s/ Edward (x) Kirksey, Winny (x) Kirksey. Proven 8 February 1797 by Joseph Jolly; John Blocker J P. Recorded 4th March 1797.

p.490-491   John Bridges, planter, to John Strother. Deed, 18 January 1797. £10 sterling, 10 acres on Mill Creek of Stephens Creek adj land formerly called Fudges old survey, sd John Bridges, land formerly called Fudges mill tract. Wit: Jeremiah Strother, Charles Banks. /s/ John (B) Bridges. Proven 8 March 1797 by Jeremiah Strother; John Blocker J P. Recorded 8th March 1797.

p.491-492   Nicholas Hill, planter, to Hodson Bennett & John Strother, planter and carpenter. Deed, 20 May 1795. 100 acres on Little Stephens Creek adj Joseph Stephens, conveyed from Drury Hearn to Nicholas Hill 1792. Wit Jeremiah Strother, George Mason. /s/ Nicholas (W) Hill. Proven 8 March 1797 by Jeremiah Strother; John Blocker J P. Recorded 8th March 1797.

p.492-493   Hodson Bennett, carpenter, to John Strother, planter. Deed, 16 December 1796, £100 sterling, to John Strother 100 acres on Little Stephens Creek adj Joseph Stevens, when run conveyed from Drury Hearn to Nicholas Hill 1792, from Nicholas Hill to Hodson Bennett 1796. Wit Jeremiah Strother, Josiah Stephens. /s/ Hodson Bennett. Proven 8 March 1797 by Jeremiah Strother; John Blocker, J P. Recorded 8th March 1797.

p.493-494   Briton Mims to Talton Mims. Deed £10, 100 acres originally granted unto Francis Sinquefield, on Cedar Creek. Wit Wm Hagins, Wm Robertson. /s/ Briton Mims. Proven 10 March 1797 by William Robertson; Richard Tutt J P. Recorded 10th March 1797.

p.495-496   Christopher Ward, planter, to William Green, planter. Deed, 13 February 1797. $150 current SC money, 50 acres on branches of Little Stephens Creek part of 500 acres originally granted to Richard Buckelew 14 Aug 1772 and by decease of sd Richd Buckelew descended to George Buckelew son & heir to sd Richard Buckelew decd, sd 50 acres adj George Buckelew, Ogden Cockeroft, William Green. Wit John Cockeroft, Ogden Cockeroft, Jacob Green. /s/ Christopher (x) Ward. Proven 11 March 1797 by Ogden Cockeroft; Rd Tutt J P. Rec 11 Mar 1797.

p.496   Martin Forest to son Jesse Forest. Bill/sale. Negro boy Caesar for £35 sterling. Wit Bartlet Bledsoe, George Mason. /a/ Martin (x) Forrest. Recorded 11th March 1797.

p.496-500   James Buckelew to William Green. L&R, 9 December 1788/10 Decr 1788, £35 sterling, 50 acres on branch of Little Stevens Creek part of 500 acres originally granted to Richard Buckalew 14 August 1772 and by decease of Richard Buckelew descended unto George Buckelew son & heir to sd Rd Buckelew decd, and by sd George Buckelew conveyed to James Buckelew. Wit Frederick (F) Buckelew, Samuel Lewis, Christopher (R) Ward. /s/ James Buckelew, /s/ Rachel (B) Buckelew. Proven 11 March 1797 by Samuel Lewis; Richard Tutt. Recorded 11th March 1797.

p.500-504   Col Philemon Waters to Jacob Pope. L&R, 22 July 1787/21 July 1787, £10 sterling of SC, 394 acres on Indian Creek of Little Saludy granted by Thomas Pinckney Esqr 5 March 1787 adj Peter Whitten, Gentry, & vacant land. Wit Hezekiah Gentry, Pleasant (+) Burnett. /s/ P Waters. Proven 23 April 1789 by Hezekiah Gentry; Russell Wilson J P.   Recorded 13th March 1797.

p.504-507   James Minge Burton to Jacob Pope. L&R, 8 October 1789/ 9 October 1789, £100 sterling, 120 acres adj sd Jacob Pope, Jno Ewing Colhoun, Philemon Waters, Burton, Nathan Melton. Wit Allen Robinson, Thomas Melton, Benjamin Etheridge. /s/ James Minge Burton. Proven 2 August 1790 by Benjamin Etheridge; James Spann J P.   Recorded 18th March 1797.

p.508-511   Oliver Toles of Craven County SC to Jacob Pope of Bladen County, North Carolina. L&R, 3 October 1772/2 October 1775, £50 SC money, 200 acres in Colleton County on Little Saluda adj Thomas Carter. Wit Solomon Pope, Joseph Goodman. /s/ Oliver Towles. Proven 7 June 1784 by Solomon Pope; P Waters J P. Recorded 13th March 1797.

p.511-512   Joseph Walker, planter, to John Blalock, planter. Deed, 20 March 1796, £12 SC money, 50 acres part of 598 acres on north side of South Edistoe, adj Lewis Clark & Streets Branch. Wit William Beads, Prescott Bush. /s/ Joseph Walker, /s/ Elizabeth (E) Walker. Proven 29 February 1797 by Prescott Bush; Van Swearingen J P. Recorded 13th March 1797.

p.512-514   William Butler & wife Behethland to Robert Allen. Deed, 14 October 1796, £10 SC money, 129 acres, part of land formerly granted unto William Butler 5 Dec 1785 by Gov Wm Moultrie, on Little Saluda near Richland Creek. Wit Barnabas F Payne, Henry Tate. /s/ Wm Butler, /s/ Behethland Butler. [Plat shows land of Rideing Grigsby, estate of Smallwood Smith, Jacob Smith, Thomas Williams]. Proven 28 October 1796 by Henry Tate; Russell Wilson J P.   Rec 18th March 1797.

p.514-516   John Bridges to John Stephens[Stevens]. Deed, 22 September 1796, £20 sterling of SC, 1500 acres on Little Stevens Creek originally granted to Hugh Rose 17 Decr 1772 by Gov of SC; 285 of sd 1500 acres conveyed to me by Hugh Young, atty of Hugh Rose by L&R 26 & 27 of May 1794, sd 130 acres being a part of my 285 acres and adj Fudges line. Wit Alexr Bean, Jonathan Esary. /s/ John (I) Bridgers. Proven 13 March 1797 by Alexr Bean; Wm Daniel J P.   Recorded 13th March 1797.

p.516-517   James & Martha Hagood to Enoch Brazeal of Abbeville County. Deed, 9 January 1797, £35 sterling, 128 acres on Bedingfield Creek, adj Wm Anderson and Reuben Monday; granted to sd James Hagood by Gov Wm Moultrie on 5 February 1787. Wit LeRoy DuCerqueil, Greenberry Roden. /s/ James Hagood. Proven 11 March 1797 by Greenberry Roden; Jas Harrison J P.   Rec 13th March 1797.

p.517-519   James and Martha Hagood of Pennelton County, SC, to Enoch Braziel [Brazeal] of Abbeville County SC. Deed, 9 January 1797, £25 sterling, 200 acres on Bedingfield Cr and road from Long Cain to Augusta at the Red Lick adj John Wallace, W Frasier, & heirs of Reuben Monday; granted to John Trice by Gov Wm Moultrie 1 May 1793, and conveyed to James Hagood. Wit Ezekiel Hudnall, Greenberry Roden. /s/ James Hagood, /s/ Martha Hagood. Proven 11 March 1797 by Greenberry Roden; Jas Harrison J P. Recorded 13th March 1797.

p.519-520   John Mobley Senr to Josiah Howell. Deed, 17 December 1796, £17, 338 acres on Pen Creek, Little Saluda R, granted to sd John Mobley Senr 7 Octr 1793 by Gov Wm Moultrie. Wit Mumford Perryman, Jeremh Mobley. /s/ John (+) Mobley Senr. Proven 4 March 1797 by Mumford Perryman; Wm Daniel J P. Recorded 13th March 1797.

p.520-522   Hezekiah Walker to Joseph Walker. Deed, 1 January 1796 £50 starling, 50 acres on North side Edisto River, being a survey granted to James Jonakin by Lt Gov Wm Bull 1765. Wit Nathan Godwin, James (I) Sillavent. /s/ Hezekiah (W) Walker. Proven 13 March 1797 by Nathan Goodwin; Rd Tutt J P.

p.522-523   Arthur Watson to John Kirkland. Deed, 6 February 1797, £2 starling, 200 acres on Dry Creek of Mine Creek originally granted to Arthur Watson in 11th year of independence, adj Snowdon Kirkland & sd Watson. Wit Arthur Rice Watson, Hezekiah Watson. /s/ Arthur (A) Watson. Proven 13 March 1797 by Hezekiah Watson; Rd Tutt J P. Recorded 13th March 1797.

p.524-525   John Catlett to Daniel McKie of Newberry County. Deed, 11 January 1797, £150 sterling, 350 acres both sides Stevens Creek of Savannah River adj George Sutherland, Greenberry Caps, Martin Gosey, being two tracts, one originally granted to William Savage & James Simpson on 9 Novr 1774 for 500 acres; the other to Thomas Lamar for 100 acres and conveyed to George Longmire 1 May 1776 and sold by Sheriff Samuel Mays to John Catlett 6 June 1794 for 351 acres 6 Aug 1794. Wit John Ryan, Geo B Moore. /s/ John Catlett. Proven 13 March 1797 by John Ryan; S Mays J P. Recorded 13th March 1797.

p.525-527   John McQueen of East Florida to William Holliday of SC. Deed, East Florida, 17 September 1792, £30, 200 acres Cuffee town Creek adj John Walker, William Davis, William Anderson, John McFarlin, Samuel Holliday, John McIntosh, Peter Youngblood. Wit Andw Atkinson, A Buyck. /s/ John McQueen. Proven 11 February 1793 by A Buyck; Jos Habersham J P. Recorded 13th March 1797. [Plat: pursuant to warrant by Lt Gov Wm Bull, and directed by John Bremar DSG 3d July 1770, laid out to Robert Bull 200 acres on Cuffeetown Creek bounded by John Walker, Wm Davis, Wm Anderson, John McFarlin, Samuel Holliday Snr, John McIntosh, Peter Youngblood. Surveyed 20 July 1770, Wm Anderson DS. At request of William Holloway we have viewed within described tract and are of opinion that the value does not exceed thirty pounds. Edgefield April 23d, 1792. John Williams S D, George Forrest. Recorded 13th March 1797.

p.527-528   William Warren to Thomas Warren. Deed, 5 April 1796. £10 SC money, 100 acres on Clouds Creek, granted unto Wm Warren by patent 4 February 1788 by Gov Thos Pinckney. Wit Wm Wright, Adam Essert[Epert?]. /s/ Sarah (x) Warren. /s/ William Warren. Proven 18 June 1796; Russell Wilson J P. Rec 13th March 1797.

p.528-531   Benjamin Waring to John Hancock Senr. L&R, 1 May 1786/ 2 May 1786,

£134 current money, 500 acres in Granville County on Stevens Creek adj Thos Carter, John Carter, David Sigler, Gosper Strouble, and granted to sd Benjn Waring 8 July 1774. Wit Geo Joor, Thos Waring. /s/ B Waring. Proven 4 May 1786 by Thomas Waring Esqr; Daniel Huger J P. Recorded 13th March 1797.

p.531-535   Robert Stark the younger and wife Mary & Alexander Bolling Stark of Orangeburgh District SC to Joseph Williams, planter. Feoffment, 7 May 1795, $300, 376 acres on the waggon road from Cambridge to Charleston below the old store on the head of Indian branch, Clouds Creek in Edgefield County, being part of 1570 acres known as Starks Old Store originally granted to James Ravenel, adj Andress & land claimed by John Jones. Wit William Bell, James McGowen. /s/ R Stark, /s/ Alexr Bollg Stark. [plat of Old Store Tract by John Abney]. Proven 13 March 1797 by William Bell; John Blocker J P.   Recorded 13 Marh 1797.

p.535-536   William Humphreys to Barrot Travers. Deed, 12 December 1796, £25 sterling, 237 acres on Mine creek of Little Saluda River, part of 312 acres granted sd Wm Humphreys 4 Decr 1786 by Gov Wm Moultrie, adj Samuel Hmphreys, Ann Bland, Wm Daniel, & sd Barrot Travis land. Wit Mumford Perryman, Samuel Humphreys. /s/ William (x) Humphreys. /s/ Ann Humphreys. Proven 13 March 1797 by Mumford Perryman; Wm Daniel J P.   Recorded 13th March 1797.

p.537-538   Joseph Lewis Junr of Georgia to William Smith. Deed, 20 June 1796, £50 Starling of SC, 200 acres Turkey Cr surveyed for Samuel Whitney & after granted 2 March 1789 to Joseph Lewis Jr, bounded by Reuben Kirklands land and land of Isaac Lewis. Wit J Wever, Elender (+) Reabon, Joseph Lewis. /s/ Joseph Lewis. Proven 6 Octr 1796 by Jonathan Weaver; Van Swearingen J P.   Recorded 13th March 1797.

p.538-544   George Buckelew to Alexander Bean, both of Colleton County, Ninety Six Dist. L&R, 17 January 1784/16 January 1784, £150 SC money, 75 acres, part of 500 acres originally granted unto Richard Buckelew by Gov Chas Grenville Montague 1772, on Little Stevens Cr, adj Garrett Buckelew, surveyed by Wm Anderson DS on 2 June 1772 and certified 17 June 1772 Rd Lambton D S and examined pr D Mazyck; sd Richard Buckelew being dead, George Buckelew his son & heir sells to Alexr Been, 75 acres. Wit Azariah Lewis, John Harkins, Garret Buckelew. /s/ George Buckelew. Proven 13 January 1797 by Garret Buckelew; John Blocker J P.   Rec 13 March 1797.

p.544-546   James Lyon of Linkhom County, Georgia, planter, to William Kill-crease of Edgefield, planter. Deed, 12 October 1796, $260, 400 acres on Beaverdam of Turkey Creek of Savannah River, adj John Logan, Wm Coursey, Jacob Bell, Abraham Martin, being part of 500 acres that I purchased from William Coursey which was part of two tracts formerly granted unto sd Wm Coursey. Wit W Coursey, Constant (O) Oglesby, Anne (=) Oglesby. Proven 13 March 1797 by Constant Oglesby; John Blocker J P. Recorded 14th March 1797.

p.546-548   William Coursey and Mary Coursey to John Daulton. Deed, 13 March 1797, $100, 160 acres part of 1000 acres granted to Edward Vann by Gov Wm Moultrie 6 May 1793, by Vann conveyed unto sd Wm Coursey 10 June 1790, Beaverdam Creek of Turkey Creek of Savannah river, adj lands of Fredk Holmes, original grant, Obediah Kilcrease, John Thurmond decd, & John Loggin decd. Wit Constant (x) Oglesby, James Lyon. /s/ Wm Coursey. Mary (S) Coursey. Proven 13 March 1797 by Constant Oglesby;

John Blocker J P.   Recorded 14th March 1797.

p.548-549   Obediah Kilcrease [Killcrease], planter, to John Daulton. Deed, 13 March 1797, $20, 8 acres part of 100 acres granted unto me by State of SC on Beaverdam Creek of Savannah river adj land of Wm Coursey, long branch, and original grant. Wit James Lyon,a Constant (+) Oglesby. /s/ Obediah (O) Killcrease. Proven 13 March 1797 by Constant Oglesby; John Blocker J P.   Rec 14th March 1797.

p.549-553   Samuel Harris and wife Martha Harris to Samuel Hill. L&R, 12 Septr 1787/12 Sept 1787, granted 2 April 1773 by Lt Gov Wm Bull to Levi Harris 200 acres on Gunnels Creek of Stevens Creek adj Saml Harris, Thomas Stephenson, Levi Harris; sd Samuel Harris now for £100 sterling paid by Samuel Hill sells sd 200 acres. Wit Henry Key, James Thomas, Jeffery (H) Hill. /s/ Samuel (x) Harris, /s/ Martha (+) Harris. Proven 23 February 1797 by James Thomas; Henry Key J P.   Rec 14 March 1797.

p.553-554   Henry, Michael & Catherine Muckenfuss & Mary Desel to Jiles Chapman. Deed, 15 November 1796, £40 sterling, 200 acres on Clouds Creek of Little Saluda. Wit Adam Efurt, Mathew Burden, Samuel Gruber. /s/ Michael Muckenfuss, /s/ Henry Muckenfuss, /s/ Katharine Muckenfuss, /s/ Mary Desel. Proven 7 Feby 1797 by Adam Efurt; Russel Wilson J P.   Recorded 14th March 1797.

p.555-556   James Wilson of Abbeville County, Inn Keeper in Cambridge, to Charles Cooper. Deed, 1 November 1796, £85 sterling, 300 acres on Ninety Six Creek of Saluda River adj land of sd James Wilson, originally granted to William Bell 6 Feby 1786, conveyed by Bell to sd Jas Wilson 16/17 May 1790. Wit Benjn Glover, J Nichols Junr. Judge Chas J Colcock certifies relinquishment of dower by Tabitha Wilson wife of James Wilson, 10 March 1797. Proven 11 March 1797 by Benjamin Glover; Jno Trotter J P.   Recorded 14th March 1797.

p.557-558   Joseph Hightower to David Quarles. Deed, 31 December 1796, $273 109 acres and 24 perches on Chavers Creek bounded by lands granted unto John Buck-halter & Richard Quarles. Wit David Glover, Dudley Carter. /s/ Joseph Hightower. Proven 11 Feb 1797 by Dudley Carter; Chas Old J P.   Rec 14th March 1797.

p.558   Michael Buckhalter to Henry Buckhalter. Deed, 6 June 1796, £50 sterling, Negroe man Charles about seventeen years old. Wit Absolam Napper, George Grigory. /s/ Michael (EB) Buckhalter. Proven 21 December 1796 by Absolam Napper; Van Swearingen J P.   Recorded 14th March 1797.

p.559-560   Michael Buckhalter to Henry Buckhalter. Deed, £50 current money, 50 acres on branch of Big Horse Creek, originally granted to John Randal 5 June 1786, from him conveyed to Michael Buckhalter, also another tract of 97 acres originally granted to Thomas Bickum. Wit Absolam Napper, George Grigory. /s/ Michael (EB) Buckhalter. Proven 21 Decr 1796 by Absolom Napper; Van Swearingen J P. Recorded 14th March 1797.

p.560-562   Benjamin Harry to Thomas Adams. Deed, 14 March 1797, £20, 100 acres originally granted to William Mosley Junr 21 May 1772 by Gov Montague and conveyed by Wm Mosley 1775 to Benjamin Harry, lying in Granville County now Edgefield, on Nobles Creek adj lands of Lawrence Rambo and John Powman White.

Wit Burrel (+) Johnson, George H Perrin. /s/ Benjamin Harry. Judge Arthur Simkins certifies relinquishment of dower by Hannah Harry wife of Benjamin Harry, 14 March 1797; Arthur Simkins. /s/ Hannah Harry. Proven 14 March 1797 by George H Perrin; Rd Tutt, J P. Recorded 14th March 1797.

p.562-563   John Perry to Jacob Isom. Deed, 24 October 1796, 30 acres Hard-labour Creek adj sd Isom and Henry Mark, £10, 30 acres, part of 100 acres whereon sd John Perry lives. Wit Abner Perrin, Philip Peter Knob, Daniel Whiteman. /s/ John (IP) Perry. Proven 14 March 1797 by Abner Perrin; Richard Tutt. Recorded 14th March 1797.

p.563-565   Young Bickham to Drury Adams. Deed, 5 October 1796, £60 sterling, 75 acres south Horns Creek adj Pinex Howlet, sd Adams, Demsey Beckham, originally granted to Thomas Beckham. Wit Dempsey Beckham, Wm (Y) Cone. /s/ Young Beckham. Proven 21 October 1796 by Demsey Beckham; Aquila Miles J P. Rec 14 Mar 1797.

p.565   Elizabeth Coursey wife of James Coursey to John McFatrick. Renun-ciation of dower, 14 March 1797, certified by Judge Arthur Simkins, /s/ Elizabeth (x) Coursey. Recorded 14th March 1797.

p.566-567   James Barentine to Thomas Walpole. Deed, 23 August 1796, £30 ster-ling, 250 acres Rockey Fork of South Edistoe, part of 687 acres originally granted to Robert Lang, adj Charles Williams. Wit Eugene Brenan, Stn Norris. /s/ James (I) Barrontine. Proven 14 March 1797 by Stephen Norris; Rd Tutt JP. Rec 14th Mar 1797.

p.567-568   Enoch Grigsby to widow Rebeckah Hogans. Bill of Sale, 22 January 1789, £41 sterling, Negro girl Mary age nine. Wit Jacob Smith, James Grigsby. Proven 10 March 1797 by Jacob Smith; Rd Tutt J P. Recorded 15th March 1797.

p.568-570   Mary Johnston sole heir of John Savage Esqr decd to John Marshall Moore. Deed, 24 January 1797, £87.10 sterling 175 acres Cuffeetown Creek, part of 250 acres granted to my father John Savage 1 June 1767. Wit William White, William Moore. Certified 24 January 1797 to John Marshall Moore by Mary Johnston. Proven 24 January 1797 by William White; W Anderson J P. Recorded 15th March 1797.

p.570-571   Mary Johnston to John Marshall Moore. Deed, 23 January 1797, £10.10 sterling, 30 acres on small branch of Cuffee town Creek, part of 130 acres originally granted to my father John Savage decd adj John McClure, John Walker, William Davis. Wit Wm Moore, Richard Moore. /s/ Mary Johnston. Certification 23 January 1797 by Mary Johnston. Proven 14 March 1797 by William Moore; Chas Old J P. Recorded 15th March 1797.

p.571-573   Joseph Fuqua, planter, to Samuel Crafton, planter. Mortgage, 8 September 1796, condition payment of £60.18.2.1 sterling with legal interest on or before 1 December 1797 secured by mortgage to Crafton of slave boys: Ned and Isaac. Wit Charles Old, Jas Baker. /s/ Joseph Fuqua. Receipt of Joseph Fuqua. Proven 14 March 1797 by Charles Old; John Blocker J P. Recorded 15th March 1797.

p.573-574   Isaac Foreman to Samuel Sotcher. Deed B/Sale, 16 January 1796. £29.3.3 sterling, sell to Saml Sotcher, Negro boy Harry. Wit Arthur (A) Watson,

Amos Watson Sotcher. /s/ Isaac Foreman. Proven 16th March 1797 by Arthur Watson;
Richard Tutt J P. Recorded 16th March 1797.

p.574-575   Fredrick Wimberley to Samuel Sotcher. Bill of Sale, 11 May 1795.
£40.16.8 sterling, Negroe girl Dianah. Wit Arthur (A) Watson, Fredrick Cullens.
/s/ Frederick Wimberley. Proven 16 March 1797 by Arthur Watson; Rd Tutt J P.
Recorded 16th March 1797.

p.575-576   Sheriff William Tennent to Samuel Crafton. Title, 7 March 1796; at
suit of William Hort and Benjamin Waring Treasurers of State against Samuel Crafton
admr/estate of Bennet Crafton decd. Sheriff Wm Tennent sold to the highest bidder
Samuel Crafton for £50 sterling ready money at Cambridge 364 acres being part of
lands formerly property of Moses Kirkland and all the right title & interest sd
Bennet Crafton at time of death had in same. Wit Chas J Colcock, Charles Tennent.
/s/ Wm Tennent Shff 96 Dst. Proven 16 March 1797 by Charles J Colcock; Rd Tutt.

p.577-578   Henry Ware[Wayr] to Daniel McKie[McKey]. Deed, 2 Octr 1792, lease
dated 1 Oct for one acre west of Stephens Creek; for 40 shillings sold the acre to
McKey. Wit Greenberry Caps, Tom McKie, Daniel McKie Junr. /s/ Henry Ware. Proven
13 March by Tom McKey; Hugh Middleton. Recorded 16th March 1797.

p.579-581   Drury Mims to Elias Blackbourn. Deed 31 January 1797, £200, 360
acres on branches of Horns Creek, Cedar Creek, and Rays Creek, being part of four
tracts; 171 acres part of two tracts granted to sd Drury Mims by Gov Chas Pinckney
that is part of 211 acre tract granted 4th May 1789 and part of 150 acres granted 6
April 1789 and 196 acres being part of above mentioned 367 acres is part of two
other tracts of land, viz part of a 100 acre survey granted to Thomas Ray 28 January 1771 and part of 150 acre survey granted unto Solomon Peters 8th February 1773
the two pieces together containing 367 acres. [Plat shows 367 acres adjoining land
of John Mims]. Line corners on land granted to Joseph Nobles, corner on Hagins.
Wit Briton Mims, John Gray Junr. /s/ Drury Mims.   Certification by Judge Arthur
Simkins of dower release by Liddia Mims wife of Drury Mims.   /s/ Liddia (x) Mims.
Proven 16 March 1797 by Briton Mims; Rd Tutt J P.   Recorded 16th March 1797.

p.582   Mathew Wills to William Spragins. Bond, 6 September 1794, £150
to Spragins, condition 150 acres purchased of Wm Spragins for £40 sterling by L&R 6
Sept 1794. Wit Jacob Brooks, Evan Brooks, Sarah (x) Wells. /s/ Math Wills. Proven
6th September 1794 by Jacob Brooks who saw Mathew Wells sign within bond to Wm
Spragins; Nathl Abney J P.   /s/ Jacob Brooks. Recorded 16th March 1797.

p.583   William B Bland to Susannah Bland. Deed of Gift, for love & affec-
tion, Negro man Joe, Negro woman Sarah, another named Venus. Wit Robert Cochran,
Sithan Cochran. /s/ Wm B Bland. Proven 14 March 1797 by Robt Cochran; Chas Old J
P. Recorded 16th March 1797.

p.524   Mrs Lucy Purdue to John Hammond. Receipt & Bill of Sale, 5th May
1795, Received of John Hammond £50 sterling in full for a Negro woman Mary and her
child Lewis. Wit Wm Covington. /s/ Lucy Purdue. Proven 11 June 1796 by William
Covington; Joseph Hightower J P.   Recorded 18th March 1797.

p.524-586   Sarah Haddocks to Moses Haddocks. Deed, 17th April 1793, £50 sterling, 200 acres, Little Mine Creek of Little Saludy, originally granted to sd Sarah Haddocks 6 June 1786. Wit Presley Bland, Ewd Bland, Wm Bland. Sarah (SH) Haddocks. Proven 10 Augt 1793 by Edward Bland; Russell Wilson J P. Recorded 21st March 1797.

p.586-587   Tolaver Bostick, Stephen Bostick, & John Norwood. Bond. In behalf of himself and his wife Nancy are bound unto Davis Bostick and Littleberry Bostick in sum of £800 sterling, dated 22 March 1797. Whereas John Bostick Senr father of the parties above mentioned lately deceased, in his lifetime made his will by which he devised his estate; said will is lost. Condition of above obligation is that if above bound Tolaver Bostick, Stephen Bostick and John Norwood in behalf of himself and wife Nancy permit sd David Bostick and Littleberry Bostick to occupy the lands of sd John Bostick decd, and that sd Tolaver Steven & John Norwood release claim to sd estate. Wit Chas J Colcock, E Ramsay. /s/ T Bostick, /s/ Stephen Bostick, /s/ John Norwood in behalf of self and wife. Proven 22 March 1797 by Chs J Colcock; Rd Tutt J P. Recorded 22 March 1797.

p.587-588   Littleberry Adams to Samuel Walker. Bill of Sale, 30 January 1797, £37.11.10 sterling, also one note of hand for $96, Negro man Harry. Wit James Cobbs, Janey Cobbs. /s/ Littleberry Adams. Proven 29 March 1797 by James Cobbs; Henry Key J P. Recorded 29th March 1797.

p.588-590   William Deen and wife Ruth Deen to Olleyman Dodgen. Deed, 6 January 1795, £20 sterling, 100 acres Balees Branch of Little Saluda adj Joel Pardues, James Cheineas, corner of land laid out to John Chanea, adj Joel Pardue, Sam Pardue, said 100 acres being part of 390 acres formerly granted to John Chenea by Gov Wm Moultrie 2 Jan 1786. Signed 6 April 1795. Wit Gideon Christian, Joshua (M) Deen. /s/ Wm (M) Deen, /s/ Ruth Deen. Proven 6 December 1796 by Gideon Christian; Russell Wilson J P. Recorded 29th March 1797.

p.590-592   Joel Pardue to Olleyman Dodgen. Deed, 12 February 1794, £50 sterling, 324 acres on Baleys branch of Big Creek originally granted to sd Joel Pardue by Gov Wm Moultrie 4 March 1793, joyning land of Wm Willson, James Cheney, Wm Deen, Samuel Mays, John Abney. Wit Reuben (R) Lisenbee, Elizabeth (x) Pardue, Henry Weaver. /s/ Joel Pardue. Proven 6 December 1796 by Reuben Lisenbee; Russell Wilson J P. Recorded 29th March 1797.

p.592-593   Thomas Sikes of Charleston to Dionysius Oliver the younger. Deed, 28 March 1721, £140 sterling, originally granted 15 July 1765 to sd Thomas Sikes, 250 acres but by a late survey thereof 180 acres near Burgess' Beaverdams a Branch of Turkey Creek. Wit Joseph Peace, James T Neilson. /s/ Thom Sikes. Deed acknowledged by Thomas Sikes; John Johnson J P. Rec 3rd April 1797.

p.594-596   John Moore, planter, to Benja Glover & Co. Mortgage for five Negroes, 27 April 1797; in penal sum £116.7.2 sterling, condition the payment of £58.3.7 sterling with lawful interest unto Benjn Glover & Co; for securing payment, deliver Negro man Mingo about forty years old, Negroe woman Tabb about 25 yrs old, also her three children: Jenny about five, Harry about three, Stepney about one year old. Wit J McKellar. /s/ John Moore. Proven 27 April 1797 by John McKellar; Julius Nichols J P. Recorded 3 April 1797.

p.596-601   Joseph Reed, planter, and Phebe his wife, of Ninety Six District to Robert Russell, planter. L&R, 7 September 1775, £50 of SC, 100 acres in Granville County surveyed by Wm Goode D S, part of a tract of 300 acres granted by Gov Wm Bull 8 July 1774. Wit Robt Bryan, David Maxwell. /s/ Joseph (I) Read. Phebe (P) Reed [plat shows 100 acres on branches of Rockey Creek of Stephens Creek]. Proven 8 September 1775 by Robert Bryan; Benjamin Tutt J P.   Recorded 10th April 1797.

p.601-602   William Rowan to his daughter Elizabeth Carson. Deed of Gift, love and affection, all his goods and estate whatsoever; Elizabeth is put in full possession by the delivery of one cow and calf. Wit Jos Wallace, John Blocker Junr. /s/ William Rowan. Proven 10th April 1797 by Joseph Wallace; John Blocker J P. Recorded 10th April 1797.

p.603-605   William Fudge and Jacob Fudge to John Howard. Deed, 14 November 1796, £500 SC money, two tracts of land on Little Horse Creek, one of 640 acres originally granted unto sd Jacob Fudge 5 June 1786 and afterward conveyed by sd Jacob Fudge to his father Jacob Fudge except what lies in the fork of little Horse Creek and Nappers branch as far as line of sd 640 acres which sd fork was willed by Jacob Fudge Senr to John Fudge and his heirs, and all our parts of 2,375 acres originally granted unto Jacob Fudge Senr 1 January 1787 adjoining the former 640 acres, all 2375 except 500 acres on the south and west side willed by Jacob Fudge Senr to sd William Fudge & 260 acres on South and SE side willed by sd Jacob Fudge Senr to John Glekler, all the land of both surveys after the aforementioned small survey comes of the same according to will of Jacob Fudge Senr which after survey is computed to be 200 acres. Wit John G Cooke, James Ouers. /s/ Wm Fudge, /s/ Jacob Fudge. Judge Joseph Hightower confirms renunciation of dower by Mary Fudge wife of William Fudge, and Catherine Fudge wife of Jacob Fudge, 14 November 1796; /s/ Joseph Hightower, /s/ Mary (x) Fudge, /s/ Catherine (x) Fudge. Proven 8 April 1797 by James Ouers; Van Swearengen J P.   Recorded 17th April 1797.

p.605-606   Bowlen Dees to Eleazar Tharp Senr. Deed of Gift, for love and good will to his brother in Christ Eleazar Tharp, schoolmaster, land sd Tharp now lives on, east side of the part sd Bolen Dees now lives on, once belonging to Rowland Williams, joining Joseph McQuinney's line, line betwixt Bowlen Dees and Eleazar Tharp is a little branch heading up to Sisters Ponds. Wit Samuel Jescoat, Hugh Britt. /s/ Bolen (+) Dees. Proven 4 March 1797 by Samuel Jescoat[Jefcoat?]; William Daniel J P.   Recorded 17th April 1797.

p.607-612   John Thomas Fairchild of Lexington County in Orangeburgh District to Alexander Bolling Stark of the same place, attorney at law. L&R, 29 December 1794/30 December 1794, £20 sterling, 7500 acres, being parcels of several tracts granted 6 October 1794 to John Thomas Fairchild, a mistake made by William Wright the surveyor in the plat scale, on Clouds Creek and Beaverdam adjoining John Thomas Fairchilds land, David McGehee, Sion Mitchell, Saluda River, Sullivans land, Thomas Williams, William Butler, also on Little Saluda River adj Sion Mitchell and Moses Prestates, Samuel Johnson, Hezekiah Cotney. Wit Jno Bynum, Jos Williams. /s/ J Thos Fairchild. Proven: Camden District, Richland County, 19 April 1797 by John Bynum; Martyn Aiken J P.   Recorded 21st April 1797.

p.612-613   John Norwood to Tolaver Bostick. Deed of gift in Trust, 18 April

1797, 5 shillings and natural love & affection, furniture and livestock, condition described goods and chattels not to be sold unless with consent of Nancy Norwood wife of sd John Norwood clearly expressed in writing, also agreed that afsd goods & chattels remain in possession of sd Nancy and under her direction during the life of sd Tolaver and at his death sd Nancy is to take full possession thereof. Wit John M Moore, Wm Glover. /s/ John Norwood. Receipt of 5 shillings from Tolaver Bostick by John Norwood. Proven 25 April 1797 by John M Moore; Rd Tutt J P. Recorded 21st April 1797.

p.614-617   William Glover of Georgia to James Rushton. L&R, 9 May 1785/10 May 1785, £85.14 SC money, 183 acres on Cuffeetown Creek adj land of John Bostick, Richard Brooks, Isaac Ramsay, part of original grant unto Elisha Brooks 12 August 1768. Wit Nathaniel Henderson, Eli Thornton. /s/ William Glover. Proven 10 March 1790 by Eli Thornton; John Moore J P.   Recorded 22nd April 1797.

p.617-618   Nathan Henderson to James Rushton. Deed, 24 March 1793, £6; 6¼ acres on Cuffey Town Creek, line between Nathan Henderson and James Rushton. Wit John Hamilton, John Henderson. /s/ Nathan Henderson. Proven 19th January 1797 by John Henderson; W Anderson JCE.   Recorded 22nd April 1797.

p.618-620   Mary Johnston eldest daughter & sole heir to John Savage deceased to James Rushton. Deed, 24 January 1797, £37.10 current money, 75 acres part of a tract on Cuffey Town originally granted to sd John Savage 1 June 1767. Wit William White, William Moore. Proven 24 January 1797 by William White; Wm Anderson JCE. Recorded 22nd April 1797.

p.620-621   Mary Moore to Andrew Pickens & Thomas Bacon admrs of James Moore decd. Bill/Sale, 18 January 1797, $992.75, Negro man Sam and his wife Hannah and their three children John, Rachel and Minder, also livestock, all purchased at the sale of James Moore decd. Wit Matt Henderson, Melines C Leavensworth. /s/ Mary Moore. Proven 4 May 1797 by Melines C Leavensworth; Joseph Hightower J P. Recorded 6th May 1797.

p.621-623   Edmund Riggs to Hezekiah Gentry. Deed, 12 August 1795, £60 sterling, to Hezekiah Jentry 150 acres on Bigg Creek branch of Little Saluda, part of original grant to Wm Moulton 1792. Wit James McKnight, David Pugh, Jesse Griffin. /s/ Edmund Riggs. Proven 14 April 1797 by Jesse Griffin; Nathl Abney J P. Recorded 10th May 1797.

p.623-625   Sampson Pope, George Pope & Elijah Pope. Bond. Land of Jacob Pope decd late of Edgefield County hath been appraised by Hezekiah Gentry, Jesse Griffin and Aron Etheridge to be worth £340 and is assented to by heirs Sampson, Elijah & George Pope. To George Pope 160 acres on south side Little Saluda. To Sampson Pope 600 acres on Indian Creek being part of a purchase made by L&R 4 & 5 January 1791 being appraised at £75. To Elijah Pope 394 acres in the Barrens between Little Saluda & Indian Creek appraised at £40. Wit Susannah Pope, Robert (x) Christie, Hazekiah Gentry trustee. /s/ Sampson Pope, /s/ George Pope, /s/ Elijah Pope. Proven 18 January 1797 by Robert Christie; Russell Wilson J P. Recorded 10th May 1797.

47

p.625-628   Cornelius Jeter to William Garrett. Mortgage, 6 February 1797, £200 SC money, 300 acres on branch of Turkey Creek granted to John Logan whereon sd Cornelius Jeter now lives, condition that land sd Garrett purchased of sd Jeter being a part of a tract granted to John Hitchcock, agreeable to bond sd Geter has given to sd Garrett. Wit Thos Jinkins, John Jaggars, Thomas Garrett Sagars. /s/ Cornelius Jeter. 6 Feby 1797 certification by Cornelius Geter that above land was his own property; Thos Jinkins J P. Proven 6 Feby 1797 by John Jaggars; Thos Jinkins J P. Recorded 10th May 1797.

p.628-633   William Hale of Charles town SC exr of Peter Stephenson deceased to Samuel Savage Esqr. L&R, 20 August 1779/31 August 1779. Will of Peter Stephenson 23 July 1773 appointed Thomas Jones and William Hale his executors; Thos Jones refused to qualify; Wm Hale alone qualified. Will directed sale of estate. £1800 current SC money, 450 acres south branch Santee River, adj Daniel Burnett original grant of same 12 June 1751 by Gov Jas Glen. Wit Thos Commander Russell, Jno Caldwell. /s/ Wm Hale. Proven 10 July 1793, Newberry County, by William Caldwell who sayeth that witness John Caldwell was wrote by John Caldwell deceased late of sd district and that this deponant was well acquainted with sd Caldwell's handwriting; Robert Gillam J P. /s/ William Caldwell. Recorded 15th May 1797.

p.633-634   Jeremiah Jones and wife Joice to John Bruton of Warren County, Georgia. Deed 17 April 1797, £25 sterling, 100 acres part of 461 acres granted to Stephen Smith and transferred by deed from sd Smith to Jeremiah Jones 25 April 1795. Wit John (x) Brooks, Joseph Ferguson Senr. /s/ Jeremiah Jones, /s/ Joyce (J) Jones. Proven 20 May 1797 by John Brooks; Chas Old J P.

p.634-637   Joseph Forguson to John Bruton. Deed, 17 April 1797, £50 sterling, 100 acres on Savannah River surveyed 10 May 1794 by Robert Lang D S., same being part of 400 acres granted to John Crookshanks decd father of Benjamin Crookshanks dated 8 March 1754 afterwards by sd John Crookshanks conveyed unto his three sons John, David & Benjamin Crookshanks 10 March 1765 and transferred by sd Benjamin Crookshanks unto Joseph Forguson 22 December 1794. Wit John (+) Brooks, Jeremiah Jones. /s/ Joseph Forguson. Proven 20 May 1797 by John Brooks; Chas Old J P.

p.637-638   Davis Moore to Wiley Glover of Cambridge town. Bond for Titles, 21 September 1793, Davis Moore and Thomas Edwards bound unto Wiley Glover in sum £100 SC money, condition title be made to 132 acres within 2 miles of Cambridge bounding land of Fredrick Glover, Thomas Livingston, James Gouedy, James Harkins, & William Robertsons land within six calendar months. Wit Patk McDowall. /s/ Davis Moore, /s/ Thos Edwards. Proven 25 April 1797 by Patrick McDowall; Wm Anderson JCE. Recorded 15th May 1797.

p.638-639   David Sigler to his son Jeremiah Sigler. Deed, 29 December 1796, $10 paid, 250 acres on Stephens Creek granted unto David Sigler as followeth: 100 acres on 29 April 1768, 150 acres to David Sigler on 23 January 1773. Wit Thomas Carter, Richard Hardy. /s/ David Sieqler. Proven 11 February 1797 by Captain Thomas Carter; Chas Old J P. Recorded 16th May 1797.

p.639-641   John Stringer to Joel Grizzel. Deed, 30 August 1796, £300 SC money, 300 acres Stephens Creek surveyed by Robert Lang. Wit Jno Slater, Enos

Morgan. /s/ Jno Stringer. Certification of release of dower rights by Ann Stringer wife of John Stringer, 21 August 1796; Joseph Hightower. /s/ Ann (x) Stringer. Certification of plat by Robert Lang, 300 acres on SW side Stephens Cr including the old place known as Stringers old place bounded by lines of John Stringer, William Stringer, Col John Purvis. Proven 17 May 1797 by Enos Morgan; Chas Old J P. Recorded 20th May 1797.

p.642   Stephen Norris to John Olliphant. Bill of Sale, 7 January 1797, £60 Negroe boy David, condition Stephen Norris hath borrowed £60 from John Olliphant, money to be paid to John Olliphant on or before 7 January 1799 or above bill of sale to be of none effect. Wit George H Perrin, Rd Tutt. /s/ Stn Norris. Proven 23 May 1797 by George H Perrin; Rd Tutt J P.   Rec 23rd May 1797.

p.243-644   Thomas Williams, John Smith & Sarah his wife & Robert O Williams and Kezia his wife, legatees of estate of William Williams decd, to Benjamin Williams. Deed/conveyance, 25 November 1796. £12 sterling to each of us paid; 150 acres; the greater part of sd land originally granted to John Scott on Chavers Cr, a branch of Stephens Creek. Wit Edmond Watson, Frances (x) Watson, Thomas Traylor, Richard Robinson, Owen Williams. /s/ Thomas Williams, /s/ John Smith, /s/ Robert Owen Williams. Proven 12 April 1797 by Edmond Watson who also saw Frances Watson sign her name; Chas Old J P. Proven 29 April 1797 by Thomas Traylor; Chas Old J P. Proven 23 May 1797 by Owen Williams who saw Robert Owen Williams sign and that he signed as witness with Richard Robinson; Chas Old J P.   Rec 24 May 1797.

p.644-646   Russell Wilson to Shepherd Spencer. Deed, 28 December 1796, £50 sterling, 255 acres on Ceder Cr originally granted unto sd Russell Wilson. Wit Benjamin Etheridge, Jesse Wilson. /s/ Russell Wilson. Proven 6 February 1797 by Benjamin Etheredge; S Mays J P.   Recorded 24th May 1797.

p.646   James Whitlock to Asa & Patsey Whitlock. Deed of Gift, 22 May 1797; for love and affection to his son Asa Whitlock, give livestock, and unto my daughter Patty Whitlock, livestock. Wit Solomon (+) Holmes, Betty Tutt. /s/ James Whitlock. Proven 25th May 1797 by Betty Tutt; Rd Tutt.   Rec 25th May 1797.

End of Book 13

p.1-3   Herman[Harmon] Gallman and wife Lucretia to Joseph Addison. Deed 1 April 1789, £50 SC money, part of two tracts, 100 acres in one on main road from Augusta to Island ford of Saluda adjoining John Addison's land, originally granted to John Rutledge being part of 200 acres originally granted to Allen Addison 20th April 1764, also forty acres adj afsd tract, John Grays land, John Bayly, being part of 400 acres originally granted to Hermon Gallman. Wit James Brown, Wm Brown. Proven 30 June 1797 by James Brown. Recorded 30th June 1797.

p.3-4   Daniel Bird, planter, to Jane Rairden. 20 May 1797; $50 paid by George Rardane and delivered unto Jane Raredane two young Negroes, one boy Jery and one girl Siller now in possession of sd Jane Rareden and at her death to descend to her three youngest children: John, Patsey and Clarisy if they should have living issue, but if they dy without heirs to descend to lawful heirs of sd Daniel Bird. Wit James Blocker, John Blocker Junr. /s/ Daniel Bird. Proven 3 June 1797 by James Blocker; John Blocker J P. Recorded 3d June 1797.

p.5-12   Jacob Fudge to Ebenetus Stephens. L&R, 4 April 1772/5 April 1772, between Jacob Futch of Greenville County, planter, and Ebenetus Stephens of afsd county, ten pounds SC money, 100 acres on Rockey Creek near Long Cane road, granted Henry Hartley alias George Hartley, 12 Sept 1768, by Gov Wm Bull. Wit Chrismas Ray, Silvenes Stephens. /s/ Jacob Fudge. Proven 23 Septr 1772 by Selvenes Stevens; Moses Kirkland J P. Recorded 5th June 1797.

p.12-14   David Glover to Joseph Hightower. Deed, 31 December 1796; $200, 109 acres 24 perches bounded by lands of John Buckhalter and Richard Quarles. Wit David Quarles, Dudley Carter. /s/ David Glover. Proven 10 June 1797 by David Quarles; Chas Old J P. Recorded 14th June 1797.

p.14-18   Solomon Fudge to Jacob Fudge. Deed, 29 May 1797, £100 SC money paid by William Fudge, sell to sd William Fudge 241.5 acres being part of three surveys of land, one of 100 acres granted unto Daniel Ellis 19 Aug 1788(?) another tract of 56 acres granted Nicholas Glasser 4 May 1775, another tract of 327 acres granted unto Jacob Fudge Senr 5 June 1786, the first hundred acres here mentioned was conveyed by sd Daniel Ellis to James Jernegen 13 Sept 1771 and by Jas Jernegan unto Jacob Fudge Senr 13 Jan 1785, and by him by will to Solomon and Richard Fudge, the afore mentioned 56 acres was conveyed by Nicholas Glasser to Jacob Fudge Senr 14 March 1780 likewise willed by sd Jacob Fudge as afsd, the other 327 acres granted unto sd Jacob Fudge 5 June 1786 likewise willed by Jacob Fudge Senr to Solomon and Richard Fudge as afsd. Wit J G Cooke, Thomas Westbay, James Guess. Relinquishment of dower rights by Elizabeth Fudge wife of Solomon Fudge, 10 June 1797; Joseph Hightower. /s/ Elizabeth (x) Fudge. Proven 10 June 1797 by J G Cooke; Chas Olds J P. Recorded 14th June 1797.

p.18-21   John Buckhalter to William Fudge. Deed, 31 May 1797; £25 SC money, swamp land on both sides Phillips branch where sd Wm Fudge erects a mill dam on sd creek. Wit J G Cooke, Thomas Westby, James Guess. /s/ John (IB) Buckelew(sic). Relinquishment of dower by Anne Buckhalter wife of within named John Buckhalter 10 June 1797; Joseph Hightower. Anne (x) Buckhalter. Proven 10 June 1797 by J G Cooke who saw John Buckhalter sign; Charles Old J P. Recorded 14 June 1797.

p.21-23   Philip Lamar to John Jones. Deed, 23 February 1797, $22.50, 45 acres below Horse Creek adj George Wallace, Peppers branch, James Jones, George Wallace, being part of 816 acres granted to Ayers Gorley and conveyed to Philip Lamar unto sd John Jones. Wit John Hart, John (OO) Low. /s/ Philip Lamar. Proven 6 April 1797 by John Hart; John Clarke J P.   Recorded 14 June 1797.

p.23-24   Philip Lamar to George Wallace. Deed, 30 January 1797, $69, 118 acres below Horse Creek adj John Jones, James Jones, Robert Lamar, part of 816 acres granted to Ayers Gorley, transferred to sd Philip Lamar, unto George Wallace. Wit John Jones, Lewis (P) Pike. /s/ Philip Lamar. Proven 6 April 1797 by John Jones; John Clarke J P.   Recorded 14th June 1797.

p.25-26   Peter McCain to William Terry, planter. Bill/Sale. £35 sterling, livestock [marks described]. Wit W Coursey, John Terry, Francis Covington. /s/ Peter McCain. Proven 17th June 1797 by John Terry; Rd Tutt J P. Rec 17 June 1797.

p.26-29   William McDaniel and wife Mary of Abbeville County to Jacob Hibler[Hebler]. Deed, 15 June 1797; £70 sterling, 107 acres on Stephens Creek part of grant to Benjamin Bell bounded by Samuel Stalnaker, Hawley, Hiram McDaniel, Richard Tutt Senr. Wit B Howorth, J Evans, Richd Tutt Junr. /s/ William (x) McDonald, /s/ Mary (x) McDonald.   Proven 16 June 1797 by Doctor Benjamin Howorth; Jas Harrison J P.   Recorded 19th June 1797.

p.29-35   Jacob Brown to William Golden. L&R, 16 May 1792/17 May 1792, £30 Sterling, 100 acres part of a survey of 300 acres on Beaverdam branch of Little Saluda granted to Edward Coe by Gov Wm Bull 18 Oct 1774. Wit Thos Deloach, Samuel McKinsey, Thomas Deen. /s/ Jacob Brown. Proven 17 June by Thomas Deen; Russell Wilson J P.   Recorded 20th June 1797.

p.35-41   Abraham Loftin Fairchild, planter, to John Davis. L&R, 13 September 1791/14 Septr 1791, £50 sterling, 150 acres on Richardsons Mill creek of South Edisto River bounding on land of James Richardson when surveyed, granted by Gov Chas Montague unto John Fairchild 10 May 1768, conveyed from John Fairchild to Abraham Loftin Fairchild 4 & 5 Nov 1768. Wit William Fairchild, Robert Fairchild, Benj (B) Hughes. /s/ Abraham Loftin Fairchild. Proven 14 September 1791 by William Fairchild; John Thomas Fairchild J P.   Recorded 20th June 1797.

p.41-44   Theodore Stark to Samuel Marsh. Deed, 18 February 1797. Whereas Harman Gallman, William Brown, Joseph Addison and Lucretia Gallman executrix of will of Harman Gallman decd by L&R date 13/14 Feb 1786 between them and Theodore Stark conveyed to sd Theodore Stark 160 acres on Horns Creek adj John Gray, public road from Augusta to Island Ford, to Da Carters line, to Thomas line, on land granted to Daniel Rogers, Mitchels line, Grays line, £99.12 paid by Samuel Marsh for land described above 160 acres. Name Allen Addison inserted by mistake as Gallman is now alive. Wit. Alexr B Stark, James Brown, John Addison. /s/ Theodore Stark. Proven 30 June 1797 by Jas Brown; Rd Tutt, J P. Recorded 30 June 1797.

p.44-48   John Davis to Charles Purkins. Deed, 19 June 1797, £50 sterling, 100 acres on Saluda River originally granted unto John Davis 25 April 1786. Wit Arthur W Davis, Benjamin Tucker, Gartrude (D) Davis. /s/ John Davis.   Proven 20

June 1797 by Arthur Davis; Russell Wilson J P.   Recorded 20th June 1797.

p.48-49   Abraham M Wade to Daniel Tillman. Bill/Sale, 30 January 1797;
$274, Negro boy Ned. Wit Matt Martin, Lewis Tillman. Proven 20 June 1797 by Lewis
Tillman; Rd Tutt J P.   Recorded 20th June 1797.

p.49-50   Hugh Middleton Junr to William Tennent. Deed, 13 February 1797;
£50 sterling, 155 acres surveyed for afsd Hugh Middleton 2 April 1792 on Savannah
River, adj Hugh Middleton Senr, John Middleton. Wit Hugh Middleton Senr, Charles
Tennent. /s/ Hugh Middleton Junr. Proven 8 March 1797 by Chas Tennent; Chas J
Colcock J P.   Recorded 26th June 1797.

p.50-54   Hugh Middleton Esqr to William Tennent Esqr. Deed, 15 February
1797, £183, two tracts of land being part of different surveys, one run out by
Richd Meadows, the other by [blank] Vann, situate on Savannah River, joining Jno
Middleton, 158 acres and 10 acres resurveyed for Jno Boyd on Deep Step Creek. Wit
Chas Tennent, John Middleton. /s/ Hugh Middleton. [Plat for Majr H Middleton and
William Tennent Esq, laid out unto sd Tennent two pieces of land containing 41.5
acres and 117 acres and 155 acres, 15 February 1797. H W Coursey D S.] Proven 8
March 1797 by Chas Tennent; Chas J Colcock J P.   Recorded 26 June 1797.

p.54-57   Abraham Holsenback to Isaac Brunson Junr. Deed, 13 January 1797,
£30 sterling 128 acres on Beaver pond Creek of Horse Creek of Savannah River, plat
by William Coursey Dep Survr being part of 178 acres granted unto sd Abraham
Holsenback by Gov Thos Pinckney 7 April 1788. Wit W Coursey, Daniel Brunson. /s/
Abraham (A) Holsomback, /s/ Jean (x) Holsomback. Proven by Daniel Brunsen; Henry
Key J P. Recorded 28th June 1797.

p.57-58   Philip Johnson to William Johnson. Bill of Sale, 12 January 1793,
£50 sterling Negro man Oliver. Wit Thos Childers, W Jeter Junr. /s/ Philip Johnson.
Proven 29 June 1797 by Thomas Childers; Rd Tutt J P.   Recorded 29th June 1797.

p.58-59   William Johnson to Littlebery Adams. Bill of Sale, 20 June 1797,
$300, Negro man Oliver. Wit Thomas Childers, Edwin Farned. /s/ William Johnson.
Proven 29 June 1797 by Thomas Childers; Rd Tutt J P.   Recorded 29th June 1797.

p.59-61   Isaac Foreman to Benjamin Hart indorsed to Nathan White indorsed
to William Hill. Bond, 18 November 1796. Isaac Foreman bound to Benjamin Hart $1000
to be paid to Benjn Hart, condition Isaac Foreman doth cause to be made lawful conveyance by 25th Decr 1797 of 160 acres on Horns Creek joining Wm Hills land, also a
tract of 28 acres joining Wm Hardins, then obligation to be void. Wit J Spann, Jno
G Snead. /s/ Isaac Foreman. Nov 30, 1796 indorsed by Benjamin Hart to Nathan White.
Proven 1 July 1797 by John G Snead; John Blocker J P.   Endorsed within bond unto
William Hill for value recd of him 3 January 1797; Wit Rd Tutt, /s/ Nathan White.
Proven 1 July 1797 by Richard Tutt; John Blocker J P. Recorded 1 July 1797.

p.61-63   John Slone & William Hill to John Monk. Covenant & Deed, 28 March
1795; 18 months after date John Sloan and William Hill covenant to pay unto John
Monk £350 sterling for his land & improvements 1150 acres, also to keep him in
peaceable possession of sd land by us untill sd money is paid; whenever that is

done possession to be given of the mills and Iron works; sd Monk is to have use of his house three months longer if he chooses and liberty to take whatever crop he may have on sd lands at that time; in case money is not paid in 18 months from date hereof sd land conveyed back unto sd Monk. Wit Isaac Kirkland, Moses Armstrong, James (+) Bannister. /s/ John Sloan, /s/ W Hill. Proven 19 January 1796 by Isaac Kirkland; Vann Swearengen. Recorded 1 July 1797.

p.63-65   Absolam Williams to Emsley Lott. Deed, 23 January 1797, £30, 100 acres on drains of Edisto and Saludy Rivers at fork of Long Cain & Savannah Road originally granted to George Alexander 21 March 1768. Wit Jesse Lott, J Spann. /s/ Absolam Williams. Proven 1 July 1797 by Jesse Lott; Vann Swearengen J P. Recorded 1st July 1797.

p.65-68   Sheriff William Tennent Esqr to John Mims Junr. Sheriff titles, 4th January 1796, by virtue of writ at suit of William Stevens against Davis Moore and Peter Chastain for sheriff to sell 150 acres to highest bidder for ready money at Cambridge, struck off to John Mims for £9.11, sd land surveyed for Joseph Thomas 30th August 1771 in county then called Granville on Loyds Creek, granted by Wm Campbell 5 May 1775. Wit Chas Tennent, Davis Moore. /s/ Wm Tennent Shff 96 Dst. Proven 3 July 1797 by Davis Moore; Rd Tutt J P.   Recorded 3rd July 1797.

p.68-69   Richardson Bartlett to William Fountain. Deed, 7 January 1797, £25 sterling, 100 acres on lines of James Durham, Thomas Marbury, heirs of Wm Hairgrove, James Durham, Willis Whatly. Wit William Durham, Thomas Marbury. /s/ Richardson (x) Bartley. Proven 3 July 1797 by William Durham; John Blocker J P. Recorded 3 July 1797.

p.70-71   Richardson Bartlett to James Durham. Deed, 7 January 1797, £25 sterling, 50 acres, lines at Dry Creek, Thmas Marbury, Robert Melton, Lusby Boid. Wit William Durham, Thomas Marbury. /s/ Richardson (x) Bartlett. Proven 3 July 1797 by William Durham; John Blocker J P.   Recorded 3d July 1797.

p.71-75   Robert Smith to William Anderson. Release, 24 April 1781, £1200 current money, 244 acres whereon Robert Smith now lives on Saludy River originally granted to James Shingelton and conveyed by Wm Seyer, from Seyer to Robert Smith. Wit Thos Anderson, Hubbard Quarles, James (0) Crow. /s/ Robert (x) Smith. Proven 1 February 1785 by Thomas Anderson; Bartlett Satterwhite J P. Recorded 3d July 1797.

p.75-78   William Anderson to Thomas Anderson Junr. Deed, 10 February 1797, £500 sterling, 640 acres on Wilsons Creek whereon my grist mill and saw mill now stands, 400 acres of which was granted to myself, and one hundred acres granted to William White and 50 acres granted to William Mossman and the remainder to Edwd Buck and William Anderson. Wit Rd Tutt, Martha Perrin, George H Perrin. /s/ Wm Anderson. Relinquishment of dower by Eliza Ann Anderson wife of Wm Anderson, 20 February 1797; Arthur Simkins JCE; /s/ Eliza Ann Anderson. Proven 3 July 1797 by George H Perrin; Rd Tutt J P.   Recorded 3 July 1797.

p.78-80   William Anderson to his daughters Rachel & Eliza Anderson. Deed, 10 February 1797, £300 sterling, 440 acres including the following grants: 140 acres purchased of Robert Lang and granted to James Myrick; also 100 acres purchased of Robert Lang and granted to Millicent Lang; 150 acres purchased of Little Berry Harris and granted to William Ellice, and 40 acres which I purchased of Samuel Sansom, bounded by James Hill, the Goose pond branch, Saludy River. Wit Rd Tutt, Martha Perrin, George H Perrin. /s/ W Anderson. Relinquishment of dower by Eliza Ann Anderson wife of William Anderson, 20 February 1797; Arthur Simkins. /s/ Eliza Ann Anderson. Proven 3 July 1797 by George H Perrin; Rd Tutt J P. Recorded 3rd July 1797.

p.81-83   William Anderson to Rebeccah Anderson. Deed, 10 February 1797; £300 sterling, 740 acres on Saluda River known as Horse Shoe Neck including following grants: 100 acres granted to John George Dorst, 250 acres granted to Joseph Johnson, 100 acres granted to Alexander Campbell, 140 acres granted to sd William Anderson, about 200 acres granted to William Anderson being a part of a 272 acre grant, also 50 acres which I purchased of Robert Anderson, being part of land which was granted to his Father Thomas Anderson. Wit Rd Tutt, Martha Perrin, George H Perrin. /s/ W Anderson. Relinquishment of dower by Eliza Ann Anderson wife of William Anderson, 20 February 1797; Arthur Simkins. /s/ Eliza Ann Anderson. Proven 3 July 1797 by George Henry Perrin; Rd Tutt J P.   Recorded 3 July 1797.

p.83-86   William Anderson to Thomas Anderson Junr. Deed, 19 September 1758; £700 sterling, 244 acres on Saluda River originally granted to James Shingleton 15 May 1751, conveyed by Jas Shingleton to William Syer, by Wm Syer to Robt Smith, by Robt Smith to William Anderson 23 and 24 April 1781, also 200 acres on Saluda River bounded by land surveyed for James Anderson, originally granted to Patrick Kelty 19 September 1758. Wit Rd Tutt, Martha Perrin, George H Perrin. /s/ W Anderson. Relinquishment of dower by Eliza Ann Anderson wife of Wm Anderson; Arthur Simkins. /s/ Eliz Ann Anderson. Proven 3 July 1797 by George H Perrin; Rd Tutt J P.   Recorded 3rd July 1797.

p.87-89   Thomas Elliott and wife Lucy to Henry Herron. Deed, 4 March 1797; £30 sterling, 123 acres on Pen Creek of Little Saludy adj Jeremiah Mobley, William Hart, Robert Starks granted by Gov Chas Pinckney. Wit Jeremh Mobley Senr, William Herrin. /s/ Thomas Elliott, /s/ Lucy Elliott. Proven 13 March 1797 by William Herrin; Rd Tutt J P.   Relinquishment of dower by Lucy Elliott wife of Thomas Elliott, 3 July 1797; Arthur Simkins. /s/ Lue Elliott.   Rec 3d July 1797.

p.89-93   Samuel Lewis to Henry Clark. L&R, 14 December 1792/15 December 1792, £35 sterling, 230 acres Red Bank Creek of Little Saluda and Little Stevens of Savannah River being part of 250 acres originally granted to Samuel Lewis 2 Octr 1786, adj lines of Brison, Parson, and old grant lines. Wit Thomas Scott, Lewis (x) Clark, Aron Clark. /s/ Samuel Lewis. Proven 3 July 1797 by Thomas Scott; Rd Tutt J P.   Recorded 3 July 1797.

p.93-96   Sheriff Jeremiah Hatcher Esqr to Jesse Puckett. Shff Titles, 5 January 1796; Davis Moore obtained judgment against Michael Blocker for £26.1.7; attested by Richard Tutt Clerk of court 17 October 1794; sheriff directed to sell real estate of Michael Blocker, 150 acres, lying on road from Martintown to McKies Mill bounded by Wm Wright, Geo Cowan, Nathan Evans, Wm Longmire; on 3d October 1795 to highest & last bidder Jesse Puckett 150 acres for £9 sterling paid by John Hammond for J Puckett. Wit Thos Butler, P Bland. /s/ J Hatcher Shff.   Proven 3

July 1797 by P Bland; John Blocker J P.   Recorded 8 July 1797.

p.96-99   Prescott Bush to Mathew Wilkinson.   Deed, 6 February 1797, £20 sterling, 300 acres surveyed by Wm Swift, granted by Gov Wm Moultrie, Little Bog branch, Buck Creek. Wit Hezekiah (W) Walker, Wm Wimberley. /s/ Prescott Bush. Proven 3 June 1797 by Hezekiah (x) Walker; Van Swearengen J P. Arthur Simkins certifies relinquishment of dower by Susannah Bush wife of Prescott Bush; /s/ Susannah (x) Bush.   Recorded 3 July 1797.

p.99-102   Richard Bush Junr to Hezekiah Walker.   Deed, 24 January 1797; £75 sterling, 70 acres adjoining Beach Creek, Edistoe, John Couch, Willm Wimberley, Edward Couch, Ezekiel Walker, originally granted to John Cronan by Gov William Moultrie 1787. Wit Wm Wimberley, Ezekiel (x) Walker. /s/ Richard Bush Junr. Judge Arthur Simkins certifies relinquishment of dower by Sarah Bush wife of Richard Bush Junr, 3 July 1797.   Proven 3 July 1797 by Wm Wimberley; Van Swearengen J P. Recorded 3 July 1797.

p.102-104   Absey Couch to Ezekiel Walker, yeoman.   Deed 24 January 1797, £20 sterling, 40 acres South Edistoe part of land originally granted to Edward Couch by Gov Chas Pinckney 206 acres, adj John Couch. Wit Wm Wimberley, Hezekiah (x) Walker. /s/ Absey her(x)mark Couch. Proven 3 July 1797 by Wm Wimberley; Van Swearengen J P. Recorded 3 July 1797.

p.104-106   Absey Couch to Hezekiah Walker Senr, yeoman.   Deed, 24 January 1797, £20 sterling, forty acres on South Edistoe, part of land originally granted to Edward Couch by Gov Chas Pinckney, and 6 acres of sd 40 acres adj John Couch. Wit Wm Wimberley, Ezekiel (x) Walker. /s/ Absey her(x)mark Couch. Proven 3 July 1797 by Wm Wimberley; Van Swearengen J P.   Recorded 3rd July 1797.

p.106-109   Richard Bush Junr to Ezekiel Walker, yeoman.   Deed, 24 January 1797, £75 sterling, 80 acres on Beach Creek of Edistoe, across Bog Branch adj Vicey Couch, Wm Wimberley, Hezekiah Walker Senr, & John Couch. Wit Wm Wimberley, Hezekiah (W) Walker. /s/ Richard Bush Junr. Judge Arthur Simkins certifies dower release of Sarah Bush wife of within named Richard Bush; /s/ Sarah (x) Bush. Proven 3 July 1797 by William Wimberley ; Van Swearingen J P.   Recorded 3rd July 1797.

p.109-112   Prescott Bush to William Wimberley.   Deed, 16 January 1797, £50 sterling, 150 acres on Beach Creek of Edisto River, part of 312 acres granted to William Swift by Gov Moultrie at Charleston 1787; adjoins sd bush's saw mill on sd creek, to road from saw mill to Richard Bush's grist mill, joining land surveyed for John Cronan, including the plantation where sd Prescott Bush now lives. Wit John Bush, Hazekiah (x) Walker. /s/ Prescott Bush. Judge Arthur Simkins certifies dower release of Susannah Bush the wife of within named Prescott Bush, 3 July 1797. Proven 3 July 1797 by Hezekiah Walker; Van Swearingen J P.   Rec 3 July 1797.

p.112-114   John Gormon[Gorman] to Gabriel Berry.   Deed, 24 March 1796, £17 sterling, two parcels of land containing 30 acres being part of 104 acres on Mill Creek and Saluda River originally granted unto John Gorman 5 Sept 1785, adj Thomas Berry Junr formerly conveyed to Thomas Berry Senr by sd John Gormon granted to Michael Abney and conveyed to sd Gorman; the other piece adj land formerly granted to Michael Abney, land conveyed by John Gormon to Thomas Berry Senr. Wit Thos Carson, Elizabeth (x) Carson, Mary (x) Spragins. /s/ John (I) Gorman. Proven 30 June 1797 by Mary Spragins; Nathal Abney J P. Recorded 3rd July 1797.

p.114-117   Abraham Richardson to Mary Ann Hammond. Deed, 27 January 1797, $1500, 650 acres on Fox Creek originally granted 500 to Sarah Baker 17 Feby 1773 joining Ephraim Sizemore, also 150 acres originally granted to Ephraim Sizemore. Wit Chas Goodwin, LeRoy Hammond. /s/ A Richardson. Proven 3 July 1797 by LeRoy Hammond; Vann Swearingen J P.   Recorded 3rd July 1797.

p.117-120   Benjamin Jernegan[Jarnagan] to Joel Dees. Deed 13 October 1796, £100 starling money, 150 acres originally granted by Gov Wm Moultrie to sd Benjamin Jarnagan 1 February 1787, 300 acres on Rockey Creek of Edistoe. Wit Thomas Swarengen, Shade Day, Isaac Kirkland. /s/ Benjamin Jernegan. Proven 24 October 1796 by Thomas Swearengen; Van Swearingen J P.   Recorded 3rd July 1797.

p.120-122   John Prior to James Otis Prentiss. Deed, 1 April 1797, £1000 sterling, 2480 acres on Town Creek adj John Gray, Nathaniel Howell, Red House tract, Herman Boozman, John Butler, Jacob Zin Junr, Thomas Lamar, Isaac Parker, on boundary line between Ninety Six District and Orangeburgh District, and tract I bought of David Zubly and on which I now live. Wit William Stewart, Henry D Ward. /a/ John (P) Pryor.   Proven 30 June 1797 by William Stewart; John Clarke J P. Recorded 23rd July 1797.

p.123-124   John Pryor to James Otis Prentis. Deed, 1 April 1797, £500 sterling, land which I purchased of David Zubly, the lower mill seat on Town Creek containing 1000 acres on division line with Orangeburgh District, adj Samuel Burges, George Miller. Wit William Stewart, Henry D Ward. /s/ John (P) Pryor. Proven 30 June 1797 by William Stewart; John Clarke J P. Rec 3rd July 1797.

p.125-127   Edward Morris of Orangeburgh District, planter, to Thomas Dalton. Deed, 19 August 1793, £10 SC money, 120 acres part of 640 acres granted to Josiah Frisbea on Middle Creek 1 Jany 1787, adj Tedders. Sd Edward Morris doth no further warrant but for himself but not warranting claims that Sarah Morris wife of Edward Morris afsd doth freely of her own voluntarily give up to her right of dower. Wit William Morris, Wm Linvill. /s/ Edward (x) Morris, /s/ Sarah (x) Morris. Proven 19 August 1793 by William Linvill; Richard Blalock J P.   Rec 3 July 1797.

p.128-131   Thomas Dalton late of Augusta and Sarah his wife to Chancey Jourdan. Deed 18 May 1797, $400, 120 acres known as Richland on Savannah River, certified for Josiah Frisbey 18th Feby 1785 by Harwood Jones DS. Wit Henry (x) Dalton, Nathan Jordon. /s/ Thomas (D) Dalton, /s/ Sarah (+) Dalton. [Plat by David Burks D S, 8 April 1797 for Chancey Jourdon purchased from Thomas Dalton, shows adj land of Joseph Tucker, Wm Anderson, & Catlet Corley.] Proven 28 June 1797 by Nathan Jordon; Henry Key J P.   Recorded 3rd July 1797.

p.131-134   Benjamin May of Wilkes County, Georgia, to William Wallace Senr of sd county & state. Deed 9 August 1794, £100 sterling, 150 acres on Savannah River, it being part of a grant to Richard Kennedy 1 Decr 1772. Wit D Burks, Nathan Gordon, William Jemison. /s/ Benjamin May. Proven 28 June 1797 by Nathan Jordon;

Henry Key J P.   Recorded 3rd July 1797.

p.134-136   Benjamin May of Wilkes County, Georgia, to William Wallace Senr of
Wilkes County, Georgia. Deed, 9 August 1794, £50 sterling, 100 acres on Savannah
River, granted to William Brooks 3 July 1786. Wit D Burks, Nathan Jordon, William
Jemison. /s/ Benjamin May. Proven 28 June 1797 by Nathan Jourdon; Henry Key J P.
Recorded 3rd July 1797.

p.137-138   William Wallace to Nathan Jordon. Deed of Gift. William Wallis of
Wilks County, Georgia, for love & affection to son Nathan Jordan and Rebeccah his
wife of Edgefield County, South Carolina, 150 acres where sd Nathan Jourdain now
lives; after their decease to my grandson Levi Jourdain; likewise another tract of
land 150 acres adj sd tract first granted to Richard Kennedy I give to sd Nathan
Jordain and his wife Rebeckah and after their decease to be equally divided among
my four granddaughters to wit Margaret Jordain, Abegal Jordain, Leah Jourdan, Sarah
Jordain. Wit John Wallace, John Chancey C Jordan. /s/ William Wallace Senr.
Proven 20 June 1797 by John Chancey Jourdan; Henry Key J P.   Rec 3rd July 1797.

p.138-141   Joshua Lockwood of Charleston and his wife Mary to John Star
[Starr]. Deed, 14 October 1796, 20 shillings SC money, 250 acres in Granville
County at Seven Springs adj sd Lockwoods land. Wit Jacob H Alison, Simon Cushman.
/s/ Joshua Lockwood, /s/ Mary Lockwood. Proven 29 June 1797 by Simeon Cushman;
John Clarke J P.   Recorded 3rd July 1797.

p.141-142   William Fountain to William Durham. Deed, 24 January 1797, £20
sterling, 100 acres, lines of James Durham, Thomas Marbury, William Hargrove,
Charles Martin. Wit Robert Melton, James Durham. /s/ William (x) Fountain.
Proven 3 July 1797 by James Durham; John Blocker J P.   Recorded 3d July 1797.

p.143   William Brooks deposition before John Blocker J P: he was present
at a contract between William Killcrease and John Dalton when sd Killcrease sold
unto sd Dalton two pieces of land, that the rights or conveyance lay one piece in
William Coursey and the other in Obediah Killcrease which sd Wm Killcrease sold sd
Dalton and sd Dalton agreed to take the titles of sd lands made by William Coursey
for the other piece the titles made by Obediah Killcrease; sworn 31st August 1796.
/s/ William Brooks.   Recorded 3rd July 1797.

p.143-144   William Courseys deposition before Henry Key Esqr to William
Killcrease; saith that some time in the Spring of 1788 which was short time after
the marriage of Wm Killcrease and Frances his wife the daughter of James Lyon he
this deponant was present in company with James Lyon, and after conversation
between sd Jas Lyon and deponant, sd Lyon told deponant that a certain negro girl
Yellow Betty he does give unto sd William Killcrease and Frances his wife the
daughter of sd Lyon and also told deponant he was to allow sd Killcrease that year
a shear in the crop for sd negroes work besides the part he was to give Killcrease
as an overseer over his hands and asked this deponant if he did not think he had
given Killcrease a verry good chance that year. Sworn 30 June 1797. /s/ W Coursey.
Recorded 3rd July 1797.

p.144-145   Mary Coursey's deposition before Henry Key Esqr to William Killcrease. Some time in Spring of 1788 after marriage of Wm Killcrease and Frances his wife the dau of James Lyon she was present with James Lyon and in discourse between James Lyon and Wm Coursey her husband she heard sd Lyon say he had given unto Wm Killcrease a negro girl Yellow Betty and he was to allow Killcrease that year a shear of the crop for sd negro and further this deponant saith not; 30 June 1797. /s/ Mary (S) Coursey. Recorded 3rd July 1797.

p.145-150   Peter McCain and his wife Dicea to Charles Martin. Deed, 31 January 1795/31 Jan 1795, £80 sterling, 116 acres Horns Creek granted to Robert Mosley by Gov Wm Moultrie 4 Dec 1786 adj Sumerall, David Mathews, John Rainesford, Charles Martin. Wit William Martin, John (P) Atwood. /s/ Peter McCain, /a/ Duca[Deeca, Dicea?] (x) McCain. Proven 31 January 1795. Proven 3 July 1797 by William Martin; James Harrison J P. Recorded 3 July 1797.

p.150-153   William Wallace of Georgia, blacksmith, and Martha his wife to Nathaniel Howell. Deed, 2 December 1796, £25 SC money, 100 acres near Town Creek of Savanna River, originally granted to James Ashberry 5 June 1786 and transferred by sd Jas Ashberry unto Wm Wallace. Wit William Headen, Nathaniel Howell Junr. /s/ William Wallace, /s/ Martha (x) Wallace. Proven 11 March 1797 by Nathl Howell Junr; John Clarke J P.   Recorded 3rd July 1797.

p.154-156   John Huffman and Lucretia his wife to Demcy Hughs. Deed, 15 December 1796, £20 sterling, 50 acres on Stevens Creek bounded on Brezeals land, Logans land. Wit Elisha (P) Palmer, Archibald McKay, George Bassey. /s/ John Huffman, /s/ Lucretia Huffman. Proven 8 March 1797 by Elisha Palmer; Henry Key J P. Recorded 3d July 1797.

p.156-159   Edmund Holleman to Richard Newman. Deed, 3 July 1797, $95, 85 acres on Loyds Creek of Stevens, bounded by lines of Hughs Moss, Edmund Holleman, John Flick, Christian Buckhalter, Capt Henry Key, which tract was granted to sd Edmund Holleman 11 July 1795 by Gov Arnoldus Vanderhorst. Wit Betty Tutt, Joseph Hightower. /s/ E Holleman. Judge Joseph Hightower certifies relinquishment of dower of Catherine Holleman wife of Edmund Holleman 3 July 1797; /s/ Catherine Holleman. Proven 3 July 1797 by Betty Tutt; Rd Tutt J P.   Recorded 3d July 1797.

p.159-161   John Killcrease to Stephen Smith. Deed, 4 July 1797, £10 sterling, 100 acres adj John Logan, James Lesueur, Stony lick Br, Abraham Holsenback. Wit Rd Tutt, E Holleman. /s/ John Killcrease. Judge Arthur Simkins certifies relinquishment of dower by Mary Killcrease wife of John Killcrease; 4 July 1797; Mary (-) Killcrease. Proven 4th July 1797 by Edmund Holleman; Rd Tutt J P. Rec 4 July 1797.

p.161-163   James Yeldell and wife Elizabeth to John George Saibart. Deed, 25 April 1797, £30 sterling, 66 acres part of 200 acres granted to James Yeldell Senr decd bounded by lines of Thomas Bacon Esqr, Robert and William Yeldell. Wit Abner Perrin, John Longmire, Henry Cooper. /s/ James Yeldell, /s/ Elizabeth (x) Yeldell. Proven 4th July 1797 by Abner Perrin; Rd Tutt J P.   Recorded 4th July 1797.

p.163-166   William Fudge to John Buckhalter. Deed, 30 May 1797, £25 SC money, 15 acres adj sd Buckhalter and John Fox. Wit John G Cooke, Thomas Westby /s/ William Fudge. Judge Joseph Hightower certifies relinquishment of dower by

Polly Fudge wife of sd William Fudge, 10 June 1797; /s/ Polly (x) Fudge. Proven 10 June 1797 by John G Cooke; Chas Old J P. Recorded 4th July 1797.

p.166-168   John Killcrease and wife Mary to James Lisuerer[Lesurur?] planter. Deed, 4 July 1797, £30 sterling, 100 acres adj Hezekiah Oden, Wm Howle Junr, Henry Key Esqr, John Killcrease, Stephen Smith, Abraham Holsenback. Wit Rd Tutt, E Holleman. /s/ John Killcrease. Judge Arthur Simkins certified dower release by Mary Killcrease, 4 July 1797; /s/ Mary (-) Killcrease. Proven 4th July 1797 by Edmund Holleman; Rd Tutt J P.   Recorded 4th July 1797.

p.168-171   Robert Samuel to John Buckhalter. Deed, 20 March 1797, £100 sterling, 50 acres on Phillis branch. Wit John G Cooke, Thomas Westbay. /s/ Robert Samuel. Judge Joseph Hightower certifies dower relinquishment of Lucy Samuel wife of Robt Samuel, 3 July 1797, /s/ Lucy Samuel. Proven 4 July 1797 by John G Cooke; Rd Tutt J P.   Recorded 4th July 1797.

p.171-173   William Fudge to John G Cooke. Deed, 30 May 1797, £25 SC money, s5 acres being part of tract willed by Jacob Fudge Senr decd to Solomon and Richard Fudge and by them conveyed to sd William Fudge where Wm Fudge now lives, adj John Buckhalter, Buckelews land sd five acres whereon sd Cooke has a tanyard. Wit Thos Westbay, James Owers, John (IB) Buckhalter. /s/ Wm Fudge. Proven 4th July 1797 by John Buckhalter; Richard Tutt J P.   Recorded 4th July 1797.

p.173-176   James Otis Prentis to John Pryor. Mortgage, 3 April 1797, £1000 sterling paid by John Prior, 2480 acres on Town Creek on lines of John Gray, Archd Howell, red house tract, heirs of Harmon Boozman, John Butler, Jacob Zinn Jr, Thos Lamar, Isaac Parker, Orangeburgh District line, land Prior bought from David Zubly and which sd Prior now lives. Another 1000 acres lower Mill Seat on District line, Samuel Burge's land, George Miller's land. Conditions, to pay unto John Prior £599 and lawful interest from date hereof and in case titles cannot be procured by Benjamin Sims of Augusta to sd Prior for lot 28 in Augusta or $2200 with interest recovered on sd sums, sd Prentis to make titles in lieu of sd titles to sd Prior and that within 18 mos from 30 Decr last, then if Prentis shall pay unto Prior $2200 before 1 April 1799 with lawful interest, this deed be of none effect otherwise shall remain in full force. Wit Wm Stewart, Henry Dillard. /s/ James Otis Prentiss. Proven 11th July 1797 by William Stewart; John Clarke J P.   Recorded 11th July 1797.

p.177-178   Samuel Dennis Senr, planter, to son Samuel Dennis Junr. Deed of Gift/ 1 July 1797, love and affection, livestock, household tools and furniture. Wit Willm Beades. /s/ Samuel Dennis Senr. Proven 3 July 1797 by William Beads; Van Swearingen J P.   Recorded 12th July 1797.

p.178-179   Mathew Henderson of Salem County, SC, to Melines C Leavensworth. Bill/sale, 18th January 1797, $500, my negro wench Dine and her child Tiner. Wit Gidn Pardue. /s/ Matt Henderson. Proven 10th July 1797 by Gideon Pardue; John Clarke J P.   Recorded 14th July 1797.

p.179-180   Gideon Pardue to Melines C Leavensworth, Bill of Sale, 18th January 1797, $500 Negro wench Venus, Negro fellow Merdeen. Wit Matt Henderson,

David Whitmore. /s/ Gidn Pardue. Proven, 10 July 1797 by David Whitmore, John Clarke J P. Recorded 14th July 1797.

p.180-181   Jacob Miller to His five Children. Deed of Gift, 14 July 1797, to Sitney, Susannah, Polly, Betsey and Nancy and future increase of my wife during my natural lifetime, the whole of my personal estate to wit one negro girl about 14 years of age named Dyedoe also negro girl about 13 named Patt, also my stock and householf furniture and tools at decease of myself and wife Elizabeth, then above mentioned personal estate to be equally divided. Wit Jas McMillan, Jas Moorison. /s/ Jacob (JM) Miller. Proven 14 July 1797 by James McMillan; Wm Robinson J P. Recorded 26th July 1797.

p.182-183   John Gordon of Northumberland County, Virginia, by his atty Thomas Pool to Dionysius Oliver of Edgefield. Deed, 27 February 1797, $500, 500 acres originally granted to Jacob Fudge on Stephens Creek, plat by Wm Coursey. Wit Frans Burt, Edward Burt. /s/ John Gorden by his atty Thos Pool. Proven 31 July 1797 by Edward Burt; Rd Tutt J P.   Recorded 31st July 1797.

p.183-186   Absolom Williams to Hardy Cornett. Deed, 18 June 1792, £100 sterling, 150 acres on Steavens Creek of Savannah River, granted to sd Hardy Cornett 22 February 1771. Wit Joab Blackwell, James Blackwell. /s/ Absolom Williams. Proven 29 July 1797 by Joab Blackwell; Henry Key J P.   Recorded 31 July 1797.

p.187-188   Fredk Rutledge to John Ryan. Deed, 22 April 1797, £162 sterling, 500 acres Racoon branch of Savannah river, adj land of John Harvey, bounty land surveyed for the Irish, land of John Ryan, and vacant land at time of original survey. Also 500 acres head of Nobles Creek of Stephens Creek adj Lacon Ryan, Benjamin Ryan, above tract, Benjamin Mazeack, Able Gibson. Wit W Anderson, J Dunlap. /s/ Frederick Rutledge. Proven 5 June 1797 by John Dunlap; Jno Trotter J P. Recorded 31st July 1797.

p.189-190   Jacob Hibbler to Richd Wetherington. Deed, 13th Feby 1797, $200, Negro boy Sam about 12 years old. Wit Garrett Longmire, Minor (W) Wetherington, Thos (W) Wetherington. /s/ Jacob Hibbler. Proven 19th July 1797 by Thomas Wetherington; Jas Harrison J P.   Recorded 4th August 1797.

p.190-192   Samuel Arnett to Thos Witherington. Deed, 16 February 1797, £10 SC money, 100 acres originally granted unto Samuel Arnett 23 November 1793 on Haspan Creek of Cuffeetown Creek adj land of Crabtree, Robart Hugens. Wit Alexander Patton, Manoa (M) Witherington, Goolds Berry (x) Garner. /s/ Samuel Arnett. Proven 19 July 1797 by Alexander Patton; Jas Harrison. Recorded 4th August 1797.

p.193-194   Richard McCary's Deposition before Henry Key Esqr. Sworn, saith that some time in 1788 this deponant swaped a negro woman named Hannah to Morris Calliham for which sd Calliham let deponant have Negro lad Samson, which Samson deponant have just reason to beleave to be property of Dudley Carter of Edgefield County, sd deponant further saith on oath that woman Hannah was delivered of a male child Ben and that deponant gave Bill/sale for Hannah to Morris Calliham during his natural life and after said Callihams death to Dudley Carter & wife, Negro child Ben to have been inserted in sd Bill/sale but through mistake Ben was omitted;

deponant believes Hannah & child Ben to be property of sd Dudley Carter. August 7th 1797; /s/ Richd McCarry; Henry Key J P.   Recorded 18 Augt 1797.

p.194-195   John G Cooke's deposition before Charles Old Esqr.   Cooke, sworn, sayeth on 13th November 1788 Dudley Carter applied to this deponant to draw a bill of sale for Negro woman Hannah that deponant understood was at that time in possession of Morris Calliham which sd wench deponant understood had a child which deponant understood to be sd Dudley Carters but was omitted being put in Bill/sale which Negro wench & child was to be Morris Callihams during natural life of sd Callaham and then to be Dudley Carters; 11 Aug 1797. /s/ John G Cooke.   Rec 18 Aug 1797.

p.195   Dudley Carter's deposition before Charles Old Esqr.   Carter, sworn, sayeth that negroe wench Hannah sworn to by Richard McCary and John G Cooke, he sd Morris Callaham sold and it was contrary to orders of sd Dudley Carter and that the deponant knew nothing of it till some time after when he went in search of her and on 17 April last he found sd Hannah in possession of Peter Partan in Georgia on the Connuchy which sd Negro this deponant never bargained or sold; 11 August 1797. /s/ Dudley Carter.   Recorded 18th August 1797.

p.196-197   Thomas Walpole to Emsley Lott. Deed, 19 August 1797, £30, 253 acres part of grant to Robert Lang 7 May 1787 adj Augusta road. Wit John Bush, William Prichard.   Proven 19 August 1797 by William Prichard; Rd Tutt J P. Recorded 19th August 1797.

p.198-199   Penelope Moseley to Daniel Mosley. Deed of Gift, 19 August 1797, for love & affection and £10 paid by a friend of his, to her son Daniel Mosley about twelve years of age, also after my decease one negro child Dick about eight months old. Wit John (x) Green, Sten Norris. /s/ Penelope (+) Mosley. Proven 19 August 1797 by Sten Norris; Rd Tutt J P.   Recorded 19th August 1797.

p.199-200   John Dees to Rachel & Neomy Dees. Deed of Gift, 5 June 1797, love & goodwill to his two daughters, mares, cows, calves. Wit John Dees Junr, Thomas (T) Ramsay, Jesse (J) Dees. /s/ John Dees. Proven 6 June 1797 by Jesse Dees; Jas Harrison, J P.   Recorded 8 August 1797.

p.200-203   Asa Hix to Jas Hunter & John Roundtree. Deed, 16 September 1796, $94.28½, 100 acres on Town Creek of Savanna River bounded at time of survey on Lamar & Evans land, Lud Williams, Joseph Hix, being part of 1000 acres originally granted Asa Hix 4 June 1792, survey of 100 acres for Joseph Hix 6 Jan 1785. Wit Philip Lamar, William Stewart. /s/ Asa Hix, Asa Hix mark. Proven 23 January 1797 by William Stewart; John Clarke J P.   Recorded 28 August 1797.

p.203-205   James Forguson & his wife Martha to Peter Morgan. Deed 1 January 1795, £100 sterling, 153 acres on branch of Stevens Creek, granted to Moses Lucas. Wit John Wright, Richard Quarles, Mourning (x) Hogg. /s/ James (x) Forguson, /s/ Martha (MR) Forgeson. Proven 25th May 1785 by Richard Quarles; Hugh Middleton J P. Recorded 28 August 1797.

p.206-208   Alexander Frazor and Rachel his wife to Peter Morgan. Deed 18 March 1795, £25 sterling, 150 acres granted unto Allen Hinton on Stevens Creek, joining land of Moses Lucas, Evans Morgan & James Carson. Wit John Wright, Enos Morgan, James Carson. /s/ Alexander (F) Frasor. Proven 9 May 1795 by Enos Morgan; Joseph Hightower J P. Recorded 28th August 1797.

p.209-211   George B Moore, merchant, to John Ryan, planter. Bill/sale, 26 August 1797, $5210, Negroes Pompy, Brister, Bob, Peter, Will, Feby, Nan, Biner, Seal, Sylus, Harry, Shadrach, Phereby, Biddy, Benjamin, Milly with the increase of females. Wit John Gray, Saml Crafton, James Borden. /s/ George B Moore. Proven 29 August 1797 by James Borden; Isaac Herbert J P. Richmond County, Augusta, 30th August 1797 Clerks office, Superior Court. Recorded, examined by Thomas Hebby for Wm Robertson Clerk. Edgefield County, SC, Proven 2 September 1797 by John Gray; John Blocker J P. Recorded 2nd September 1797.

p.212-214   Christian Gomillian to John Street. Deed, 16 March 1797, $85.71 100 acres part of 165 acres granted by Gov Wm Moultrie 1794. Witness Drury Mims, Stephen Norris, Andrew Gomilan. /s/ Christian (x) Gomilion. Proven 2 September 1797 by Drury Mims; John Blocker J P. Recorded 2 Septr 1797.

p.214-216   John Anderson to George Delaughter. Deed, 4th September 1797. $60, 25 acres on Stephens Creek part of land granted to Philip Goode, bounded when surveyed by Solomon Newson, Chatten, George Anderson. Wit Steuwart Minor, George Anderson. /s/ Jno Anderson. Proven 1 August 1797 by George Anderson; Joseph Hightower. Judge Joseph Hightower certifies dower renunciation of Elizabeth Anderson wife of John Anderson, 31 August 1797. /s/ Elizabeth Anderson.

p.217-223   John Anderson and wife Elizabeth to George Delaughter. Deed 21 February 1797, £80 SC money, 122 acres part of tract originally granted to Solomon Newsom on Stephens Creek bounded by Goode, George Delaughter, Peter Hitt, Jas Rhodes. Wit James Carson Senr, James Carson Junr, James Bruwer, Robert Carson. /s/ Jno Anderson. Within mentioned land is my part of land of Ricard Pace decd which I have sold to George Delaughter for £65 sterling, 21 Feb 1797. Wit James Brewer, James Carson, Robert Carson. /s/ Jno Anderson. Renunciation of claim to sd land by coheirs James Rhodes and Ludbrook Lee, day & year above. Wit James Carson Senr, James Carson Junr, James Brewer, Robert Carson. /s/Ludbrook Lee, /s/ James Rhodes. Proven by James Carson 9 May 1797; Chas Old J P. Proven 9 May 1797 by James Carson Junr; Chas Old J P. Judge Joseph Hightower certifies renunciation of dower by Elizabeth Anderson wife of John Anderson, August 1797; /s/ Elizabeth Anderson. Judge Joseph Hightower certifies release of dower by Mary Rhodes wife of James Rhodes and Charlotte Lee wife of Ludbrooke Lee, 21 February 1797; /s/ Charlotte (I) Lee, /s/ Mary (-) Rhodes. Recorded 4th September 1797.

p.223-224   Pennix Howlett to John Buckhalter. Deed, 26 May 1789, £70 sterling, negro wench Rose, age 25. Wit David Buckhalter. /s/ Pennix (P) Howlett. Proven 2 September 1797 by David Buckhalter; Aquila Miles J P. Rec 5 Sep 1797.

p.224-230   Doctor Joseph Fuller to Meshack Wright. L&R, 4 June 1792, £15 SC money, 100 acres on Savanna River near Red House, being part of 338 acres granted Joseph Fuller 15 February 1791, sd 100 acres adjoins Mr Williams, Mr Lockwood, Mr Downers. Wit Cradk Burnell, Casper Nail Junr. /s/ Joseph Fuller. Proven 1 April 1797 by Cradock Burnell; John Clarke J P. Recorded 5th Septr 1797.

p.231-233   Nicholas Shaffer, planter, & wife Mary to Meshack Wright. Deed October 1796, $88.93, 300 acres on Hollow Creek in Winton County, Orangeburgh Dist, being one moiety of 1000 originally granted 2 October 1786 to David Zubly now decd and conveyed by Ann Zubly extx/estate of sd Zubly decd to Nicholas Shaffer by deed 25 July 1792, sd 300 acres adj land sold to Charles Ransay by sd Nicholas Shaffer. Wit Cradk Burnell, Abram Ardis. /s/ Nicholas Shaffer, /s/ Mary (x) Shaffer. Proven 1 April 1797 by Cradock Burnell; John Clarke J P.   Rec 5 Sept 1797.

p.234-237   Joseph Wood to Joseph Hix. Deed, 9 December 1796, $76, 52 acres near Musterfield Branch opposite Beech Island originally granted to Robert Lang depy surveyor, conveyed to sd Joseph Wood, adj his own land, by Parsons, land supposed to be James Grays. Wit Giles Bowers, James Fox. /s/ Jos Wood.   Proven 2 September 1797 by Giles Bowers; John Clarke J P.   Recorded 5th Sept 1797.

p.237-239   William Evans to John & Jinsey Lyon. Deed, 30 March 1797, for love & affection unto daughter Jinsey and son in law John Lyon, give one negro wench Amy and negro girl Tyro. Wit J Evans, James Martin. /s/ William Evans.   Proven 29 August 1797 by John Evans; John Blocker J P.   Recorded 7th Septr 1797.

p.239-241   Amasa Baugh to Drury Adams. Deed, 16 August 1797, £60 sterling, 87¼ acres adj lands of Pinix Howlet, Alexander Edmonds, Aquila Miles Esqr, Caleb Neblet, Drury Adams, on Horns Creek, 51¼ acres of sd land originally granted to Aquila Miles on 6 Feb 1786, and 36 acres of sd land originally granted to Thomas Beckham. Wit Daniel Flandigame, Joshua Marcus. /s/ Amasa Baugh.   Judge Joseph Hightower certifies release of dower by Pashia Baugh wife of Amasa Baugh, 17 August 1797. /s/ Pashia (x) Baugh.   Proven 8 September 1797 by Daniel Flandigame; Aquilla Miles J P.   Recorded 9th Septr 1797.

p.241-246   Caleb Holloway to John Newton of Newberry County, SC. Deed, 31 December 1792, 10 shillings, 150 acres by grant 10 April 1771 by Lt Gov Wm Bull granted unto Obed Holloway 150 acres on Halfway Swamp Creak of Saluda River. Wit Richard Lanier, Wm Crenshaw, Nancy (x) Lanier. /s/ Caleb Holloway.   Proven 8 August 1796 by Nancy Lanier; Wm Robinson J P.   Recorded 9th Septr 1797.

p.247-248   Thomas Williams, planter, to William Morris. Deed 9 September 1796, £10 sterling, 100 acres on Stevens Creek adj Jolly, Augusta road. Wit Thos Williams, James Morris, Joseph (I) Morris, Thomas Allenden. /s/ Thomas Williams. Recorded 9th September 1797.

p.248-250   Thomas Williams, planter, to Joseph Morris, planter. Deed, 1 October 1796, £20 sterling, 150 acres branch of Little Stephens Creek adm land of Odom, Joseph Morris, Thomas Williams, granted to sd Williams. Wit George Mosley, James Morris, Joseph (x) Tally. /s/ Thomas Williams. Proven 9 September 1797 by James Morris; Rd Tutt J P. Recorded 9 September 1797.

p.250-251   William Morris to James Morris. Deed 9 September 1797, £10, 50 acres part of 200 acres originally granted to Joseph Lewis on 6 Aug 1787 adj land of John Still, Jacob Utz. Wit Rd Tutt, Joseph (I) Morris. /s/ William (+) Morris. Proven day & year above by Joseph Morris; Rd Tutt J P.   Recorded 9 September 1797.

p.252-254   Sheriff Jeremiah Hatcher to John Boyd. Deed, 5 August 1797, suit of Thomas Beckam assignee against John & Martha Boyd extr & extx of William Talbot deceased, sheriff to sell to highest bidder for ready money at Edgefield Court House, struck off to Henry Key for $60 he being highest and last bidder for same. This indenture, sd Jeremiah Hatcher for $60 paid by John Boyd, sold to John Boyd 1592 acres originally granted William Talbot deceased adj Butler, Gibar, Thomas Freman. Wit Eugene Brenan, Wm Burtt. Proven 7 October 1797 by Eugene Brenan; Rd Tutt J P. Recorded 7th October 1797.

p.254-256   John Youngblood to Conrad Gallman. Deed, 9 May 1797, £60, 220 acres granted sd Youngblood 5 June 1786 by Gov Wm Moultrie. Wit Thomas McDaniel, James Brown. /s/ John (X) Youngblood. Judge Arthur Simkins certifies release of dower by Catherine Youngblood wife of John Youngblood, 18 Sept 1797. /s/ Catherine (X) Youngblood. Proven date above by Jas Brown; Arthur Simkins. Rec 7th Octr 1797.

p.256-258   Thomas Warren to Thomas Mann. Deed, 19 February 1797, $500, 250 acres in two tracts, one of 150 acres Clouds Creek adj Wm Johnson and John Watts Mann, Widow Johnson, Butlers land, which was granted to John Watts Mann 1 March 1775; the other of 100 acres being part of 150 acres on Clouds Creek adj Jno Watts Mann 13th August 1774, conveyed to sd Thomas Warren 7 March 1796. Wit Wm Norris, Stephen Williams. /s/ Thomas (x) Warren. Proven 10 June 1797 by William Norris; Jno Bond J P. Recorded 10 Octr 1797.

p.258-261   John Itson and Patience his wife to Edward McCartey. Deed, 14 July 1795, £16 sterling, 198 acres on Dry Creek of Mine Creek granted to sd John Itson 7 January 1788 by Gov Thos Pinckney adj James Cox, heirs of Michael Watson. Wit Michael (x) McCarty, Arthur Rice Watson, Richmond Watson. /s/ John Edson [Eitson], /s/ Patience (x) Edson. Proven 2 Feby 1796 by Michael McCarty; Russell Willson J P. /s/ Michael (x) McCartey. Recorded 10th Octr 1797.

p.261   Edgefield County, David Gains sworn sayeth that the mark of his stock of cattle & hogs is a swallow fork and underkeel in each ear. 10 Octr 1797; John Blocker J P. /s/ David Gains. Recorded 10th Octr 1797.

p.262-265   Bailey Crouch and wife Mary to Michael McCartey. Deed, 27 June 1795, £40 sterling, 300 acres on Richland Creek of Little Saluda River being part of 400 acres granted to Joseph Allen 7 July 1788 by Gov Thos Pinckney, adj Golover Crouch referring to original plat. Wit Edward McCartey, Francis Davis, Samuel Sentell. /s/ Bailey (x) Crouch, Mary (x) Crouch. Proven 2 Feby 1796 by Edward McCartey; Russell Wilson J P.   Recorded 10th October 1797.

p.265-267   William Boulware[Boler] and wife Rachel to Jas Courtney. Deed, 19 January 1796, $28.50, 170 acres on Big Creek of Little Saluda R, being part of a tract of 350 acres granted to William Boaler 5 January 1789 by gov Thos Pinckney, adj John Mosley, Spencer Bowler, Joseph Mosely. Wit Rutherford Boulware, Spence Boulware. /s/ William Boulware, /s/ Rachel (x) Boulware. Proven 4 Feby 1797 by Spencer Boleware; Nathaniel Abney.   Recorded 10th Octr 1797.

p.267-270   Thomas Mann to Stephen Williams. Deed, 1 February 1797, $500, 250 acres being two tracts one of 150 acres part of 250 acres on Clouds Creek adj Wm

Johnston, John Watts Mann, where Widow Johnson now lives. The other 100 acres being part of 150 acres on Clouds Creek bounding on John Watts Mann at time of granting where widow Mann now lives, which was granted to Jno Watts Mann 13th August 1794, sd Thomas Mann being eldest son and heir to Jno Watts Mann deceased. Wit Wm Norris, Thos (x) Warren. /s/ Thos (x) Mann. Proven 10 June 1797 by William Norris; John P Bond J P. /s/ William Norris. Recorded 10th Octr 1797.

p.270-271   William Anderson to William Cox. Deed 20 February 1797, £25, 103 acres run by Martin Gardaner on Edisto bounded by Benjamin Lawless(?), Benjamin Burton, Jacob Read, R Stark. Witness Jas Perry, William Bell, Rolan Williams. /s/ Willis Andison. Proven 10 Oct 1797 by James Perry; John Blocker. Rec 10 oct 1797.

p.272-274   James Huston to Alexander Paterson. Deed 29 January 1796, 10 shillings SC money, 150 acres on Little Saluda [surveyed] 1774 adj William Brisan, [blank] Friday, sd James Huston, Wm Adams. Wit John Sadler, William Sample. /s/ James Huston. Recorded 10 October 1797.

p.274-276   Henry Day of Columbia County, Georgia, to Robert Gardner. Deed, 4 October 1797, $100, 250 acres Stephens Creek part of tract originally granted unto Henry Day Senr 17 August 1771 of 300 acres but 50 acres by sd Henry Day Senr willed to his daughter Mary Bennett. Wit West Cook, Names Fletcher. /s/ Henry Day. Judge Joseph Hightower certifies that Elenor Day wife of Henry Day relinquished dower, 6 October 1797; /s/ Elender (x) Day. Proven 4 October 1797 by West Cook; Joseph Hightower. Recorded 10th October 1797.

p.276-279   James Huston to Alexander Paterson. Release, 1 February 1796, £37 .10 sterling, 300 acres of date 1774 on Little Saluda, sell to Alexr Paterson 150 acres of sd tract adj William Brisan, Friday, James Huston, Stark, William Adams. Wit John Sadler, Wm Sample. /s/ James Huston. Proven, Fairfield County, 24 September 1796 by John Sadler; William Daniel J P. Recorded 10 October 1797.

p.279-282   Azariah Lewis to William Buckhalter. Deed, 13 May 1793, £30 sterling, 188 acres Sleepy Creek of Savannah river, granted unto Azariah Lewis 2 Octr 1786. Wit William (~) Maurice, Jeremiah (I) Youngblood, Samuel Lewis. /s/ Azariah Lewis. Proven 1 May 1794 by Samuel Lewis; Henry King J P. Rec 9 Sept 1797.

p.282-283   Richard Freeman to Paul Williams. Deed 14 September 1797, $34, 450 acres granted unto me on Cuffeetown and Hard Labour creeks adj Jno Wallace, Absalom Williams, Jno Clam, Benjamin Blake, Jno Anderson. Wit Jas Sanders, Thomas (II) Freeman. /s/ Richard (R) Freeman. Proven 19 Sept 1797 by James Sanders; Rd Tutt J P. Recorded 19th September 1797.

p.283-284   Lucy Exums dower. Judge Joseph Hightower certifies Lucey Exum wife of Field Pardue decd when release was signed appeared and relinquished dower rights unto within named Thomas Herron, 8 September 1797. /s/ Lucey Exum. Recorded 25 Sept 1797.

p.284   Mary McQueen's dower. Judge Joseph Hightower certifies relinquishment of dower by Mary McQueen wife of Jas McQueen unto within named William F Taylor, 13 June 1797. /s/ Mary (+) McQueen.   Rec 21 Septr 1797.

p.284-287   Shadrach Rozar to Zachariah Lamar. Deed 23 August 1788, £100 SC money, one quarter acre lot #27 in Campbelltown. Witness Peter Chastain, Francis Settle, Thomas Hunt. /s/ Shadrach Rozar. Proven Burke County, GA, 25 Sept 1795 by Peter Chastain; James Stubbs J P. Certification 4 June 1796 by Gov Jarad Irwin, appeared James Stubbs who was a J/P, Burke County, Georgia, at time of deed.

p.287-289   John Quattlebaum to Peter Uttz. Deed, 29 May 1788. 2 shillings sterling, 100 acres originally granted unto Johanas Flick by Wm Bull Esqr and transfered unto Deterigh Uttz by L&R 15 & 16 July 1784 and by sd Deterigh Uttz to sd John Quattlebaum 7 & 8 Sept 1784. Wit Henery Croft, Samuel Lewis, Peter (-) Torst. /s/ John Quattlebaum "wrote in Dutch." Rec 28th Sept 1797.

p.289-294   John Quattlebaum to Peter Uttz. Release, 30 May 1788, land granted 30 August 1765 by Lt Gov Wm Bull unto Johanas Flick, 450 acres on Little Stevens Creek, sd property transfered unto Deterigh Utz and by sd Deterigh Utz 100 acres being part of above mentioned tract being transfered unto sd John Quattlebaum 7 & 8 Sept 1784, now for £20 sterling sell unto Peter Utz. Wit Henery Croft, Samuel Lewis, Peter Dorst. /s/ John Quattlebaum "wrote in Dutch.". Proven 28 Sept 1797 by Henry Croft; Richard Tutt. Recorded 28th Sept 1797.

p.294-296   Julius Scruggs to admrs of Grigsby. Release, 2 October 1797, Tennesee, Jefferson County, £400 Virginia currency paid by Mary Grigsby admx and Samuel Mays and Rhydon Grigsby admrs of Enoch Grigsby decd, action pending in Courts of South Carolina by admx & admrs sd Enoch Grigsby defendants. Wit Lodwich Hill, James (x) Scruggs, Richard (x) Scruggs. /s/ Julius Scruggs. Proven 12 Oct 1797 by Lodwich Hill; Rd Tutt. Rec 12th Octr 1797.

p.296-298   Jonathan Clegg & wife Phimba & John Coursey to Peter Utz. Release, 30 June 1796, £50 sterling, 16 acres taken off a prior grant of James McCreelus the remainder containing about 440 acres on Mountain and Sleepy creek of Savannah River bounded by sd McCreelus, John Rutledge Esqr, John Jacob Messer Smith decd, granted unto Jonathan Clegg for 456 acres by Gov Arnoldus Vanderhorst 5 January 1795. Wit John Henry Croft, Henry (x) Timermann. /s/ Jonathan Clegg, Pharaba (x) Clegg, John (IC) Coursey. Proven 28 Sept 1797 by John Henry Crofft; Rd Tutt. Rec 28 Sept 1797.

p.299-302   Macartan Cambell/Campbell Esqr of city of Charleston to Shadrach Rozar. Deed, 11 June 1787, £30 current money, lot #27 containing one half acre in Campbellton. Wit Danl Md Sturges, James Stewart. /s/ Macartan Campbell. Proven 19 Nov 1796 by James Stewart; Rd Tutt. Rec 21st September 1797.

p.302-304   Thomas Heron of Augusta, Georgia, to William F Taylor. Deed, 28 April 1797, $150, lot 23, ¼ acre in Campbellton. Wit Joseph Hightower, G Leslie. /s/ Thomas Heron. Proven 20 Sept 1797 by G Leslie; Chs Old J P. Rec 21 Sep 1797.

p.304-308   Maccartan Campbell Esqr of Richmond County, Georgia, and Sarah his wife, to Field Pardue of Edgefield County, planter. Release, 8 February 1793, £20 SC money, lot 23 in Campbellton. Wit David Sandrige, John Anderson. /s/ Maccartan Campbell, /s/ Sarah Campbell. Proven 31 Aug 1797, David Sandrige; Joseph Hightower. Certification by Dalziel Hunter J P, Richmond County, Georgia, that Sarah wife of Maccartan Campbell relinquished dower right; D Hunter J P. Recorded 21st Sept 1791.

p.308-311   Agreement between R Gantt and John Chastain, 10 June 1797, negro man Harry property of sd John Chastain has been levied on at instance of Davis Moore, sd Negro now in possession of Sheriff of Ninety Six Dist; John Chastain sells Harry upon terms, $400, &c. Wit Osmanus Allen.   /s/ R Gantt, John Chastain. Receipt 10 June 1797 $15 part of first sum of $150. Proven 22 Septr 1797 by Osmanus Allen; Richard Tutt J P.   Recorded 22nd Sept 1797.

p.311-312   William Anderson to stepdaughter Eliza Ann Purves. Deed of Gift, 10 July 1797, for 5 shillings and natural love & affection, Negroe girl Lenah about five years old and her increase. Wit Wm Prichart, Thos Anderson.   /s/ W Anderson. Proven 3 August 1797 by Wm Prichard; John Blocker J P.   Rec 27th Sept 1797.

p.313-321   Elizabeth Baseheart single woman to John Henry Grofft/Graff, shoemaker. Lease/Release, 2 July 1790/3 July 1790, £20 sterling, granted 200 acres on 30 August 1785 by LtGov Wm Bull unto Peter Coon adj Harling, Andrew Marks, conveyed 1780 unto John Baseheart who died intestate, sd Elizabeth Baseheart, lawfull daughter of sd Baseheart decd, 100 acres on Little Stevens Creek. Wit Henry (x) Timmermann, Peter (x) Timmermann. /s/ Ann Elizabeth (x) Baseheart. Proven 15 February 1796 by Peter (P) Timmermann; John Blocker J P. Recorded 28 September 1797.

p.321-328   Zachariah Lamar of Hancock County, Georgia, to Alexander Kevan of Campbellton, SC. Lease, 19 June 1795/20 June 1795, £5 SC money, lot 27 one quarter acre in Campbellton. Wit J H McPherson, West Cook. /s/ Zachh Lamar. Proven 17 August 1795 by West Cook; Joseph Hightower. Recorded 28 Sept 1797.

p.329-322   John Addison to Samuel Marsh. Deed, 28 September 1797, £100, 150 acres on Horns Creek of Savannah River, being part of two tracts one granted to Allen Addison father of afsd John Addison[Adderson], it being the part that fell to him by heirship, the other part was granted unto John Bailey and conveyed by Clejamiry(?) Bailey after decease of John Bailey to Harman Coleman and from him to John Addison, tract adjoining Decosper, John Gray, Marshels Creek, Fair Hill tract. Wit Patsey (x) Stott, Abdell(x) Stott. /s/ John Addison. Judge Arthur Simkins certifies relinquishment of dower by Amy Addison wife of John Addison, 28 Sept 1797; Arthur Simkins; /s/ Amy Addison. Proven by Abdell (x) Stott; Arthur Simkins. Recorded 28 September 1797.

p.332-334   John Coursey to Peter Utz. Deed, 8 July 1797, $15, 75 acres on branches of Mountain Creek of Turkey, adj Messer Smith, granted unto sd John Coursey by Governor [blank] 17[blank] adjoining Rutledge, Andrew Seannel, Smith. /s/ John (IC) Coursey, /s/ Elizabeth (-) Coursey in presence of John Henry Groff, Adam (x) Harter. Proven 28 Sept 1797 by John Henry Grafft; Richard Tutt J P. Recorded 28 Sept 1797.

p.335-337   Lydia Leech spinster to John Henry Grafft. Deed, 8 March 1796, £17 sterling, 75 acres part of tract originally granted 200 acres but lacks 50 granted Peter Khoon 13 Aug 17[--] situate on Little Stevens Creek adj Harling, land granted to Andrew Marks transferred by sd Khoon unto John Baseheart 1780; sd John Baseheart died intestate, one half sd land descended to sd Lyddy Leech lawfull granddaughter of sd John Baseheart. Wit Burges White, James Blocker. /s/ Lydda (x) Leach. Proven 26 April 1796 by James Blocker; John Blocker J P.   Recorded 28 Sept 1797.

67

p.337-342   John Blocker to Adam Bruner.   L&R, 10 February 1795/ 11 Feb 1795, £14 sterling, 200 acres on branches of Mountain Creek bounded on land surveyed for John Heator, Thomas Gray, being part of 1000 acres granted John Jacob Messer Smith decd 6 May 1793 by Gov Wm Moultrie and left by will unto sd John Blocker. Wit Wm Vanse[Fann], Jacob Lahr, Johann Henry Graff. /s/ John Blocker. Proven 28 Sept 1797 by John Henry Crofft; Rd Tutt J P.   Rec 28 Sept 1797.

p.342-344   Dudley Carter to James Mundy.   Release, 2 June 1797, £50 sterling, 50 acres on Chaveses Creek adj lands of Thomas Burnett, James Butler, Capt John T Louis. Wit John G Cooke, Zachariah (x) Smith. /s/ Dudley Carter. Relinquishment of dower right by wife of within named, 1797 [date & name are obliterated]. Proven 20 August 1799 by John G Cook; Rd Tutt. Recorded 20th August 1799.

p.345-347   James Reshton[Rushton] to Young Allen. Deed, 4 May 1795, £20 sterling, 100 acres on Manchester Branch of Little Saluda river, bounded by land of Daniel Greenwood, originally granted to John Reshton, decd, on bounty warrant 13 April 1769 by Gov Chas Montagu. Wit John (x) Reshton, Edward Mobley. /s/ James (x) Reshton. Proven 9 October 1797 by Edward Mobley; Wm Daniel J P.   Rec 10 oct 1797.

p.348-349   John Wells to Jonathan Weever[Weaver]. Deed, 20 March 1797, $500, 500 acres on Turkey creek of Savannah River adj James Gunnells land, granted by Gov Arnoldus Vanderhorst 7 Sept 1795. Wit Joseph Lewis, Demsy Weaver. /s/ John Wells. Proven 7 October 1797 by Demcy Weever; Wm Daniel J P.   Recorded 11th Octr 1797.

p.349-350   Joseph Lewis to Jonathan Weever[Weaver]. Deed, 20 March 1797, $500, 500 acres on Turkey Creek and Mine Creek of Savannah and Saluda Rivers, adj Capt Jonathan Weaver, granted by Gov Vanderhorst 7 Sept 1795. Wit John Wells, Demcy Weaver. /s/ Joseph Lewis. Proven 7 October 1797 by Demcy Weever; Wm Daniel J P. Recorded 11th Octr 1797.

p.351-354   John Cockerham, Mary his wife and Sarah his mother to Shederick Holmes. Deed, 22 May 1795, £50 sterling, 100 acres in fork of Stephens and Turkey creeks, bounded by John Garrett, Nimrod Shinolt, Widow Cobb, Thomas Pennington, Robert Killcrease, Big Stephens Creek, laid out by William Coursey Deputy Survr, being part of 305 acres granted unto Sanfort Keziah 23 June 1794 by LtGov Wm Bull, sd 100 acres transfered by sd Sanfort Keziah by L&R 1795 under William Reed and by sd Reed conveyed by L&R 1776 unto Benjamin Killcrease and by decease of sd Benjamin Killcrease descended to Robt Killcrease son and heir to sd Benjn Killcrease decd and by Robt Killcrease unto Benjamin Cockerham and by decease of Benjn Cockerham the right of sd 100 acres descended unto above sd John Cockerham son and heir to sd Benjamin Cockerham decd. Wit Morris Calliham, Jones Holmes, Edward Holmes. /s/ John (I) Cockerham, /s/ Mary (I) Cockerham, /s/ Sarah (I) Cockerham. Plat by W Coursey D S. Proven 25 February 1796 by Morris Calliham; Henry Key J P. Rec 11 Oct 1797.

p.354-356   Richard Bush Senr Pherebee[Phereby] Colley. Deed, 10 March 1797, £10, 85 acres, granted by patent 27 February 1777 by Wm Bull Esqr to Jessee Lott Sr, Brices Creek adj land of Mark Lott when granted. Wit John Bush, Emslay Lott, Lewis Ezard. /s/ Richard Bush. Proven 29 July 1797 by John Bush; Van Swearingen J P. Recorded 11th October 1797.

p.356-358   Ezekiel Perry to Lewis Wimberley. Deed of Gift, 30 July 1795, for love & goodwill to loving son Lewis Wimberly, Negroes Fillis and her increase, girl Luvey about 15 and her increase, boy Hardy 10, boy Taf age 8, gal Harty 6, boy George 4, gal Hagar 4 months old & her increase. Wit Ezekiel Perry Junr, Frederick Wimberley. /s/ Ezekiel Perry Senr. Proven 20 Jan 1797 by Ezekiel Perry Junr; Wm Daniel J P.   Recorded 11 October 1797.

p.358-363   William Taylor, planter, to Rufus Inman, blacksmith. Release, 4 September 1793, £25 sterling, 150 acres on Halfway Swamp creek being part of land surveyed for sd William Taylor 10 Decr 1786, granted by Gov Chas Pinckney 7 June 1790 adj land of Rufus Inman. Wit Joseph Culbreath, Isaac Norrell. /s/ William (x) Taylor, /s/ Mary (-) Taylor. (Plat shows McConneco's land adjoining). Proven 21 July 1794 by Isaac Norrell; Russell Wilson J P.   Recorded 11 October 1797.

p.363-365   Patsey Pardue to William Moore. Bill of Sale, 18 September 1797, £13.13.3 sterling money, Negro man Mingoe, livestock and household goods. Wit Wm (x) Carter, Jas (x) Little. /s/ Patcey (his + mark) Pardue. Proven 9 October 1797 by James Little; Nathaniel Abney J P.   Recorded 11 October 1797.

p.365-367   John Thos Fairchild of Orangeburgh District to John Frederick of Edgefield County. Deed, 1 February 1797, £5 lawfull money, 316 acres off a tract of 500 acres it being that part as joines sd John Fedricks land which was granted to John Thomas Fairchild 5 January 1795. Wit Machun Whitney, William Courtney, Stephen Elmore. /s/ J Thom Fairchild, /s/ Mary (c) Fairchild. Proven 1 February 1797 by Machun Whitney; J Thos Fairchild J P.   Rec. 11 Oct 1797.

p.367-369   James Frazier to Josiah McDaniel. Deed, 12 March 1797, $50, 125 acres on Paces branch of Shaws Cr of Edisto R adj Mezeck originally granted to William Frazier decd 4 June 1792, fell to afsd James Frazier by heirship being eldest brother of afsd deceased. Wit William Vann, Mark (x) Nobles, Joseph Jones. /s/ James Frazier. Proven 7 Oct 1797 by Wm Vann; Van Swearingen J P. Rec 11 oct 1797.

p.369-370   Sarah Smith to Benjamin Williams. Judge Joseph Hightower certifies that Sarah Smith wife of John Smith relinquished dower rights to 30 acres on Chaves Cr part of 150 acres originally granted to John Scot, sold by John Smith to Benjn Williams by conveyance 25 Novr 1797 and was returned to clarks office 24th May last. Signed 10 June 1797 Sarah (+) Smith.   Rec 11 Oct 1797.

p.370-372   Nancey Bland to John Wells. Deed, 14 January 1797, $100, 100 acres on road from Purkins ford on Saluda to Edgefield Court House, being part of 350 acres originally granted to William Brown by Gov Wm Moultrie 1 January 1787. Sd 350 acres conveyed from Wm Brown to Nancy Bland; sd 100 acres adj Wm Daniel Esqr. Wit John Daniel, Wormley Bland. /s/ Nancy (x) Bland. Proven 4 March 1797 by John Daniel; Wm Daniel J P.   Recorded 11 Octr 1797.

p.373-375   John Killcrease, planter, to Shadrack Holmes. Deed, 10 August 1797, £15 sterling, 129 acres on Turkey Cr bounding lands of Logan, John Duley, Benjamin Kilcrease, George Blair, granted by Gov Chas Montague unto John Logan 1774. Wit Jones Homes, Edward Homes. /s/ John Killcrease. Proven 1 Sept 1797 by Edward Homes; Henry Key J P. Recorded 11 Oct 1797.

p.375-379   Benjamin Williams to David Roper.   Deed, 30 May 1797, $300, 120 acres it being my part of 150 acres survey originally granted to John Scott and by sd Scott conveyed to Jacob Summerall and by Summerall to William Williams Senr and by sd Williams Senr by will conveyed to William Williams Junr, now deceased and by heir of sd Wm Williams conveyed to Benjamin Williams, sd land both sides Chaves Cr a branch of Stevens Cr.   Witness David Boswell, Benjamin Roper, John M Roper. /s/ Benjamin Williams.   Proven 10 June 1797 by David Boswell and Benjamin Roper; Chas Old J P.   Judge Joseph Hightower certifies relinquishment of dower rights by Kezia Williams wife of Robert O Williams, she freely released unto Benjamin Williams by deed of conveyance 25 Novr 1796. /s/ Kezia Williams.   Recorded 11 Oct 1797.

p.379-385   Willis Anderson & wife Patience to Lewis Wimberley[Wimbley]. L&R, 28 March 1793/29 March 1793, £75 sterling, 150 acres Clouds Cr bounded by land of Willis Anderson, Jacob Adams, Mary Watson, Willis Watson, Jacob Reed. Wit Ezekiel Perry, Elisha Watson, Thos (x) Lakey. /s/ Willis Anderson, /s/ Patience (x) Anderson.   Proven 15 May 1793 by Ezekiel Perry; Henry King J P.   Rec 11 Oct 1797.

p.385-387   John Chaney to John Moulden, planter, of Laurens County. Deed, 14 October 1797, £90 sterling, 215 acres on Red lick branch of Big Creek, adj land of Williams; sd land was granted to John Cheney by Gov Wm Moultrie 25 March 1785. Witness William White, Joshua (--) Dean. /s/ John Cheney.   Proven 12 October 1797 by William White; Russell Wilson J P.   Recorded 11 Octr 1797.

p.387-389   Francis Walker to Phereba Colly. Deed, July 1797, £40, 100 acres being part of land granted to sd Francis Walker by patent 2 Sept 1793 adj land of Buckner Blaylock, Wm Smith, Jesse Lott, Absalom Posey. Wit Prescott Bush, [---]ac Bush. /s/ Francis Walker.   Proven 29 July 1797 by Prescott Bush; Vann Swearingen J P.   Recorded 11th Octr 1797.

p.389-392   Richard Bush and wife Mary to Sion Mitchell. Deed, 10 March 1797, £100 sterling, 200 acres on Clouds Cr of Little Saluda R, adj lands of Slywenters, David McGehee, sd survey certified 10 Decr 1774 granted 10 Feb 1775, examined pr Wm Nisbett DS, sd land granted to Francis Jones & Francis Jones to sd Richard Bush. Wit John Mitchell, Betty (x) Bush. /s/ Richard Bush, /s/ Mary (+) Bush. Proven 7 April 1797 by John Mitchell; Elkanah Sawyer J P.   Rec 11 Oct 1797.

p.392-399   Adam Brooner, planter, to Michal Utz, planter. L&R, 12 June 1791/ 30 June 1791, £15 sterling, 100 acres Turkey Creek of Stevens Cr, adj Henry Middletons old line, certified by John Lyon mathematitioner, part of larger tract originally granted Adam Brooner. Wit John Lyon, John Henry Croff. /s/ Adam (x) Brooner. /s/ Michal (c) Utz. [Plat certified by John Lyon, Mathern Milloner] Proven 15 February 1796 by John Hennery Craff; John Blocker J P.   Recorded 12 Oct 1797.

p.400   Pierce Butler to Hankinsons Heirs. For one penny received before signing, sold my right in one undivided moiety of land of Robert Hankinson decd for their benefit. Wit A Darby, Danl Jas Ravenel. /s/ P Butler. Proven 16 Feb 1797 by Daniel James Ravenel; John Samford Dart J P. Pierce Butlers and Robert Haninsons Grant for 230 acres recorded in Grant Book 2222 p 292 and examined by John Vanderhorst, secy. Recorded 10 Octr 1797.

p.401-403   John Anderson to George Anderson.   Titles, 22 March 1797, £300 lawfull money, 300 acres formerly granted to Jas Noldbey & Philip Goode, on Stevens Creek bounded by Geo Delaughter, John Hancock Sr, David Seqler, John Dooleys heirs, Nicholas Minor, Matthew Stoker, Stephens Cr. Wit James Rhodes, David Boswell, Allan Sanderson. /s/ John Anderson.   Receipt, 22 March 1797, £300 sterling. Wit: David Boswell, John Hancock, Stewart Minor. /s/ John Anderson. Proven 9 May 1797 by James Rhodes; Charles Olds J P.   Proven 9 May 1797 by Stewart Minor; Charles Olds J P. Judge Joseph Hightower certifies relinquishment of dower by Elizabeth Anderson wife of John Anderson, 31 August 1797; /s/ Elizabeth Anderson.   Recorded 10 Oct 1797.

p.404-408   Francis Jones to Richard Tate.   L&R, 25 June 1790/26 June 1792, £7 sterling, 22 acres mouth of Fosetys Cr of Saluda River, originally granted unto sd Francis Jones 1 August 1785. Wit Rebekah Abney, Thomas Spragins. /s/ Francis Jones. Proven 9 October 1797 by Thomas Spragins; Nathl Abney J P.   Rec 11 Oct 1797.

p.408-410   Robert Christie to Sampson Pope, planter.   Deed, 9 February 1796, £30, 135 acres on Indian Creek of Saluda River granted by Lt Gov William Bull unto Benjamin Tutt 31 August 1774, from whom sd land conveyed 15 & 16 April 1789 unto sd Robert Christie. Wit James Grisby, Elijah Pope. /s/ Robert (x) Christie.   Proven 18 May 1797 by James Grigsby; Russell Wilson J P.   Rec 13 Oct 1797.

p.410-413   William Coursey, Deputy Surveyor, to Obediah Kilcrease, planter. Deed, 10 January 1795, £10 sterling, 60 acres on Lick branch of Beaverdam Cr branch of Turkey Creek of Savannah River; adj land of sd Killcrease, on Thurmond & Coursey land held for Daniel Brunson from original grant, being part of a tract granted to Edward Vann for 1000 acres by Gov Wm Moultrie at Columbia 6th May 1793, sd 1000 acres transfered by sd Vann unto sd Coursey 16 June 1793. Wit Robert Lyon, John (I) Witt. /s/ Wm Coursey. [Plat shows 60 acres adj lands of Obediah Williams, Mimler, Thurmond, Jno Wills, Danl Brunson.] Proven 23 May 1795 by Robert Lyon; Henry Key J P.   Recorded 13 Octr 1797.

p.413-415   William Donoho, yeoman, to John Walker Senr.   Release, 10 February 1797, £50 sterling, 246 acres part of 400 acres on Rocky and Beech creeks of South Edistoe, sd 400 acres a part of 700 acres originally granted to Elvington Squires by Governor William Moultrie; sd 246 acres bounded upon lands of John Walker Senr, James Tomlin Senr. Wit James Tomlin, Thomas (T) Fares. /s/ William Donoho. Proven 18 March 1797 by Thomas Fares; John Blocker J P.   Rec 12 Octr 1797.

p.415-420   Matthew Wills, carpenter, to Richard Tate, planter. L&R, 15 January 1793/16 January 1793, £10 sterling, 81½ acres on Toselys Creek of Saluda River, part of 175 acres granted to Sarah McQueen who has since married William Davis on 6 February 1786 from Gov Wm Moultrie; William Davis & Sarah his wife who was Sarah McQueen, to sd Matthew Wills by indenture 7 & 8 December 1786; adj land of Andrew Brown, Wm Stewart, Richard Tates old survey line, belonging to Jones Wills. Wit John Abney, Jones Wills, Thos Spragins. /s/ Matthew Wills. Proven 9 October 1797 by Thomas Spragins; Nathl Abney J P.   Recorded 11 Oct 1797.

p.421   Peter Freneau of Charleston City to Craddock Barnell. Deed, 1 March 1797, $25, 25 acres in Ninety Six in township of New Winsor, being half of a tract granted to sd Peter Freneau on 4 July 1785, bounded by lands of Conrad

Andrew, Leonard Bruder, Hansarcher, Conrad Lutz, being half of a tract of 50 acres, the other half of which sd Peter Freneau has already sold to sd Craddock Barnell. Wit J McIver, Peter M Neusville. /s/ Peter Freneau. Proven, Edgefield, 2 March 1797 by John McIver; A[?] Cunnington J P.   Recorded 14th Oct 1787.

p.423-424   Joseph Fuller, physician, to George Bender, planter. Deed 12 July 1797, £80 sterling, two tracts, one of 140 acres granted to Thomas Rogers 23 August 1724 adj Adam Hyles, the other of 72 acres, 40 acres of which is supposed to be in an old survey granted to sd Thos Rogers 2 Oct 1786, sd tracts conveyed by sd Thomas Rogers to Simeon Cushman and by Simeon Cushman and Judah his wife to Joseph Fuller. Wit Casper Nail, [blank] Tobler, Fredk Cradk Burnell. /s/ Joseph Fuller. Proven 12 Oct 1797 by Casper Nail; Rd Tutt J P.   Rec 12 Oct 1797.

p.424-427   Nicholas H Bugg, of Georgia, to Alexander Smith, of Edgefield. Deed, 5 September 1797, $200, 200 acres on Little river, land of Tutt, and land of Winter where James Tutt now lives. Witness James Fox, Eliza Fox, Joseph Hutchenson, Abram Jones. /s/ N Bugg. N H Bugg warrants land against all persons except Mrs. Susannah Winter so far as respect her third therein. Georgia, Justice Joseph Hutchenson certifies that Charlotte the wife of Nicholas H Bugg relinquished dower right 5 Sept 1797. Proven 13 Oct 1797 by James Fox; Rd Tutt J P.   Rec 13 Oct 1797.

p.427-430   Nicholas H Bugg, of Georgia, to Alexander Smith, of Edgefield. Deed 12 August 1797, $150 SC money, 150 acres adj sd Smith, Savannah river, Doct Delahaw which is known by name of Horns Lookout where sd Smith now resides. Wit James Fox, Nicholas Fox, J Malone. /s/ N H Bugg. Georgia, Richmond County, 14 Aug 1797, Justice Abram Jones certifies that Charlotte, wife of Nicholas H Bugg, relinquished dower rights. Proven 13 Oct 1797 by Jas Fox; Rd Tutt J P.   Rec 13 Oct 1797.

p.430-432   Alexander Oden and Elisha his wife to Luke Sharpton. Deed, 1797, 40 acres on Gunnels Creek of Stevens Creek adj David Hopkins, Robert Collins, and Alexander Oden. Wit Zachariah Lunday[Sunday?], Abraham M Wade. /s/ Alexander Oden. /s/ Elisha (x) Oden. Receipt, 7 Sept 1797, $60 in for for within debt of conveyance. Proven 13 Oct 1797 by Zachariah Lunday; Rd Tutt.   Rec 13 Oct 1797.

p.432-435   Mitchel Dooly of Lincoln County, Georgia, to Samuel Clayton of sd county. Deed, 13 October 1797, £50 sterling, 100 acres on Stevens Creek granted to Mary Summerville, transfered by L&R to Col John Dooly. Wit A Smith, Thos Broughton. /s/ Mitchell Dooly. Proven 13 Oct 1797 by Alexander Smith; Rd Tutt J P. Recorded 13 October 1797.

p.435-441   Thomas Shilles of Creaven County to Nathan Mellton, planter. L&R, 3 May 1773/4 May 1773, £100 SC money, 225 acres in Barkley County on Indian Creek of Little Saludy, part of 450 acres granted to Thomas Shiles 13 October 1772 by Gov Chas Montague, bounding on William Whitakers land. Wit John North, William (N) Tomson, William (N) West Junr. /s/ Thomas Shiles, /s/ Ann (x) Shiles.   Proven 17 November 1773 by William West Junr; John Fairchild J P.   Rec 13 Oct 1797.

p.441-443   Philip May Senr, planter, to James May. Deed, 14 October 1797, £5 sterling, Negro girl about two years of age named Syllah.   Witness James Campbell, Frances Pickett. /s/ Philip May. Proven 14 Oct 1797 by James Campbell; Rd Tutt.

Recorded 14 October 1797.

p.443-445   John Slater Senr to Jeremiah Stringer. Deed, 5 April 1797, £40,
100 acres adj William Stringer. Wit John Stringer, William Stringer. /s/ John (x)
Slater Senr. Proven 25 Sept 1797 by William Stringer; Chas Old, J P. Recorded 14th
October 1797.

p.445   Thomas Murrah's deposition for John Kimbrel. 16 October 1797
before Rd Tutt J P, Thomas Murrah sworn, saith that in an affray on 23 Sept last
between John Kimbrel and Allan Baily, deponant saw Allan Baily bite a part of sd
John Kimbrel's right ear off; Rd Tutt. /s/ Thomas Murrah. Rec 16 Oct 1797.

p.446-448   Charles Fralick to Adam Stalnaker. Deed, 26 September 1796, £40,
200 acres on Dry fork of Mine Creek of Little Saluda River, adj George Smith's
land, granted to sd Charles Fralick 1789 by Gov Chas Pinckney. Wit John Harrod,
Hannah Williams, Robert (x) Hattox. /s/ Charles Fralic. Proven 16 October 1797 by
Robert Haddocks; William Daniel J P. Recorded 17 October 1797.

p.448-455   Arthur Watson, planter, to Anderson Winzor, planter. L&R, 28 May
1795/29 May 1795, £10 SC money, 180 acres part of 450 acres granted 7 January 1788
to sd Arthur Watson in Ninety Six Dist on Underwoods branch of Mine Creek of Little
Saluda. Wit Arthur Rice Watson, Adam Stalnaker, Isaac Coe. /s/ Arthur (A) Watson.
Proven 16 Oct 1797 by Adam Stalnaker; Wm Daniel J P.   Rec 17 Oct 1797.

p.455-457   David Gains to William Gains. Bill of Sale, 4 April 1797, $200,
all my livestock, household furniture. Wit D Henderson, Wm Vann. /s/ David Gains.
Proven 6 April 1797 by David Henderson; John Blocker J P.   Rec 17 Oct 1797.

p.457-463   Rolan Williams Senr to Benjamin Melton. L&R, 5 June 1792/6 June
1792, £50 sterling, 206 acres on Dry Creek of Little Saluda river granted to Rolan
Williams 3 October 1792 by Gov Charles Pinckney adj lands of George Smith, Arthur
Watson, William Hearing. Wit Matthew Melton, William Frederick, Sampson Williams.
/s/ Rolan Williams. Proven 30 May 1794 by Matthew Melton; Henry King J P.
Recorded 17 October 1797.

p.463-464   Tom's Indenture to Daniel Bird. Tom a Negroman said to be free
hath bound himself as a servant under Daniel Bird for ninety nine years or during
his life, to obey sd Bird in all things as a servant ought to do his master, and sd
Bird is to find sd Tom sufficient clothes during his servitude. 4 May 1797. /s/
Tom (+). John Blocker J P. Recorded 10th October 1797.

p.464-470   Arthur Watson to Absalum Shurley. L&R, 27 March 1795/28 March
1795, pursuant to will of Michael Watson decd between Arthur Watson executor of sd
will and Absalum Shurley of sd county. £13.5 paid, 150 acres originally granted to
Isaac Lindsay and conveyed to William Daniel and by sd Daniel to John Roberts and
by sd Roberts to Michael Watson decd, on Dry Creek of Little Saluda River. Wit
Arthur Rice Watson, Adam Stalnaker. /s/ Arthur (A) Watson. Proven 25 April 1795 by
Adam Stalnaker; William Daniel J P.   Recorded 10 Oct 1797.

p.470-472   Zephaniah Harvey of Hancock County, Georgia to James Shepperd of

Washington County, Georgia. Deed, 8 April 1797, $30, 14¼ acres on Savannah river in Edgefield County formerly Granville County, part of a grant to Job Red [surveyed by?] Wm Lang. Wit Jones Griffin, John Harvey. /s/ Zepheniah Harvey. Proven 26 April 1797 by Jonas Griffin; Chas Old J P. Recorded 21 Octr 1797.

p.472-474   James Shepperd, Washington County, Georgia, to Hardy Jones, Edgefield County. Deed, 9 May 1797, $30, 14¼ acres on Savannah river, part of grant to Job Red, laid off by Mr Lang. Wit Mills Woodard, Jonas Griffin. /s/ James Sheppard. Proven 16 May 1797 by Jones Griffin; Hugh Middleton J P.   Rec 21 Oct 1797.

p.474-475   Hardy Jones to Samuel Scott. Deed, 14 May 1797, $30, 14¼ acres on Savannah River, upper part of tract granted to Job Red joining land granted to Samuel Fry. Wit William S Wright, John Griffin. /s/ Hardy Jones. Proven 21 Oct 1797 by William S Wright; Hugh Middleton J P.   Recorded 21 Oct 1797.

p.475-477   Zepheniah Harvey & Nancy his wife, Hancock County, Georgia, to Samuel Scott. Deed, 27 April 1797, $800, 200 acres on Savannah river in Edgefield, formerly Granville, originally granted about 1751 to Samuel Fry and by him sold to John Harvey since deceased and by him devised by will to his son William Harvey since deceased, and sold according to law by the executors of sd Willm Harvey decd to his son Zephaniah Harvey party hereto. Wit Edward Prince, Lucey Prince. /s/ Zephaniah Harvy, /s/ Nancy (+) Harvy. Proven 25 May 1797 by Edward Prince; Hugh Middleton J P.   Recorded 17th October 1797.

p.477-479   John, Thomas & James Lamar, Hancock County, Georgia, sons & heirs of Jeremiah Lamar decd, to Jonas Griffin, Edgefield. Deed, 28 April 1797, $800, 200 acres in Edgefield formerly Granville, on Savannah river, half of which was conveyed by James Dyer to sd Jereh Lamar, the other half by sd Dyer to Derby Minefin[?] and by him to sd Jereh Lamar decd, being the lower part of 300 acres originally granted to sd James Dyer in 1750s, adj land of Samuel Fry, John Lamar, Edward Prince.   Wit Edward Prince, Lucy Prince.   /s/ John Lamar, /s/ Thomas Lamar,/s/ Betsey Lamar, /s/ James Lamar, /s/ Frances (+) Lamar. Proven 15 May 1797 by Edward Prince; Hugh Middleton JP.   Recorded 21 Octr 1797.

p.480-481   Jonas Griffin & wife to Samuel Scott. Deed, 2 May 1797, $800, 200 acres conveyed by John Lamar, Thomas Lamar, James Lamar 8 April 1797 to Jonas Griffin, and is lower part of 300 acres originally granted to James Dyer, adj Samuel Fry, John Lamar, Edward Prince. Wit J Grinage, H Middleton Junr. /s/ Jonas Griffin, /s/ Jennet Griffin. Proven 2 May 1797 by Hugh Middleton Junr.   Rec 21 Octr 1797.

p.482-487   Harman Galman & wife Lucretia to John Addison. L&R, 4 November 1790/5 November 1790, £100 S C money, 250 acres in two tracts of land, one of 100 acres where sd John Addison now lives being part of 200 acres originally granted to Allen Addison containing 150 acres, near Fairhill on Horns Creek, 150 acres being part of 200 acres originally granted to John Bailey, at death of sd John Bailey fell to Elijah merry Bailey his eldest surviving brother, and conveyed by L&R by Elijahmerry Bailey and Leah his wife the 26th July 1785. Wit William Brown, Conrad Gallman. /s/ Harman Gallman, /s/ Lucretia Gallman.   Proven 21 Octr 1797 by Conrad Gallamn; Rd Tutt J P.   Recorded 21 Octr 1797.

p.487-490   Ezekiel Glover to George Slater of Claradon County, SC.   Deed, 20 October 1797, £15 sterling, 100 acres Cuffeytown Cr original grant to sd Ezekiel Glover 29 Sept 1796, adj John Adams, Robert Brown, John Pitman, Wm Coursey, Buckhalter, Henry Glover. Wit Dempsey Davis, Levy (+) Weathernton. /s/ Ezekiel Glover. Proven 21 October 1797 by Demsey Davis; Aquilla Miller J P.   Rec 28 Oct 1797.

p.490-491   John Reynolds to Silas Sellers. Bill/Sail, 19 October 1797, Negro Daniel about age 21, yellowish complexion. Wit: J Walker, Isaac Arledge.   John (m) Renolds. Proven 24 Oct 1797 by Isaac Arledge; Rd Tutt J P.   Rec 24th Octr 1797.

p.491-492   Silas Sellers to John Ryan. Bill/Sale, for $300, Negro Daniel. Wit Eugene Brenan, John Simkins, Briton Mims. /s/ Silas Sellers. Proven 24 Oct by Briton Mims; Rd Tutt J P.   Rec 24 Oct 1797.

p.493-495   Drury Mims to Talton Mims. Deed, 25 October 1797, £10 sterling, 38 acres on branches of Cedar Creek adj John Mims, land Talton Mims bought of Briton Mims. Wit Wm Robertson, Wm Hagens. /s/ Drury Mims. Proven 28 Oct 1797 by William Robertson; Richard Tutt J P.   Recorded 28 Oct 1797.

p.495-497   John Mims Senr to Talton Mims. Deed, 24 January 1797, £10, 72.5 acres being part of 450 acres originally granted to Solomon Peters lying on branch of Cedar Creek & adj sd Mims. Wit Wm Robertson, Wm Hagens. /s/ John (I) Mims. Proven 28 Oct 1797 by William Robertson; Rd Tutt J P.   Rec 28 Oct 1797.

p.497-499   Philip Lamar to Christain Rountrie. Bill of Sail, 6 July 1797, Negro girl Rachel age 16 for $162; condition that Philip Lamar pay $162 before 6 July next ensuing, then Bill/sale void. If sd Rachel should dye before 6 July, it shall not be the loss of Christain Rountrie but sd Lamar agrees to repay her sd $162 by 6 July as above mentioned. Witness: John Rountrie, Andrew Glover. Time of payment extended untill 6 September next. Time of replayment extended untill 6 Nov insuing. /s/ Christain Rountrie. Proven 30 Oct 1797 by Andrew Glover; Rd Tutt. Recorded 30th Octr 1797.

p.499-503   Isaac Kirkland to Joseph Vann. Deed, 3 October 1797, £25 or $107, 59 acres being part of 200 acres on Shaws Creek originally granted to Peter Hillard and from sd Hillard conveyed to Thomas Swearingen; from sd Swearingen to sd Isaac Kirkland, sd grant dated 28 Sept 1784. Wit Edward Vann Senr, Josiah (x) McDaniel, Delilah (x) Bettice. /s/ Isaac Kirkland. Certification by Judge Joseph Hightower of release/dower right by Mary Kirkland wife of Isaac Kirkland; /s/ Mary (x) Kirkland. Proven 11 Oct 1797 by Josiah McDaniel; Van Swearingen J P. Rec 4 Nov 1797.

p.503-506   Isaac Kirkland to James Vann Junr. Deed, 3 October 1797, $107 a son of Edward Vann, 58 acres on Shaws Creek being part of 200 acres originally granted to Peter Hillard 28 Sept 1784; from sd Hillard conveyed to Thomas Swearingen, by L&R conveyed to sd Isaac Kirkland, adj 59 acres sold to Jos Vann. Wit Edward Vann Senr, Josiah (+) McDaniel, Delilah (+) Bettice. /s/ Isaac Kirkland. Judge Joseph Hightower certifies relinquishment/dower by Mary Kirkland wife of Isaac Kirkland. /s/ Mary (x) Kirkland. Proven 7 October 1797 by Josiah McDaniel; Vann Swearingen J P.   Recorded 4 Novr 1797.

p.506-508   Hannah Bullock to Benjamin Watson.   B Sale, 6 December 1797; £350 sterling; Negro man James, wench Amy, girl Nan, small girl Ruth, boy Abram, also livestock, foodstuff, farm equipment, household goods. Wit James Ogilvie, Wm Ogilvie. /s/ Hannah Bullock. Proven by Wm Ogilvie; William Daniel. Rec 6 Nov 1797.

p.508-511   David Gains, farmer, to Samuel Humphries.   Deed, 1 October 1797, £33, 100 acres being part of 300 acres granted to Arthur Fort 2 May 1770, by Arthur Fort willed to Owen Fort heir at law, sd Owen Fort conveyed 150 acres to William Humphreys; sd Wm Humphreys conveyed 100 acres to said David Gains, also 30 acres granted to Henry Boulten 19 Aug 1784, likewise 70 acres part of 312 granted to Willm Humphrey 4 Decr 1786 on Mine Creek of Little Saluda; adj Boltons land, Joseph Nunns land. Wit: D Henderson, William Humphreys. /s/ David Gains, /s/ Sibliah (+) Gains. Proven 23 Oct 1797 by D Henderson; Wm Daniel J P.   Rec 9 Nov 1797.

p.511-513   William Morgan to Elias & John Morgan, Margaret Morgan, Martha Morgan, Nancy Morgan, Elias Morgan, Polley Morgan, Lucy Morgan. Deed of Gift, 19 August 1797, for divers good causes, all my Negroes: Tom, Nance, James, Amey, Silvey, my goods, chattels, livestock, household stuff whatsoever, to live on till John Morgan is twenty one years old and then to be equally divided, also to Elias & John Morgan I give my land and plantation whereon I live to be equally divided between them or disposed of at her[wife?] & their pleasures. Wit Elias Morgan, Sam (x) Waller, Lucy (e) Waller. /s/ William Morgan. Proven 1 September 1797 by Elias Morgan and Samuel Waller; Aquilla Miles J P. Rec 9 Novr 1797.

p.513-516   Frederick Swearingen to Benjamin Jonnakin Junr. Deed, 10 November 1797, $100, 100 acres Shaws Cr adjoining James Vann Junr, sd Swearingen. Wit Joseph Vann, Thomas (T) Sely. /s/ Fredk Swearingen. Judge Arthur Simkins certifies relinquishment of dower by Sarah the wife of Frederick Swearingen, 10 Nov 1797. Proven 10 Nov 1797 by Joseph Vann; Vann Swearingen J P.   Rec 10 Nov 1797.

p.516-520   Conrad Gallman to James Brown. Deed, 5 June 1797, £35 sterling, 180 acres part of tract sold to satisfy a judgment obtained by John Smith against Kemp T Strawther and Henry Hunted recorded in Book N p 225, bounding on Judge Simkins and Landrums land & dwelling house on Log Creek. Wit John (+) Youngblood, Jacob Youngblood, Jacob Youngblood Junr. /s/ Conrad Gallman. Judge Arthur Simkins certifies relinquishment of dower by Susannah Gallman wife of Conrad Gallman, 18 Sept 1797. Proven by John Youngblood; Arthur Simkins.   Rec 13th Novr 1797.

p.520-523   Michal Shaver, farmer, and wife Mary to Henry Timmerman. Deed, 2 June 1795, for 20 shillings sterling, 1¼ acres on Sleepy cr of Turkey Cr a prong of big Stevens cr of Savannah R; being part of 60 acres granted unto Michal Shaven by Lt Gov Wm Bull. Wit Peter (U) Utz, Peter (J) Timmerman, William Coursey. /s/ Michael (x) Shaver, /s/ Mary (+) Shaver. Proven 15 Nov 1797 by Peter Utz; Rd Tutt J P. Recorded 15th Novr 1797.

p.523-525   Hugh Middleton to daughter Eliza Middleton. Deed/Gift, 15 August 1797, for love & affection, Negroes Agg, Rachel, Johanna together with their future increase. Wit: William Tennent, Chas Tennent. /s/ Hugh Middleton. Proven 17 Novr 1797 by William Tennent; Rd Tutt J P.   Recorded 17 Nov 1797.

p.525-526   Wm Anderson to daughter Rebeccah Anderson. Deed of Gift, 24 February 1796; for love & affection, Negro girl Fany about six years old. Wit Jno Anderson, Mathew Sullivan. /s/ Wm Anderson. Proven 15 May 1797 by John Anderson; S Mays J P. Recorded 10 Nov 1797.

p.526-529   William English and wife Sarah to William Moore. Deed, £75 sterling, 113 acres N side Little Saluda originally granted to Robert Davis decd 15 May 1772 bounding on land of Moses Kirkland; also 200 acres being part of 1200 acres originally granted to Benjamin Mayzyck bounding on above tract. Wit Thomas Butler, Gilson Yarbrouth. /s/ William (x) English. Proven 31 October 1797 by Jilson Yarbrough; Nathaniel Abney J P. Recorded 25 Novr 1797.

p.529-532   Caul Collins and wife Elizabeth to Zacheus Thorp, preacher. Deed, 7 January 1796, £50 sterling, 100 acres on Crooked run a branch of Turkey Cr, adj Evelys land, Taylors land; plat by William Coursey Deputy Surveyor, being part of 200 acres granted to Ward Taylor by Lt Gov Wm Bull 9 Sept 1774, conveyed by Ward Taylor unto Nery Taylor, by Nery Taylor unto Call Collins by L&R 5 January 1787. Wit Elejar Thorp, Moses Taylor. /s/ Caul Collins, /s/ Elizabeth (+) Collins. Proven 13 January 1796 by Moses Taylor; John Blocker, J P. Rec 29 Nov 1797.

p.532-533   Jacob Capeheart to Johnson Hagood. Assignment, of right & title to land to Johnson Hagood & his heirs in payment of $118 which he has this day lent me, if same is not returned him or settled in six months from this date, 22 Jan 1796, Charlestown. Wit S A Greenland. /s/ Jacob Capeheart. Proven, Charleston District, 16 October by Samuel A Greenland; Jarvis Henry Stephens J P. Recorded 29th Nov 1797.

p.533-536   Joshua Deen to William Moore. Bill of Sale, 13 January 1796, £53.3.10.5 money of SC. Negro wench Luce, 21 or 22 years of age; if Joshua Deen pay to sd Wm Moore £53.3.10.5 & financial arrangements by 25 Nov ensuing, then deed/sale of none effect. Wit: George Deen, D Gooch. /s/ Joshua (XX) Deen. Received 13 Jan 1796 of Wm Moore sd sum; /s/ Joshua (XX) Deen. Proven 7 Novr 1797 by Daniel Gooch; Nathaniel Abney J P. Rec 29th Novr 1797.

p.536-537   John Rockett to Negro Peter. John Rockett in consideration of £90 sold Negro man Peter to himself, 30th December 1796. Wit Zacheus Middleton, James Carson. /s/ John Rockett. Proven 8 December 1797 by James Carson; Chas Old J P. Recorded 28 Decr 1797.

p.537-538   Joseph T Bell's receipt. Received of Joseph T Bell, Negro girl Fillis and her child Candes, 8 March 1797. Wit Benj Ryan. /s/ Joseph T Bell. Proven 5 December 1797 by Benjamin Ryan; Rd Tutt J P. Rec 5th Decr 1797.

p.538-546   William Clarkson and Nathaniel Russell executors/will of Aaron Loorock decd, dated 14 April 1791, to John Thornton, planter, of 96 District. L&R, 18 October 1796/19 October 1796, £30 SC money, 250 acres on Reedy branch of Cuffytown bounded at time of grant to Peter Leger 3 April 1775 by vacant land. Wit Geo A Gordon, Patrick Meur. Proven, Charleston, 23 January 1797, by Patrick Meur; John Mitchell J P. Recorded 14 December 1797.

CONVEYANCE BOOK 14: 1797 - 1799

p.546-548   John Thornton to John Hamilton. Deed, 11 December 1797, £15 sterling, 100 acres being part of tract of 250 acres originally granted to Peter Ledger
3 April 1775, on old road from Cambridge to McCoys ferry on Savannah river. Wit Wm
(x) Jordon, John Jordon. /s/ John Thornton. Proven 11 November(sic) 1797 by
William Jurdin; James Harrison J P. /s/ Wm (x) Jourdin. Rec 14 Decr 1797.

p.548-551   Lewis Jernagin, planter, to son Mudy Jernagin. Deed of Gift, 7
December 1797, for love and $10, gelding, household furniture, livestock, tools,
condition he permit sd Lewis Jernagin to use sd articles so long as sd Lewis shall
live. Wit Ezekiel McClendon. /s/ Lewis (+) Jernagan. Proven 16 Decr 1797 by
Ezekiel McClendon: Rd Tutt J P. Rec 16th December 1797.

p.551-554   Shadrack Rozar, constable, to George B Moore. Bill of Sale, 8 May
1794, at suit of John Gresham, Rozar to levy of goods of Thomas Lamar for debt of
£21.19.4; executed on three female Negroes, Cate and her two children Hannah and
Agg, struck off to highest bidder George B Moore for £45 sterling. Wit Morgan
Murrah. /s/ Shadrach Rozar, constable.   Proven 16 Dec 1797 by Morgan Murrah; Chas
Old J P. Recorded 18 Decr 1797.

p.554-556   Barrot Travis and wife Ann to James Wolf. Deed, 8 December 1797,
$15, 10 acres on Mine Creek, on roads Cambridge to Charlestown, and Lees ferry on
Big Saluda to Edgefield Court House, William Daniels line, Rober Blands line, being
part of 312 acres granted to William Humphreys 4 Decr 1786, and by him conveyed to
us. Wit Samuel Humphries, D Henderson. /s/ Barrot (I) Travis, Ann (+) Travis.
Proven 21 December 1797 by D Henderson; Wm Daniel J P. Rec 21 Dec 1797.

p.556-559   Wilson Conner, planter, to Ezekiel McClendon, planter. Deed, 18
October 1796, £10 sterling, 570 acres on branch of Beaverdam Creek of Big Horse
Creek, granted to Mike McKie 31 July 1792 by Gov Chas Pinckney, adj land of Daniel
Makick, by sd Mike McKie conveyed to sd Wilson Conner 11 of present Oct. Wit Thos
Swearingen, Demsea (x) Commoner[?]. /s/ Wilson Conner. Proven 2 December 1797 by
Thomas Swearingen; Vann Swearingen J P. Rec 21 Decr 1797.

p.559   Gabriel Tutt, Abbeville County, to Barnard Caffery, of Edgefield.
Deed, 21 January 1794, £60 sterling, 60 acres on Savannah river, being part of 200
acres granted 29 April 1760. Wit John Searls, Joseph Tucker. /s/ Gabriel Tutt.
Proven 6 Nov 1797 by Joseph Tucker; Russell Wilson, J P. Rec 22 Decr 1797.

End of Book 14

p.1-2   Francis Drinkard, Abbeville, to Barrott Travis of Edgefield.
Mortgage, 10 February 1797, for $150, mortgaged unto Barrott Travis a Negro boy
James, $150 with legal interest to be paid. Wit Mumford Perryman, Benjamin Mobley.
/s/ Francis ()) Drinkard. Proven 30 Dec 1797 by Mumford Perryman; Wm Daniel J P.
Rec 1 Jan 1798.

p.2-4   Henry Wray & wife to son Masten Smith. Deed, 22 August 1797, for
love & good will, two tracts on Richland Creek of Little Saluda, one granted to
Lewis Powel 4 May 1771, the other adjoining land of Jacob Smith originally 200
acres granted to Smallwood Smith 8 July 1774. Wit Philip Rayford, D Henderson. /s/
Henry Ray, /s/ Elizabeth Ray. Judge William Anderson certifies relinquishment of
dower by Elizabeth Ray wife of Henry Ray, 22 August 1797. /s/ Elizabeth Ray.
Proven 20 Oct 1797 by Philip Raiford; William Daniel, J P.   Rec 1 Jan 1798.

p.4-7   Christain Buckhalter & wife to John Griffith. Deed, 2 May 1797,
$275, 50 acres part of 200 acres granted to sd Buckhalter on Loyds Creek branch of
Stephens Creek. Wit John Boyd, Floodde (M) Mitchell, William (x) Flinn. /s/
Christain (C) Buckhalter. Plat shows adj land of H Key, J Killcrease, Wm Howl, C
Buckhalter, John Flukes; certified by John Boyd D S. Judge Arthur Simkins certi-
fies relinquishment of dower by Mary Buckhalter wife of Christain Buckhalter, 2
Jany 1798; /s/ Mary (x) Buckhalter.   Proven 3 May 1797 by John Boyd; H Middleton
J P.   Rec 2 January 1798.

p.7-10   Martin Williams to James and Samuel Saxon, sons of Ben Saxon. Deed
13 November 1788; £100 SC money, on Deep Creek of Little Saluda River being part of
land granted to William Bridge by Lt Gov Wm Bull 21 April 1775; by William Bridge
conveyed to sd Martin Williams 9 July 1786. Wit L Yancey, James Yancey. /s/ Martin
Williams. Proven 13 Nov 1788 by James Yancey; Charles Saxon J P.   Rec 30 Jan 1798.

p.10-13   James and Samuel Saxon and wife Mary all of Laurens County to
William Cason. Deed, 17 September 1793; £45, 300 acres on Deep Creek of Little
Saluda, originally granted to Wm Bridges by Lt Gov Wm Bull 21 April 1775, adj
Chaney at time of survey, other sides vacant; conveyed to Martin Williams 9 June
1786, and by Martin Williams to James and Samuel Saxon 13 Nov 1788. Wit Jehs
Walker, B H Saxon, Robt Ross. /s/ James Saxon, /s/ Samuel Saxon, /s/ Mary Saxon.
Relinquishment of dower by Mary Saxon, 14 Oct 1793. /s/ M Saxon. Proven in Laurens
County, 14 October 1793, by Robert Ross; William Hunter J P.   Rec 30 Jan 1798.

p.13-14   West Cook, of Village of Campbellton, Edgefield County, to David
Quarles. B/Sale, 20 March 1797, £35 sterling, a Negro girl Jude about eight years
old with her future increase. Wit George Leslie. /s/ West Cook. Proven 20 March
1797 by George Leslie; Charles Old J P.   Rec 2 January 1798.

p.14-22   Charles J Colcock to Thomas Radcliffe executor of Andrew Williamson. L&R by way of Mortgage, 7 August 1797/8 August 1797, penal sum £29.3.4 for
payment of £14.11.8 with interest thereon, 100 acres on Sleepy Creek originally
granted to F Beckman on 13 August 1765. Wit Thomas Levingston, Charles Tennent,
William Tennant. /s/ Chas J Colcock. If debt be paid, everything herein contain
shall be utterly null and void. Proven in Charleston District, 19 December 1797 by
Wm Tennent; John Trotter J P.   Recorded 2d Jan 1798.

p.22-31   Samuel Mays to Thomas Radcliffe executor of Andrew Williamson
decd. L&R, 7 August 1797/8 August 1797, penal sum £324.1.8 with condition for
payment of £162.10 with interest thereon, further sums, 40 acres in Granville
County, Ninety six dist on Rocky Creek of Stephens Creek bounding on John
Heart[Hart], James Miscampbell; also 250 acres near Cuffee Town & Stevens Creek adj
Daniel Rogers, Charles Williams, & Thomas Goode; also 72 acres in Granville County,
Ninety Six Dist on Rocky Creek of Stevens Creek bounding on Margaret Fulton, on
Walter Bell. Wit Thomas Levingston, Chas Tennent, Wm Tennent. /s/ S Mays. Proven
19 Decr 1797 by William Tennent; Jno Trotter J P.

p.31-33   Truman Wightt, John Wightt both of Edgefield & John Flint of
Georgia & wife to Edward Mitchel. Release, 17 April 1797, $630.25, 282 acres on
Nobles Creek, one tract of 225 acres originally granted James Thomas; one tract of
57 acres originally granted to Lancelot Warren. Wit Richard Burton, Lilestun
Pardue, Starling Mitchel. /s/ Truman Wightt, /s/ John Wightt, /s/ John Flint. Judge
Joseph Hightower certifies relinquishment of dower by Nancy Flint wife of John
Flint; /s/ Ann Flint. Proven 3 January 1798 by Lilestun Pardue; Rd Tutt J P.
Recorded 3 January 1798.

p.34   John Addison to Gasper Gallman. Receipt, 6 January 1798. Gasper
Gallman paid in full $400 for Negro fellow Peter. Wit Samuel Marsh, David Donald-
son. /s/ John Addison. Proven 6 Jan 1798 by David Donaldson; Richard Tutt J P.
Recorded 6 Jan 1798.

p.34-37   Hezekiah Gentry to Robert Brooks. Deed, 9 October 1797, $1000,
350 acres on Indian Creek of Little Saluda river; 200 acres of which adj Hezekiah
Burnett, Starlings branch, Runnel Gentry, James Petty, John Griffin, Robert Gentry,
Anthony Lear[?in binding]; the 350 acres are part of four surveys: first granted
by Gov Bull 21 April 1775 to Peter Whitten for 1200 acres; second granted by Wm
Moultrie for 100 acres to Bartholomew Corley 3 April 1795; third granted by Gov Wm
Moultrie to Hezekiah Gentry for 521 acres 6 Feb 1786; fourth not known being not at
hand now; all having been sold to Hezekiah Gentry but what was granted to him. Wit
Thomas Largent, Jesse Samford. /s/ Hezekiah Gentry, /s/ Catherin (x) Gentry. A plat
shows 150 acres on Indian Creek & Martins Branch, land of Robert Brooks, Hezekiah
Burnett, Elijah Worthington, James Nichols, Runnel Gentry. Proven 29 December 1797
by Thomas Largent; Nathaniel Abney J P.   Rec 6 Jany 1798.

p.37-39   John Williams to son Samuel Williams. Power/attorney, 4 January
1798, power to follow legal courses to recover matters and things due to me in
state of Georgia. Wit Eldred Simkins, Abdell Stott. /s/ John Williams. Proven 4
Jan 1798 by Eldred Simkins; Arthur Simkins J P.   Rec 8th Jan 1798.

p.39-41   Elijah Stone and Susannah his wife of Laurence County SC to Thomas
Lively of Edgefield County. Release, 4 December 1797, for $150, 169 acres,
bounding on William Thomas, the Great Survey, on Ready Creek and Cuffeetown Creek,
granted to Elijah Stone 5 Jan 1789 by Gov Thomas Pinckney. Wit William Thomas,
Richard Hogen, Dennett Hill. /s/ Elijah Stone, Susannah C Stone. Proven 23
December 1797 by William Thomas; Jas Harrison J P.   Rec 10 Jan 1798.

p.41-43   John Simkins to William Little, planter. Deed, 8 January 1798,

£43.6.8 sterling, 300 acres on Saluda River, being part of 608 acres originally granted to sd John Simkins by Gov Wm Moultrie 2 May 1785. Wit Eugene Brenan, Wm Burt. /s/ John Simkins. Judge Arthur Simkins certifies relinquishment of dower by Sally Simkins wife of John Simkins: /s/ Sally Simkins. Proven 17 Jan 1798 by Eugene Brenan; Rd Tutt J P. Recorded 17 Jan 1798.

p.44   John & Mary Clem to Eliza Blake. Receipt, 1 January 1798. Received of Elizabeth Blake five shillings the full of within bond, being my part of estate of Benjamin Blake decd both real and personal; Jno Clem. Wit John Anderson, Matthew (B) Barrett. 6 January, received of Elizabeth Blake five shillings, it being in full of within bond being my part of estate real & personal of Benjamin Blake decd; Mary Clem. Wit Jno Anderson, Matthew (B) Barrett. Proven 30 January 1798 by Matthew Barrett; James Harrison J P. Rec 5 Feb 1798.

p.44-46   James Thomas to Joseph Summerall. Deed, 11 August 1797, $400, 150 acres Stephens Creek granted to Isaac Hudson 5 March 1770, conveyed by Isaac Hudson to Abenezer Starns 8 June 1771, by sd Ebenezer Starns to James Thomas 20 Dec 1785. Wit John Boyd, Patsy (+) Boyd. /s/ James Thomas. Proven 16 December 1797 by John Boyd; Henry Key J P. Recorded 5th Feby 1798.

p.46-51   William Dorris and wife of Abbeville County to Benjamin Blackey of Edgefield. L&R, 21 September 1787/22 September 1787, £15 sterling, 100 acres in Colleton County now Edgefield on Hardlabour Creek granted to sd William Dorris 25 May 1774. Wit James Stefel, Barbara (x) Schildknecht. /s/ William Dorris, /s/ Maria (x) Dorris. Proven 29 January 1798 by Barbary Shelknot now Barbara Bell; James Harrison J P. /s/ Barbara (x) Bell. Recorded 5 Feby 1798.

p.51-53   William Holley of Laudon County, Virginia, to William Daniel of Granville County, SC. Power/attorney, 23 September 1797, to pay all taxes or quit rents or other charges due on 500 acres in Granville County, SC, on Cuffeytown and Hardlabour Creeks of Stevens Creek bounding on Mr Cannodies, Charles Williams, Benjamin Tutt, James Wilson, William Rowins, Benjamin Bell, Daniel Rogers, certified by a warrant from Hon Lord G Montague Gov, 5 Jan 1773, deed from Lt gov Wm Bull 25 April 1774, also memorial in Bk 12 examined pr William Nisbett D S. Wit George Thomas, Stephen Coy[Lay?]. /s/ William Holley. Proven 18 Oct 1777 by George Thomas; William Daniel J P. Rec 6 Feb 1798.

p.53-57   Benjamin Blackey and wife Elizabeth to John Clem. L&R, 13 January 1793(sic)/13 January 1793, [blank], 200 acres on Hardlabour Creek being part of 518 acres granted to sd Benjamin Blackey 6 March 1786, examined by John Vanderhout secy. Wit Jno Channing, James Miller. /s/ Benjamin Blackey, Elizabeth (+) Blackey. Proven 15 February 1793 by John Channing; James Harrison J P. Rec 6 Feby 1798.

p.57-61   Benjamin Blackey and wife Elizabeth to James Yelden. L&R, 13 January 1793/13 January 1793, [blank], 100 acres on Hard Labour Creek granted to sd Benjn Blackey 6 March 1786 being half of 200 acres granted unto sd Benjn Blackey, examined by Jno Vanderhout, the other half part Mary Clem of same county afsd holds and has titles for. Wit Jno Channing, James Miller. /s/ Benjn Blackey, /s/ Elizabeth (x) Blackey. Received 13 January the within consideration in full. Proven 15 February 1793 by John Channing; James Harrison J P. Rec 6 Feb 1798.

p.61-63   Ephraim Brown and Betsy his wife to Melines C Levensworth. Deed, 18 August 1797, $300, 250 acres on Stump Branch of Big Horse Creek. Wit Thos Lamar, Jas Jno Martin, J Hatcher. /s/ Ephraim Brown, Betsy (+) Brown. Proven 8 Feby 1798 by Jeremiah Hatcher; Richard Tutt J P.   Rec 7 Feb 1798.

p.63-67   Drury Pace to David Pace. Release, 24 November 1788, £10 sterling, being grant made 5 June 1786 unto Drury Pace from Lt Gov Wm Moultrie, 200 acres on Savannah river. Wit John Owens, William (+) Jonson, Mary Pace. /s/ Drury Pace. Proven 26 January 1798 by William Johnson & Mary Pace; Henry Key J P. Recorded 15th February 1798.

p.67-70   William Covington & Phebe Covington to James Baker. Deed, 28 August 1797, £10 sterling, 100 acres on road from Campbellton to Ninety Six, formerly granted to Sime[blank]tin by Gov Wm Moultrie 5 Sept 1785 and since conveyed by sd Martin to Allen Hinton & from Hinton to Samuel Wright and from Wright to William Covington; adj land of Daniel Gill, William Morgan, John Pierce, John Hammond decd. Wit Alexr Kevan, James Leslie.   /s/ Wm Covington, /s/ Phebe Covington.   Proven 6 December 1797 by Alexr Kevan; Charles Old J P.   Rec 16 Feb 1798.

p.70-73   John Carter to John Hall. Deed, 2 September 1797, £130 sterling, 857 acres on Poplar branch except 80 acres that was said to belong to estate of James Ray. Wit John G Cooke, Thomas Lamar. /s/ John Carter. Judge Joseph Hightower certifies relinquishment of dower by Elizabeth Carter wife of within named John Carter, 14 February 1798; /s/ Elizabeth (x) Carter. Proven 27 January 1798 by John G Cook; Chas Old J P.   Recorded 16 Feby 1798.

p.73-80   Richard Johnson and of Ninety Six District, gentleman and his wife Mary, to Thomas Glasscock Esqr of Augusta, Georgia. Deed, 11 April 1785/12 April 1785, £500 SC money, two adjoining plantations, being part of the lands lately known by name of the Chickesaw lands described in general plat thereof by #7 & #8, 159 acres and 156 acres; conveyed to Richard Johnson by John Bowie and Thomas Darington commissioners of forfeited estates in SC on 9 and 10 July 1783. Wit Th Carr, Nathl Cocke. /s/ Richard Johnson, /s/ Mary Johnson. Plat certified 9 July 1783 by Bennett Crafton D.S. Plat 5 July 1783 certified by Bennett Crafton D.S. Proven 14 April 1785 by Thomas Carr; John Sturzenegger J P. Rec 22 Feb 1798.

p.80   Polley Bibb to Henry Parkman. Relinquishment of rights & title to Negro girl Hanah to Henry Parkman. Wit Sarene Parkman. /s/ Polly Bibb. Proven 26 February 1798 by Sarane Parkman; Rd Tutt J P.   Rec 26 February 1798.

p.81-87   Edmond Whatley and wife Phillis to Alexander Edmonds. L&R, 14 October 1793/15 October 1793, £100 SC money, 100 acres part of 250 acres originally granted to Wm Moore on Lick fork of Horns Creek, bounding on Penix Howlets land, Aquila Miles line, P Miles land, Rock Spring. Wit Penix (P) Howlet, Ankrig Howlet. /s/ Edmund Whatley, Phillis (+) Whatley. Proven 3 Feb 1794 by Penix Howlet; Aquila Miles J P.   Recorded 24 February 1798.

p.87-88   James Bibb to Henry Parkman. Bill/sale, Negro girl [no name] five years old, £30 SC money. Wit John Spratt, Thomas Spratt. /s/ James Bibb. Proven 9 January 1798 by John Spratt; Jas Harrison, J P.   Rec 26 Feb 1798.

p.88-90   Churchill Gibson to William Walls of Newberry County, SC. Deed, 18 January 1797, £5 sterling, 130 acres South side of Big Creek of Little Saluda river, being part of 370 acres of which 240 were granted to William Riley. Wit Samp Butler, Zacheriah (S) Brooks, James Maddocks. /s/ Churchill Gibson. Proven 20 May 1797 by James Mattocks; Nathl Abney J P.   Rec 6 March 1798.

p.90-92   Churchill Gibson to William Riley of Newberry County, SC. Deed, 5 January 1797, £100, 240 acres on Big Creek of Little Saluda river, bounded by lines of John Gibson, John Cawley, Jacob Reed, Benjamin Guerard, Thomas Clark. Wit John Blalock Senr, James (I) Mattocks, John (x) Riley. /s/ Churchill Gibson. Proven 20 May 1797 by James Mattocks; Nathl Abney J P.   Rec 6 March 1798.

p.92-94   Absalom Williams to John Vardel. Deed, 17 January 1798, £10 sterling, on Hard Labour Creek on Halles line, [acreage not stated]. Wit John Wallace, James Yeldell, John Stewart. /s/ Absalom Williams. Proven 24 Feb 1798 by Capt John Wallace who saw Absalom Williams sign deed, likewise did see Absalom Williams sign receipt, and also did see James Yelding and John Stewart with himself subscribe their names as witnesses; James Harrison J P. Recorded 10 March 1798.

p.94-97   William Nichols to Drury Napper. Deed, 12 March 1796, £100 sterling, 50 acres on Chaveses Creek adj James Harris, John Herndon. Wit Henry Ware Junr, Lillestun Pardue. /s/ W W Nichols. Judge[blank] certifies relinquishment of dower by Elizabeth Nichols wife of within named William Nichols; [date is blank]. Receipt 14 Oct 1788, of Drury Napper one sorrel horse to value of £15 sterling in full for 15 acres granted to John Herndon being part of 50 acres joining sd Nappers land. Test Abraham Napper. /s/ William Nichols. Proven 10 Nov 1797 by Lillestun Pardue; Vann Swearingen J P. /s/ Lillestun Pardue.   Rec 10 March 1792.

p.97-102   John Pusley & Moses Pusley exrs of John Clackler decd to Flood Mitchell. L&R, 22 January 1794/23 Jan 1794, £20 SC money, 100 acres on Stephens Creek bounding on Christain Buckhalter, Abraham Martin; formerly granted by Lord Chas Granville Montague 7 July 1772 to Mary Flick; conveyed from her to Christain Buckhalter. Wit Butler Williams, John Mitchell. /s/ John (x) Pusley, Moses Pusley. Proven 11 March 1794 by John Mitchell; James Harrison J P.   Rec 12 Mar 1798.

p.102-108   Christain Buckhalter to John Clackler. L&R, 21 November 1785/22 November 1785, £21.8.6 SC money, 100 acres Stephens Cr adj sd Buckhalter, Abraham Martin; granted by Gov Montague 7 July 1772 to Mary Flick; sold by her to Christain Buckhalter. Wit Frances (x) Carver, John Martin, George Martin. /s/ Christain (x) Buckhalter. Proven 3 Apr 1794 by Jno Martin; Aquilla Miles JP. Rec 19 March 1798.

p.108-110   John Spragens Gormon Junr to John Bulger. Deed, 30 December 1797, £120 sterling, 300 acres, parts of different tracts of land: part of 200 acres originally granted to Michael Abney 1772 by Gov Chas G Montague; part of 104 acres granted to John Gormon Senr 1785 by Gov Wm Moultrie; also part of 300 acres granted to sd John Gormon Senr 1786 by Gov Wm Moultrie; adj Major Thomas Butler, James Carson, Samuel Abney, Thomas Young Berry Junr, Thomas Berry Senr, George Lewis Patrick, John Gormon Senr, Samuel Abney, and land formerly claimed by Mathew Wills decd. Wit Thomas Berry Senr, Thomas Young Berry, Gabril Berry. /s/ John Gormon. Proven 13 February 1798 by Thos Young Berry; Nathl Abney J P.   Rec 12 March 1798.

p.111-113   Joseph Trotter to Thomas Berry Senr. Deed, 30 December 1797, £100, 85 acres on Mill Creek being part of 150 acres originally granted to Charles Carson Senr in 1778 and conveyed by sd Carson to his son James Carson & from sd Carson to John Webb, and from sd Webb to Joseph Trotter; bounding on land of Moses Walton, George Lewis Patrick, sd Thos Berry Senr, Jerremiah Trotter. Wit John Bulger, James Carson, Wm (x) Turner. /s/ Joseph (x) Trotter. Proven 13 Feb 1798 by John Bulger; Nathl Abney J P.   Rec 12 March 1798.

p.113-114   Johnson Rainey of Laurance County SC to James Hart. Deed, 20 November 1797, $50, 110 acres Little Saluda granted to Wm Humphreys, surveyed for Humphreys 28 Apr 1788 by John Abney Depy Surveyor; bounded by land of Widow Lewis, Widow Bland, Joseph Nunn. Wit Mumford Perryman, John Rany. /s/ Johnson Rainey. Proven 9 March 1798 by Mumford Perryman; Wm Daniel J P.   Rec 12 March 1798.

p.115-117   John Spragins Gormon to Thomas Young Berry Junr. Deed, 13 December 1797, £80, 150 acres part of two tracts; tract of 200 acres granted originally to Michael Abney in 1772 by Gov Chas G Montague; part of 104 acres granted to John Gormon Senr by Gov Wm Moultrie in 1785; sd 150 acres bounded by land conveyed by sd Gormon to John Bulger, Thomas Berry Senr, George Lewis Patrick, land conveyed by John Bulger to John Coleman, and by land conveyed by sd Gormon to John Bulger. Wit Thomas Berry Senr, John Bulger, Gabriel Berry. /s/ John S Gormon. Proven 13 Feb 1798 by John Bulger; Nathl Abney J P.   Recorded 12 March 1798.

p.117-119   Thomas Berry Senr to William Turner Junr. Deed, 30 December 1797, 200 acres on Big Creek orginally granted to John Chaney in a platt of 400 acres; sd 200 acres is bounded by land of one Gray, William White, John Kay, Nathan Trotter. Wit John Bulger, James Carson, Joseph (x) Trotter. /s/ Thomas Berry. Proven 10 March 1798 by James Carson; Nathl Abney J P.   Rec 12 March 1798.

p.119-121   John Gormon Senr to son John Spragens Gormon Junr. Deed, 28 December 1797, £100, 100 acres, part of 200 acres granted to Michael Abney in 1772 by Gov Chas Montague; also part of 104 acre tract granted to sd Jno Gormon Senr 1785 by Gov Wm Moultrie; sd 100 acres bounded by lands of James Carson Senr, Samuel Abney, Thomas Berry Senr, Mathew Wills decd, [illeg] Abney, land conveyed by Jno Gormon Senr to sd John Spragens Gormon Junr. Wit Nancy Gormon, John Bulger. /s/ John (I) Gormon Senr. Proven 13 Feb 1798 by John Bulger; Nathl Abney J P. Recorded 12 March 1798.

p.121-123   William Williams to Asa Hix. Deed, 24 October 1797, $200, 12 acres bounded on all sides by land of Thomas Galphin. Wit Charles Ranzey, William Lewis. /s/ William (W) Williams, Marr (X) Williams. Proven 5 March 1798 by William Lewis; John Clarke J P.   Rec 12 March 1798.

p.123-126   Thomas Golphin to William Williams. Deed, 23 March 1797, £6, 12 acres bounded on all sides by land of sd Thomas Golphin. Wit Isaac Bush Junr, Thomas Newman. /s/ Thos Golphin. Plat of 12 acres being part of a tract of 305 acres belonging to sd Golphin, bounded on SE by land of William Dix, surveyed 16 March 1795 by William Minor D.S. Proven 26 Feby 1798 by Thomas Newman; John Clarke J P.   Rec 12 March 1798.

p.126-128   Edward Kirksy, planter, to James Morris. Deed, 11 September 1796, £14 sterling, 80 acres on Horse Pen Creek of Savannah River adj tract Jeremiah Allen bought of Kirksy. Wit Jeremiah (x) Allen, Joseph (x) Jolley. /s/ Edward (x) Kirksy. Proven 10 March 1798 by Joseph Jolley; John Blocker JP. Rec 12 March 1798.

p.128-131   Thomas Williams to Joseph Morris. Deed, 6 January 1798, £40 sterling, 250 acres on Little Stephens Creek adjoining Benjamin Eddins, William Norris, Augusta Road, Mr Jolley, William Odum(Odom), on sd Joseph Morris, it being part of 1000 acres granted to sd Thomas Williams. Wit James (x) Morris, James Eddins. /s/ Thomas Williams. Judge Joseph Hightower certifies the relinquishment of dower by Rebeckah Williams wife of Thomas Williams, 12 March 1798. Proven 12 March 1798 by James Morris; John Blocker J P. Rec 12 March 1798.

p.131-132   William Nichols to Drury Napper. Receipt, 14 October 1788, recd of Drury Napper one sorrel horse to value of fifteen pounds in full for 15 acres granted to John Herndon being part of 50 acres joining sd Napper's land on south side Chaves Creek. Wit Absalom Napper. /s/ William Nichols. Proved 10 March 1798 by Absalom Napper; Vann Swearingen J P.   Rec 12 March 1798.

p.132-134   James Bruton, saddler, to friend Moses Holstun, planter. To demand or receive from Willis Anderson of Orangeburgh District SC a settlement concerning 90 acres conveyed from Willis Anderson to James Bruton from him to Moses Holstun, to recover as I myself might or could do. Wit William Houlstun, Benjamin Bruton. /s/ James Bruton. Proven 10 March 1798 by William Holstun; William Daniel J P.

p.134-137   Jonathan Esary to Cammel Clegg. Deed, 17 January 1798, $90 sterling money, 24 acres, part of 1000 acres granted to Thomas Pinkett in 1769, transferred from him to William Robertson, from him to Thomas Youngblood and from Thos Youngblood to Jonathan Essery, bounded by Sleepy Creek, John Kirksey. Wit James McCrelass, Joseph (x) Jolley. /s/ Jonathan Esery. Judge Joseph Hightower certifies relinquishment of dower by Mary Esery wife of Jonathan Esery, 12 March 1798. Mary (x) Esery. Proven 12 Mar 1798 by Jos Jolley; John Blocker JP. Rec 12 March 1798.

p.137-139   James & Susannah Bruton to Moses Holstun[Houlstun]. Deed, 16 February 1798, £40, 90 acres part of 113 acres on both sides of Charleston waggon road on Horse creek of South Edisto, bounded by land of Benjamin Loveless, Jacob Odum, Willis Anderson, Jacob Read, & by land formerly Martin Garners; which was granted to Edward Couch 15 January 1792, and conveyed to Willis Anderson 26 Feb 1796, and from him to James Bruton 5 March 1796. Wit Benjamin Bruton, Elizabeth (x) Bruton, William Holstun.   Proven 10 March 1798 by William Holstun; William Daniel JP. Recorded 12 March 1798.

p.139-144   Benjamin Loveless, planter, and wife Constant to Moses Holstun. L&R, 5 May 1793, £30 sterling, 100 acres including the plantation where sd Moses Holstun now liveth, part of 678 acres granted by Gov Thos Pinckney unto Thomas Leher. Wit William Holstun, John Loveless, Joshaway (x) Loveless. /s/ Benjamin (x) Loveless, Constant (x) Loveless.   Proven 16 November 1793 by William Holstun; Russell Wilson J P.   Rec 12 March 1798.

p.144-147   John Moore & wife Martha to William Moore Junr. Deed, 24 January

1798, £70 sterling, 150 acres on a branch of Ninety Six Creek originally granted to Robert Cuningham 17 Feb 1767, from sd Cuningham conveyed to sd John Moore 22 & 23 July 1772, sd land joining lands of Culbert Sanderson and John Cunningham at original survey. Wit Green Moore, James Ramsey, Salley Ramsey. /s/ John Moore, Martha (M) Moore. Judge William Anderson certifies relinquishment of dower by Martha Moore wife of John Moore, 3 February 1798. /s/ Martha (M) Moore. Proven 5 February 1798 by Green Moore; William Robertson J P.   Rec 12 March 1792.

p.147-150   Edward Kirksey or Edward Cearxy to Camel Clegg. Deed, 9 February 1798, $66 sterling money, 50 acres being part of a tract of 250 acres belonging to Edward Cearxy bounded by Sleepy Cr, Long Branch, John Kirkseys and a 24 acre tract that Jonathan Esery did own but sd Camel Clegg do own now. Wit Jeremier (x) Allen, Joseph Esery. Edward (x) Kirksey. Judge Joseph Hightower certifies the relinquishment of dower by Winey Kirksey wife of Edward Kirksey; 12 March 1798. /s/ Winey (x) Kirksey. Proven 12 Mar 1798 by Jeremiah Allen; John Blocker JP. Rec 12 March 1798.

p.150-156   John Kershaw to John Adams. Colonel Joseph Kershaw deceased about 21 Feb 1790 seized of good estate, hereby to be sold; William Ancrum, Edward Darrell, James Fisher, Robert Henry, James Kershaw five of the creditors and trustees of sd Joseph Kershaw set forth that Joseph Kershaw was justly indebted to them and to sundry others which he was unable then to pay, agree he should sign over to them all his property in trust. These creditors hold letter of attorney bearing date 20 February 1794 which is now in full force authorizing John Kershaw for them to contract for disposition of whole or any part of lands of sd Joseph Kershaw decd. Now sells unto John Adams 200 acres in Colleton County on Cuffeetown Creek bounding at time of original grant made to Edmond Petrie by lands of James Harris, Field Pardue, James Gray, Samuel Anderson, Daniel Sullivan. Also 200 acres in Granville County on Stephens Creek bounding at time of original grant on lands of Peter Leger, Joel Crafford. Wit Absam Childes, Jos Cain. /s/ John Kershaw. Proven Kershaw County 16 December 1797 by Absm Childers; Francis Boykin JP. Recorded 12 March 1798.

p.156-159   Daniel Ramsay of Abevil County to Patrick Sullivan. Deed, 4 November 1797, £50 sterling, 116 acres part of 300 acres originally granted to George Wever in Edgefield on Rockey Creek of Turkey Creek, Stephens Creek, adjoining land of John Sprat. Wit Alexander Hall, William Anderson. Proven 10 March 1798 by Alexander Hall; James Harris J P.   Rec 12 March 1798.

p.159-161   Richard Pond to William Pond. Deed, 20 February 1798, $60, 150 acres on Chalk Hill on head of Foxes Creek. Wit Francis (x) Gentry, James McQueen. /s/ Richard Pond. Plat certified 5 July 1794 by Charles Banks D S shows 274 acres granted to Richard Bond on Chalk Hill fork of Foxes Creek adjoining land of Joseph Hightower, Joshua Hammond, William Buller. Proven 20 February 1798 by James McQueen; Joseph Hightower. Rec 12 March 1798.

p.162-164   Joseph Hightower to William Bond. Deed, 23 September 1797, $50, 509 acres near Foxes Creek, part of lands granted unto Joseph Hightower on 6 Sept 1790. Wit John Tarraner, Richard Pond. /s/ Joseph Hightower. Proven 21 February 1798 by John Tarrener; Chas Old JP.   Rec 12 March 1798.

p.164-165   West Cook to Nancy Doby. Deed, 18 February 1798, $400, Negro girl Dilce about 15 years old. Wit Richardson (x) Bartlett. /s/ West Cook. Proven 12 March 1798 by Richardson Bartlett; Rd Tutt JP.   Rec 12 March 1798.

p.165-167   Jiles Letcher to John Hardy of Lincoln County, Georgia. Deed, 13 March 1798, $130, 159 acres in Edgefield County on Turkey Creek part of 350 acres granted to James Letcher. Wit Wm Burk, John Boyd. /s/ Jiles Letcher. Plat shows 159 acres adj land of Canfield, Letcher, Charles Aire. Proven 13 March 1798 by John Boyd; Rd Tutt J P.   Rec 13 March 1798.

p.168   Nancy Bussey or Vancey Bussey to Elizabeth and Charles Bussey. Receipt. Received of Elizabeth and Charles Bussey admx and admr of estate of Edward Bussey decd one Negro boy named Jack and $8 cash, ackd to be in full my right of dower of above estate. Wit James Howerton. /s/ Vancy Bussey. Proven 7 March 1798 by James Howerton who saw Nancey Bussey sign her name to within receipt; Chas Old J P.   Rec 15th March 1798.

p.168-170   Elisha Knight to Elisha Knight. Deed to Mary Wilson, 15 December 1797, £10 SC money, 203 acres part of 453 acres granted to James Allen by Gov Chas Pinckney at Charleston 2 Feb 1789 and joining land of Mary Young, Wilams Butler, Jacob Smith, Thomas Wilams. Wit Jacob Smith, William Prescot, James Brooks. /s/ Elisha (x) Night. Received ten pounds full consideration for tract of land I say red by me, Elisha (x) Night; wit Jacob Smith, Samuel Brooks, William Prescot. Proven 2 February 1798 by William Prescot; Elkanah Sawyer J P. /s/ William Prescoat. Recorded 12 March 1798.

p.170-173   John Whittle and wife Winney to Thomas Warren. Deed, 4 March 1794, £100 SC money, 100 acres being part of 202 acres on Cruceid Creek joining William Holson originally granted to John Whittle by Gov Chas Pinckney at Columbia 7 June 1790. Wit Thomas Walker, John Gregory, Elizabeth (x) Gregory. /s/ John (x) Whittle. /s/ Winney (x) Whittle. Proven 22 August 1795 by John Gregory; Elkanah Sawyer, J P. Recorded 12 March 1798.

p.174-175   John Blocker Junr, planter, to Matton Mays, planter. Deed, 10 February 1798, $100, 132 acres on Waggoners Branch of Cuffeetown Creek bounded by Peter Jones, Glover, William Coursey, & Arnet, originally granted to sd John Blocker 2[?] March 1797. Wit Jesse Blocker, Thomas (x) Hatcher. /s/ John Blocker Junr. Proven 10 February 1798 by Thomas Hatcher; John Blocker. Rec 2 March 1798.

p.175-178   John Hancock to Freeman Hardy. Deed, 26 January 1798, £108 sterling, 180 acres part of land granted unto Benjamin Warring 8 July 1774 bounded John Hancocks land, James Quarles land, plat drawn by Robert Lang DS 30 March 1797. Wit Peter Hancock, James Hardy. /s/ John Hancock. Judge Joseph Hightower certifies relinquishment of dower by Ann Hancock wife of John Hancock; 9 March 1798. Proven 26 January 1798 by James Hardy; Joseph Hightower.   Rec 12 March 1798.

p.178-180   Seth Howard to Enos Howard. Deed, 10 March 1798, $200, 43 acres part of two tracts granted unto John Mitchell & Morris Calleham and bounded on Chaves Creek. Wit Richard Bush, John (x) Pursley. /s/ Seth Howard. Proven 12 March 1798 by Richard Bush; John Blocker JP. Rec 12th March 1798.

p.180-183   Elijah Watson, planter, to Job Padget. Deed, 11 August 1796, £2 SC money, 10 acres on Clouds Cr of Little Saluda River, being part of land formerly granted unto Elias Daniel of 300 acres by Gov Wm Bull, conveyed to Michael Watson deceased; now Elijah Watson heir to Michael Watson decd conveyes to Job Padget 10 acres. Wit William Wright, Thomas Deloach./s/ Elijah Watson. Plat by Wm Wright DS. Proven 13 May 1797 by Thos Deloach; Elkanah Sawyer J P.   Rec 13 March 1798.

p.183-187   John Bostick of Abbeville, planter, to William Anderson. Deed, 29 January 1798, £37.10, 60 acres part of land originally granted to Patrick Welsh, bounded by Little Berry Bostick, William Anderson, Wilsons Creek. Wit Stephen Bostick, L Bostick, Thomas Anderson. /s/ John Bostick. Plat 29 January 1798 measured unto John Bostick 60 acres agreeable to his Father John Bostick; W Anderson DS. Jane Bostick widow of John Bostick decd certifies her approval of sd sale; certifies £10 paid to her by Wm Anderson and relinquished right of dower & inheritance; 9 March 1798. Wit Davis Bostick, Thomas Anderson. /s/ Jean Bostick.   Judge James Mayson certifies relinquishment of dower by Martha Bostick wife of John Bostick; 9 March 1798. /s/ Martha (x) Bostick.   Proven 10 March 1798 by Thomas Anderson; Julius Nichols J P.   Recorded 13 March 1798.

p.187-189   Hezekiah Watson to Richard Halman. Deed, 21 December 1797, $225, 150 acres on Dry Creek of Mine Creek of Little Saluda River, part of land granted to James Cock 1774 adj land of Arthur Watson. Witness Arthur Rice Watson, Benjamin Arrinton. /s/ Hezekiah Watson.   Proven 26 January 1798 by Benjamin Arrington; William Daniel J P.   Recorded 13 March 1798.

p.189-191   James Perry to John Eidson. Deed, 30 October 1797, $70, 37 acres being part of 150 acres granted to William Dooly on Peters Creek in 1770. Wit Arthur Rice Watson, Arthur (A) Watson. /s/ James Perry. Proven 16 March 1799 by Arthur Watson; Rd Tutt JP.   Rec 13 March 1798.

p.191-193   George Harris and wife Martha to William Suddeth of Spartanburgh County, SC. Deed, 13 March 1794, £80 sterling, [acreage not stated] lying in fork of Red Bank and Pen Creeks, adjoining lands of John Douglass; being part of 400 acres originally granted to Thomas Deloach by Gov Wm Bull 31 Aug 1797. Wit Richard Lewis, John Lewis, Jos N (x) Lewis. /s/ George (x) Harris, /s/ Martha (x) Harris. Proven 29 Dec 1797 by John Lewis; Russel Wilson J P.   Rec 18 March 1798.

p.194-196   Daniel McKie of Newberry County to Jeff Sharpton. Deed, 5 March 1798, £125, two tracts on Stephens Creek 351 acres taken in execution as the property of John Garrett and by sheriff conveyed to John Hallett highest bidder, and by Hallett to Daniel McKie. Wit William Sattewhite, Rebekah Satterwhite. /s/ Daniel McKie. Judge Jacob Roberts Brown certifies relinquishment of dower by Frances McKie wife of Daniel McKie; 15 March 1798. /s/ Frances McKie.   Proven 5 March 1798 by William Sattewhite; Ja Brown judge.   Rec 18 March 1798.

p.196-199   Hezekiah Gentry to Hezekiah Burnett. Deed, 3 March 1798, $1000 SC money, 100 acres being part of survey of 1200 acres originally granted by Gov Wm Bull unto Peter Whitten 21 April 1775 and sold by Peter Whitten to James Minge Burton, and part thereof by sd James Minge Burton conveyed to me 11 October 1793; first mentioned hundred acres being part of that part which sd Jas Minge Burton conveyed to me on both sides of Indian Creek of Little Saluda River bounded by land of Robert Brooks. Wit Anthony (x) Leech, James (x) Corly. /s/ Hezekiah Gentry. Proven 9 March 1798 by James Corley; Russell Wilson JP. Rec 18 March 1798.

p.199-201   Hezekiah Burnett & his mother Anne Burnett to Anthony Leech. Deed, 5 March 1798, $1000 SC money, 120 acres on Indian Creek of Little Saluda bordering Elijah Pope original grant to Colonel Philemon Waters by Gov Thos Pinckney 5 March 1787, from sd Philemon Waters to Pleasant Burnett decd the father of Hezekiah Burnett. Wit James (x) Corley, Robert (x) Gentry. /s/ Hezekiah Burnet, /s/ Anne (+) Burnet. Proven 9 March 1798 by James Corley; Russell Wilson JP. Rec 13 March 1798.

p.201-204   William Pitman and wife Elizabeth to William Gutrey. Deed, 19 October 1797, 45 sterling money of State, 100 acres, part of a tract exclusive of prior granted lands now in possession of Peter Jones, sd land was granted to Allen Glover 2 November 1795 on Cuffeetown Creek and Mountain Creek, grant for 340 acres, conveyed by Allen Glover and Lidda his wife by deed to sd William Pitman 26 June 1796 bounded by Peter Jones, road Cambridge to Augusta. Wit Shadk Stokes, Peter Jones. /s/ William Pitman, Elizabeth (x) Pitman. Relinquishment of dower by Elizaeth Pitman wife of Wm Pitman; Joseph Hightower, 13 March 1798. Proven 13 March 1798 by Shadrack Stokes; Jas Harrison JP.   Recorded 18 March 1798.

p.204-207   Adam Brooner to John Coursey. Deed, 1 October 1795, £12 sterling, 100 acres on branches of Mountain Creek of Stephens Creek, bounding on Thomas Gray, Davis Williams, Jonathan Cleggs, conveyed unto sd Brooner 20 & 21 Feb 1795 by John Blocker Esqr, being part of 500 acres bequeathed unto John Blocker by will of John Jacob Messer Smith decd, which was part of a tract of 1000 acres granted John Jacob Messer Smith by Gov Wm Moultrie 6 May 1793; shown on plat by William Coursey D S. Wit W Coursey, Samuel Hopkins. /s/ Adam (x) Brooner. Proven 24 November 1795 by William Coursey; John Blocker J P.   Recorded 13 March 1798.

p.207-208   James Lyon to son Robert Lyon. Deed/Gift, 13 March 1798, love & goodwill, Negro boy Harry. Wit Samuel Stalnaker, James Coursey. /s/ James Lyon. Proven 14 March 1798 by James Coursey; Jas Harrison JP. Rec 14 March 1798.

p.208-209   Philip Lightfoot & Joseph Tucker to James May. Bill/Sale, 12 February 1798, $200, Negro boy Tom about seven years old. Wit Jesse Stone, C Cargill. /s/ Philip Lightfoot, /s/ Joseph Tucker. Proven 13 March 1798 by Clement Cargill; Richard Tutt J P.   Rec 13 March 1798.

p.210-211   Edward Vann to Russell Wilson. Deed, 13 March 1798, $25 SC money, 75 acres in Orangeburg District on Shaws Creek of South Edisto River, surveyed for John Pannihill 20 October 1784 and granted 5 June by Gov Wm Moultrie 1766, conveyed by Andrew Pennihill heir of John Pennihill to sd Edward Van. Wit C Cargill, John Roberts, James (I) Barrintine. /s/ Edward Van Senr. Proven 13 March 1798 by Clement Cargill; John Blocker J P.   Rec 13 March 1789.

p.211-213   Charles Goodwin to Gilliam Rainey. Deed, 10 October 1797, £60 sterling, 178 acres formerly granted unto Wm Rhodes 5 June 1780 bounded by branch of Cedar Creek of Horns Creek. Wit Wm Robertson, John Glover. /s/ Chas Goodwin. Proven 13 March 1798 by Wm Robertson; Rd Tutt JP.   Rec 13 March 1798.

p.213-216   Peter Jones & wife Mary to William Gutrey. Deed, 19 October 1797, £45, 400 acres granted to Moses Jones 28 October 1795 and sold by Moses Jones and wife Elizabeth to sd Peter Jones 16 Sept 1797, lying on Mountain Creek & Horsepen Creek excepting two acres where a meeting house is begun near branch of Mountain Creek; also 38 acres part of 500 acres granted to Menoah Witherington on 17 August 1796, by sd Menoah & wife Susanna sold to Peter Jones 19 October 1797, bounding on land granted to Allen Glover, road from Cambridge to Augusta, branches of Mountain Creek and Cuffeetown Creek. Wit Shadk Stokes, Goldsberry (+) Garner. /s/ Peter Jones, /s/ Mary (x) Jones. Proven 13 March 1798 by Shadrack Stokes; Jas Harrison JP. Recorded 13th March 1798.

p.216-219   Thomas Caison to Triplet Caison. Deed, 12 January 1798, $100, 100 acres part of 400 acres granted to David Calliham on Stephens Creek adj land of John Burris, Henry Cox, sd Thos Caison, as in plat by John Boyd D S. Wit John Boyd, Jemima (x) Caison, Thomas Caison Junr. /s/ Thomas Caison. Plat certified 2 August 1796 by John Boyd D S. Proven 28 Feb 1798 by John Boyd; Henry Key J P. Recorded 13 March 1798.

p.219-220   Garrett Freeman to Richard Freeman. Bond, 3 December 1797. Garret Freeman bound unto Richd Freeman in sum £200 sterling paid unto Richd Freeman, condition Garrett Freeman to make title to land where sd Richd Freeman now lives of 150 acres on Savannah River joining Tolberts land, and land held by Dilih---. Wit James Freeman, Jesse Copeland. /s/ Garret Freeman. Proven 12 March 1798 by Jesse Copeland; Henry Key J P. Rec 18 March 1798.

p.221-223   Burgess White & wife Martha to Robert White. Deed, 13 June 1796, £20 sterling 100 acres on branches of Beaverdam of Turkey Cr, bounding on land of Lewis Youngblood, part of 204 acres granted unto John Garrett by Gov Thos Pinckney at Charleston 1 Oct 1787 and by sd John Garrett conveyed unto Burgess White 10 June 1788. Wit Wm Coursey, Frederick White. /s/ Burgess White, /s/ Martha (x) White. Proven 13 March 1798 by William Coursey; Vann Swearingen J P. Rec 13[?] Mar 1798.

p.224   James Lyon to son-in-law Benj Tutt and daughter Rachel Tutt. Deed of Gift, 13 March 1798, love & goodwill, Negro girl Jude. Wit Saml Stalnaker, James Coursey. /s/ James Lyon. Proven 14 March 1798 by James Coursey; James Harrison JP.

p.225   Ellender Warren to son John Charles Warren. Deed/Gift, 18 March 1798, natural love, all stock, household furniture. Wit M Mims, Drury Mims Junr. /s/ Ellender (+) Warren. Proven 14 March 1798 by Mathew Mims; Rd Tutt JP. Recorded 14 March 1798.

p.226-227   Nancy Bland to Elisha Bland. Deed, 14 November 1797, $50, 100 acres part of 250 acres conveyed to sd Nancy Bland by Wm Brown situate on new road from Purkins ferry on Big Saluda to Edgefield Court House and on south side big road from Charleston to Cambridge binding on William Daniels land, John Wells's and M Brown. Wit D Henderson, Wormly Bland. /s/ Nancy (x) Bland. Proven 15 January 1798 by Wormly Bland; William Daniel J P. Recorded 14 March 1798.

p.227-229   Joshua Deen to William Moore. Deed, 14 March 1798, £30 sterling, 280 acres on Big Creek of Saluda River bounded by heirs of Isaac Crowther, originally granted to Rawling Coatney 21 January 1785. Wit Eugene Brenan, G Leslie. /s/ Joshua (--) Deen. Proven 14 March 1798 by Eugene Brenan; Richard Tutt. Recorded 14 March 1798.

p.229-232   John Adam Summers of Orangeburgh District, farmer, and Mary his wife to John Still. Deed, 23 February 1798, £10 sterling paid by John Still, £10 paid by Jean Still executrix of sd John Still deceased at delivery of these presents, both in County of Edgefield, 140 acres surveyed for Summers 9 June 1786 on Rocky Creek of Little Stephens Creek, originally granted to sd John Adam Summers by Gov Wm Moultrie at Charleston 6 Nov 1786. Wit J S Houseal, John Pope, George Summer. /s/ John Adam Summers, /s/ Mary (x) Summers. Proven 14 March 1798 by John Pope; John Blocker J P. Recorded 14 March 1798.

p.232-233   Thomas Gray to William Todd. Power attorney. Logan County, 10 November 1796, Thomas Gray of Logan County, Kentucky, appoints friend William Todd of Edgefield SC to transact my business in Edgefield, make sail of my lands in my name. Wit Joseph Dawson, John (IC) Corsey, Samuel Hopkins. /s/ Thomas Gray. Proven 10 March 1798 by John (IC) Coursey; Jas Harrison J P. Rec 14 March 1798.

p.233   William Swift to Edmund Martin. Received, 4 May 1787, of Edmund Martin Esqr one bay mare value £7 in full consideration for title which I possess of 103 acres surveyed for Mordecai Mattock and granted to me 5th Feby 1787 on road from Cambridge to Augusta. /s/ William Swift. Personally appeared John Dunlap before Richard Tutt JP swears within writing is handwriting of William Swift; 15 March 1798. Recorded 15th March 1798.

p.233-235   Richard Lewis to John Duglass. Deed, 21 May 1796, £15 SC money, 30 acres Pen Creack on North side of rode from Cambridge to Charleston bounding on William Suddeth. Wit John Lewis, Gilson Yarbrough. /s/ Richard Lewis. Proven 8 March 1798 by John Lewis; Russell Wilson JP. Rec 15 March 1798.

p.235-236   Precious Bussey & Elizabeth Bussey & Charles Bussey. Received 7 March 1798 of Elizabeth Bussey admx and Charles Bussey admr of estate of my father Edward Bussey deceased one Negro girl named Cate at £35, also a bed & furniture at £6.6, also $23 in cash in full consideration my part of estate of my Father Edward Bussey. Wit John Boyd. /s/ Precious (x) Bussey. Proven 15 March 1798 by John Boyd; Richard Tutt J P. Rec 15 March 1798.

p.236-237   John Salter Senr to John Salter Junr. Deed, 3 November 1796, $45, 88 acres it being part of a tract containing 188 acres on Richland branch of Little Saluda river granted 7 December 1793 unto sd John Salter Senr by Gov Chas Pinckney. Wit Henry King, James (x) Eidson. /s/ John Salter. Proven 25 April 1797 by James (+) Eidson; Russell Wilson JP. Rec 15 March 1798.

p.238   Winifred Richardson to Joseph Hightower. Renunciation of Dower. Judge Arthur Simpkins certifies dower relinquishment by Winifred Richardson wife of Abraham Richardson, 8 & 9 January 1794, given this 15th March 1798. Winifred (x) Richardson. Recorded 16 March 1798.

p.238-241   William Tennent Sheriff to John Boyd. Title, 6 November 1797;

suit of Treasurer against estate of William Tolbert decd, Sheriff Wm Tennent executed on land, sold to highest bidder for ready money at Cambridge, struck off to sd John Boyd for £1.1.6; tract on Swift Creek of Savannah River 1000 acres being part of 2792 acres granted to sd William Tolbert. Wit Thos Anderson, Alexr Stewart. /s/ Wm Tennent Sheriff 96 District. Proven 6 Nov 1797 by Thomas Anderson; Jno Trotter J P. Rec 16 March 1798.

p.241-244   Plowdon Weston and wife Marian to Jesse Johnson. Deed, 1 November 1797, £200 sterling, three tracts of land, about 580 acres, one tract of 250 acres near West Creek of Saluda then bounding on John Hall, William Norris, Goodridge Hughes, John Caldwell, originally granted to Charles Harrison 5 May 1773; also 150 acres on small branch of West Creek originally granted to Goodridge Hughes 5 March 1770; also 250 acres granted 13 October 1759 but now reduced to 180 acres on branch of Little Saluda River bounding on Conrad Hansler. Wit Stephen Ravenel, William Norris. /s/ Plowdon Weston. Proven 11 April 1798 by William Norris; John Bond J P. Justice Stephen Ravenel certifies relinquishment of dower by Marian Weston wife of Plowdon Weston; 1 November 1797; /s/ Marian Weston.   Recorded 16 March 1798.

p.244-246   Absalom Napper to Solomon Fudge. Deed, 10 October 1797, £50 currant money, 300 acres on Good Spring Créek a branch of Horse Creek of Savannah River adjoining lands of Col Purves, Majr John Hampton, John Herndon. Wit Henry Burckhalter, Jacob Wise. /a/ Absalom Napper. Judge Joseph Hightower certifies re-linquishment of dower by Rebeckah Napper wife of Absalom Napper; 23 March 1798. /s/ Rebeccah (R) Napper. Proven 24 February 1798 by Henry Buckhalter; Chas Old JP. Recorded 29 March 1798.

p.246-250   Daniel Bird, planter, to Arnoldus Vanderhorst & Thomas Waring Senr sole executors of will of John Vanderhorst late of Charleston. Release by way of Mortgage, 16 February 1798. Daniel Bird bound unto Vanderhorst & Waring in penal sum £284.3.6 sterling with interest; consideration: payment of £142.3.6 sterling security 242 acres late property of Moses Kirkland on Turkey and Little Stephens Creeks adjoining Lines of Heters, Freeman, & vacant, sum to be paid unto sd Vanderhorst & Waring on or before the day appointed for payment which shall cause this indenture to become of none effect. Wit S Butler, S R Norris. /s/ Daniel Bird. Proven 29 March 1798 by Sampson Butler; John Blocker J P. Recorded 29 March 1798.

p.251-256   Edward Vann and wife Mary to Robert Mosely. L&R, 10 July 1793/11 July 1793, £95 sterling, 100 acres on a path from Cedar Creek to Turky Creek originally granted unto David Duncan 1 September 1768, by sd Duncan to Richard Latham 26 & 27 Feb 1769, by Latham to Edward Vann 12 September 1778. Wit John Waldrom, Joseph Vann, Wm Robertson. /s/ Edward Vann, /s/ Mary (M) Vann. Proven 4 April 1794 by Joseph Vann; Aquilly Miles J P.   Rec 31 March 1798.

p.256-258   James Eidson[Hidson] to James Gilland. Bond, 24 February 1796. James Hidson bound in sum of 30 bushels of good sound dry corn to be paid on or before 26 November next ensuing and to give sd James Gilland 4 acres of standing fodder to get himself when ready this year and so on from year to year every year the same thirty bushels of corn and 4 acres of standing fodder during the life of sd James Gilland; if sd James Gilland should dye any time after the corn is laid by the rent to be paid that year to his successors and them to lease. Wit Isaac Coe,

Snowden (x) Kirkland. /s/ James (x) Hidson. Memorandom on 19 July 1796 appeared Snowden Kirkland and made oath he saw James Eidson sign within bond, and deponant further sayeth that sd James Eidson was only to have the south side of Dry Creek and no part of the North side at any rate though through oversight writer forgot to make mention of it in the obligation; Russell Wilson J P. At same time appeared Wm Burgess who was the writer of within obligation; duly sworn saith that at time the two parties contracted there was no other part of land mentioned but the south side; Russell Wilson J P. Recorded 6th April 1798.

p.258-260   John Tarrance, Mary Tarrance, Jean Tarrance, Henry Wise to Joseph Hightower. Deed, 14 November 1797, £100 sterling, 640 acres granted unto William Tarrance decd 6 Feb 1786 adj John Glover. Wit William Hall, William (W) Dinkins. /s/ John Tarrance, /s/ Mary Tarrance, /s/ Jean Tarrance, /s/ Henry Wise. Proven 24 March 1798 by William Hall; Chas Old J P. Rec 7 April 1798.

p.260-263   James Frazier to William Crane. Deed, 19 March 1798, £40 sterling, 128 acres on Beaver Dam Creek of Stephens Creek adj land formerly held by Daniel Rogers now by John Simkins, land formerly held by John Logan now by Pressley Bland, originally granted to John Frazier 6 March 1786. Wit John Kenady, Hezekiah Williams. /s/ James Frazier. Judge Arthur Simkins certifies relinquishment of dower by Sarah Frazier wife of James Frazier; /s/ Sarah Frazier. Proven 4 April 1798 by Pressly Bland; Van Swearingen J P. Recorded 7 April 1798.

p.263-264   William Rountree of Burk County, Georgia, to Frederick Holmes. Power atty, 10 March 1798, to recover or sue Jonas Holmes & Edward Holmes exrs of William Holmes for money due from estate. Wit William Nichols. /s/ William (x) Rountree. Proven 7 April 1798 by William Nichols; Rd Tutt J P. Rec 7 April 1798.

p.264-266   Samuel Beaks to John Riley. Deed, 2 February 1798, £65, 100 acres on Persimon Creek of Big Creek of Little Saluda River, where afsd Beak now lives, being part of the tract originally granted unto Ann Dean adj land of Richard Tear, Cols Mais Dennet Abney William Abney and James Rutherford. Wit William (x) Riley, James Rutherford. /s/ Saml Beaks, /s/ Sarah (x) Beaks. Proven 15 Feb 1798 by Wm Riley; Nathl Abney J P. Recorded 11th April 1798.

p.266-272   Frances Sinquefield of Granvill County to William Curtling of Colleton County. L&R, 27 June 1772/28 June 1772, £50 SC money, 100 acres in Colleton County bounding on Moses Powels land, land supposed to be estate of Mr Crawford of Charlestown deceased, other sides vacant at time of original survey 10 September 1767, granted to John Kinny 24 August 1770 by Lt Gov Wm Bull. Wit Thomas Lamar, Aaron (x) Sinkfield/Sinquefield, Basel Lamar. /s/ Frances Sinquefield. Proven 14 Feb 1775 by Basel Lamar; LeRoy Hammond J P. Rec 14 April 1798.

p.272-274   William Kirkland to Michael Watson. Bond, 5 March 1776, Wm Kirkland obliged unto Michael Watson £600 SC money, condition Wm Kirkland to make title to 100 acres, part held by Jno Dooly, part by Wa Crawford of Charlestown, sd land was laid out on warrant of John Kinney unto Michael Watson 1 Sept next ensuing. Wit Mark (x) Lott, James (x) Lott. /s/ Wm Kirkland. Proven 25 Jan 1790 by Mark Lott Senr; Russel Willson J P. Rec 14 April 1798.

p.274-276   Plowdon Weston to William Norris.   Deed, 1 November 1797, £100,
1000 acres originally granted to Plowdon Weston 8 July 1774 on branch of Clouds
Creek of Little Saluda bounding on land claimed by Goodridge Huse, John Sawers,
John Caldwell, John Hall. Wit Stephen Ravenel, Jesse Johnston. /s/ Plowden Weston.
Justice Stephen Ravenel certifies relinquishment of dower by Marian Weston wife of
Plowdon Weston, 1 November 1797. /s/ Marian Weston. Proven, Orangeburgh District,
11 April 1798 by Jesse Johnston; Jno Bond J P.   Rec 16th April 1798.

p.276-279   Joseph Griffin to Eugene Brenan.   Deed, 9 January 1798, £5 sterling, 205 acres Beaverdam Cr adj James Frazier, William Frazier, part of 400 acres
originally granted to Samuel Marsh by Gov Wm Moultrie in 1786. Wit William Simkins,
Saml Walker. /s/ Joseph Griffin.   Judge Joseph Hightower certifies relinquishment
of dower by Jemimah Griffin wife of sd Joseph Griffin, 6 Jan 1798. /s/ Jemima (x)
Griffin. Proven 18 April 1798 by William Simkins; Rd Tutt.   Rec 18 Apr 1798.

p.279-282   Hugh Douglass of Abbeville County to John & William Walker. Deed
of trust, 14 October 1797, $145 paid by John Walker the younger and Wm Walker both
of Edgefield trustees to Elizabeth Stedham now a minor have granted unto John & Wm
100 acres granted to Hugh Douglass in 1774, bounded on Turky Creek, Keablers land,
Kirklands land, to the proper use and behoof of sd Elizabeth Stedham. Wit William
Walker, J McCraeton. /s/ Hugh Douglass. Justice Charles Jones certifies relinquishment of dower by Jean Douglass wife of Hugh Douglass. /s/ Jean (x) Douglass.
Proven 5 March 1798 by William Walker; James Harrison J P.   Rec 19 April 1798.

p.283-284   Nicholas Vaun of Laurens County to Ann Lee widow. Deed, 20 January
1798, agreed between them that sd Ann Lee shall retain for her sole and seperate
use not withstanding marriage and subject to her own disposal all real & personal
estate now possessed; said Nicholas Vaun at all and any time during sd marriage
permit sd Ann Lee his intended wife to make deed or will for conveying afsd estate
as she shall think fit. Wit Cullen Lark, Snn Lee. /s/ Nicholas (x) Vaun. /s/ Ann
(x) Lee. Proven 20 April 1798 by Cullen Lark; Nathl Abney J P.   Rec 20 Apr 1798.

p.284-286   Nancy Lee to Cullen Lark. Bill/Sale, 8 December 1797, $300,
mulatto girl aged about 17 or 18. Wit G Lewis Patrick, Suth Lee. /s/ Nancy (x)
Lee. Proven 3 Jan 1798 by George Lewis Patrick; Nathl Abney J P. Rec 20 Apr 1798.

p.286-288   Richard McCary to John Lewis Gervais. Mortgage, 9 January 1798,
bond conditioned for payment of 25,000 of inspected tobacco delivered at Campbellton warehouse for John Lewis Gervais of City of Charleston, now secures bond by
releasing unto John Lewis Gervais 550 acres on Bird Creek, signed 9 February 1798.
Wit Sinclair David Gervais, Paul T Gervais. /s/ Richard McCary. Proven Abbeville
County by Sinclair D Gervais; John Bowie J P.   Recorded 23d April 1798.

p.289   Chas J Colcock to Edmund Martin. Receipt. 23 November 1793 Recd
of Edmd Martin an order on Messrs Leslie and Campbell for £14.15.8 which when paid
will be much in part of a Negro wench Flora; also £15.9.1 in part of sd wench
leaving balance due £14.15.3. /s/ Ch J Colcock. Proven 21 April 1798 by William
Nibbs who proves handwriting of within instrument; J Nichols J P. Rec 24 Apl 1798.

p.289-296   James Harris to Samuel Marsh. L&R, 21 May 1787/22 May 1787, £20 sterling, 50 acres being part of 206 acres on Beaverdam Cr of Turky Cr granted unto sd Jas Harris by Gov Wm Moultrie in 1787, adj John Fraziers line, Mudy branch, on Samuel Marsh's line to John Fraziers old line. Wit Saml Marsh Junr, Shiles Marsh, William Marsh. /s/ James (H) Harris. Proven 5 May 1798 by Samuel Marsh Junr; Rd Tutt, J P. Recorded 5 May 1798.

p.296-298   John Wallace to Philip Holt, planter. Deed, 1 June 1797, £50 sterling, 100 acres granted to sd Wallace by patent 1 February 1797 on Savannah River bounding on lands of Ruben Munday. Wit Jos Wallace, William Shellnutt. /s/ John Wallace. Proven 8 July 1797 by Joseph Wallace; Jas Harrison J P. Rec 10 May 1798.

p.298-299   Richard Lewis & wife Mary to Lodowick Hill. Deed, 16 October 1797, £30 sterling, 85 acres north side Pen Creek of Saluda river bounded by sd Lodowick Hills land, Charleston Road, John Douglass, part of 190 acres orginally granted to Wright Nicholson 6 March 1786. Wit Adkins Corley, Solomon Nobles, Jesse Forest. /s/ Richard Lewis, /s/ Mary Lewis. Proven 10 May 1798 before William Robertson J P.

pp.300-301 certificate of missing pages. [See p.98. Filmed out of order]

p.302-303   ...Saluda river, land belonging to estate of Clabourn Gormon, across Mill Creek, William Spragins land. The other tract being part of the tract whereon the above mentioned Mathew Wills lived at the time of his decease, bounding on land of Thomas Berry, Samuel Abney, Nathaniel Abney, estate of Clabourn Gormon decd, William Carters line, William Spragins land, conveyed unto John Coleman. Wit Chesley Davis, Susanna Davis. /s/ John Bolger. Proven 14 April 1798 by Chesley Davis; Nathl Abney J P. Rec 19 May 1798.

p.304-305   Dannett Abney to George Abney. Deed, 20 December 1797, $150, 150 acres on Persimon Lick Creek originally granted to sd Dannett Abney, whereon sd George Abney now lives, adj Joseph Griffins land, Simon Brooks, line dividing sd George Abney and his brother Samuel Abney. Wit Joel Abney, Esau Brooks. /s/ Dannett Abney. Proven 5 Jan 1798 by Joel Abney; Nathl Abney JP. Rec 29 May 1798.

p.305-306   Robert Russel to Thomas Walton. Power atty, 17 June 1797, appts Thos Walton of Georgia to collect the within account with Eneas Cooper. Wit Henry Key JP. /s/ Robert (X) Russel.   Eneas Cooper to Robert Russel: D. To boarding your wife and three children from fall untill February following pr contract 5.0.0. To boarding yourself and son and two horses fifteen days pr contract   1.0.0. To note of hand on Owen Shannon put into the hands of your wife in 1785 which she has since collected for   1.7.0.
                                                                                                £ 7.7.0.
Proven 17 June 1797 by Robert Russell; Henry Key J P.   Rec 29 May 1798.

p.306-308   James Cocks to Hezekiah Watson. Deed, 20 December 1797, $450, 300 acres on Dry Creek of Mine Creek of Little Saluda River granted to James Cocks in 1774, binding on lands of John Eidson, Arthur Watson. Wit Arthur Rice Watson, Henry Holeman, Matthew McLemore. /s/ James (x) Cocks, /s/ Jenny (+) Cocks. Proven 6 March 1798 by Arthur Rice Watson; William Daniel JP. Rec 1 June 1798.

p.309-311   Arthur Watson to Lydia Watson. Deed, 23 July 1796, $10, 125 acres
on Fall Creek being part of original grant to Robert Pringgle Esqr about 26 July
1774 joining lands of Hezekiah Watson, Rice Watson, Absalom Watson, Thomas Fortner,
James Daniel. Wit Arthur Rice Watson, Britain Partain. /s/ Arthur (A) Watson.
Proven 16 August 1796 by Britain Partin; Russel Wilson JP. Rec 1 June 1798.

p.311-312   Christain Curry to James & Bevaly[Vevaly] Easter. Deed of Gift, 3
May 1798, for love and goodwill toward two grandchildren sons of Thomas Easter, at
his decease 100 acres originally granted to Arthur Watson bounded by land of Mathew
Bettis. Wit Arthur Rice Watson, Arthur (A) Watson. /s/ Christain (x) Curry. Proven
1 June 1798 by Arthur Watson; Richard Tutt. Rec 1 June 1798.

p.312-315   Edward Prince and wife Lucy to Samuel Scott. Deed, 16 December
1797, $2143, 150 acres bounded at time of survey by James Dyer, originally granted
24 April 1752 to Joseph Nelson, and by him and wife sold 17 August 1758 to Elias
Stallings decd, conveyed by Frederick Stallings son and heir of sd Elias decd to
Robert Middleton 21 October 1778 (not recorded) thence by sd Middleton and wife
sold to Edward Prince, party hereto, 6 July 1786. 100 acres being upper part of a
300 acre tract originally granted to sd James Dyer lying on Savannah River which
land was sold 1 October 1773 by Henry Dyer son and heir of sd James Dyer decd to
Thomas Harrey recorded in Charleston 17 December 1778, thence sold by sd Harrey &
wife to sd Edward Prince 18 Nov 1782, bounded by river, by land since granted to sd
Prince, land since granted to afsd Joseph Nelson. Likewise all that other tract of
land containing 65 acres granted to Edward Prince 5(6?) Sept 1785 adj the other two
tracts first mentioned, lastly all that other tract of land containing 279 acres
granted to sd Edward Prince 6 November 1786 adjoining the other last mentioned
tract. Wit Edward Prince Junr, Morris Calliham. /s/ Edward Prince, /s/ Lucy Prince.
Proven 19 December 1797 by Morris Calliham; H Middleton JP. Rec 2 June 1798.

p.315   Jacob Parrish Deposition before Judge Arthur Simkins swears he
knew the Father and Mother, Grand Father and Grand Mother which was called the
parents and Grandparents of the present Charles Holley of Horse Creek when they
lived on Black Creek of Contentne of North Carolina, who were always considered as
people not being mixed with any Negro blood whatever, but what mixture was supposed
was always considered from Indians; 26th July 1794; Arthur Simkins. /s/ Jacob (x)
Parish. Recorded 23 June 1798.

p.316-317   John Gray Senr to daughter Harriet Gray. Deed of Gift, 2 June
1798, £10 SC money, Negro slaves Jacob age 3, Nelly age 2, Leah age 2 and their
increase to Harriet if any she should have arriving to mature age, and if deceased
without heirs above slaves shall return to sd John Gray Senr. Wit S Butler, Wm
Burt. /s/ John Gray. Proven 2 June 1798 by Sampson Butler and Wm Burt; John
Blocker JP. Recorded 2d June 1798.

p.317-319   Charles Old to Cook & Garrett. Mortgage, 6 January 1798, $300,
Negro fellow Frank age between 25 and 30, condition that if Charles Old pays unto
Cook & Garrett $300 by 6 Jan 1800, claim to be nul & void; should sd Negro die
before expiration of two years from date, Charles Old makes good to Cook & Garrett
the sum of $300. Wit William Wash, Joseph Hackney. /s/ Chas Old. Proven 31 May
1798 by Joseph Hackney; Joseph Hightower JCE.   Rec 2 June 1798.

p.319-320   Benjamin Putman, Chatam County, Georgia, to West Cook. Bill/Sale, 11 March 1798, $400, Negro fellow Nedd about age 30. Wit James Garrett   /s/ Benj Putman. Proven 31 May 1798 by Jas Garrett; Joseph Hightower JCE. Rec 2 June 1798.

p.321-322   Joseph Covington to West Cook. Bill of Sale, 3 January 1798, $400, Negro fellow Tom between 25 and 30 years of age. Wit Jehu (x) Adkins. /s/ Jas Covington. Proven 31 May 1798 by Jehu Adkins; Joseph Hightower. Rec 2 June 1798.

p.322-323   Robert Cammack to Cook & Garrett. Bill of Sale, 28 April 1798, $80, bay horse 14 hands high 8 yrs old. Wit Jos Hackney. /s/ Robert Cammack. Proven 31 May 1798 by Joseph Hackney; Jos Hightower JEC. Rec 2 June 1798.

p.323-324   William Covington of Abbeville County to West Cook. Bill of Sale, 16 March 1798, Negro fellow Tall age about 30. Wit James Garrett. /s/ Wm Covington. Proven 30 May 1798 by James Garrett; Jos Hightower JEC. Rec 2 June 1798.

p.324-325   George Shaver to his father Michael Shaver. Bill of Sale, 17 June 1798, £60 sterling, 130 acres, horse, gunn, furniture. Wit John Henry Croft, Henry (x) Timmerman. /s/ George (x) Shaver. Proven 9 June 1798 by Henry Timmerman; John Blocker JP.   Rec 11 June 1798.

p.325-326   John Anderson, Allen Anderson, George Anderson, & Jesse Meachum in behalf of himself & his wife Rachel. Agreement other to other in just sum £800 sterling; 8 February 1798; John Anderson Senr father of parties above died intestate; agreed to make division of personal estate, have this day received each their distributive share in full of the same. Wit Mathew Stoker, Arthur Rhodes. /s/ Jno Anderson, /s/ Allan Anderson, /s/ George Anderson, /s/ Jesse Meachum. Proven 10 March 1798 by Mathew Stoker; Chas Old JP.   Rec 23 June 1798.

p.327-328   John Blalock Senr to Richard Tear of Newberry County. Deed, 26 January 1798, £80, 100 acres where sd Blaylock now lives on Simmon Creek of Big Creek of Little Saluda River binding on sd Simmon Creek, James Rutherford, Saml Beak, Docasters land, Smith Brook, being part of survey originally granted unto Ann Dean. Wit John Blalock Junr, William (x) Riley. /s/ John Blalock Senr. Proved 29 June 1798 by William Riley; Nathl Abney JP.   Rec 30 June 1798.

p.329-335   Stephen Collins to Samuel Abney.   L&R, 1 April 1774/2 April 1774, £1000 SC money, 150 acres in Colleton County in Ninety Six District bounded by land of Widow Brown, granted by Gov Chas Montague 21 February 1772.   Wit William Hill, Charles Simmons, Nat Spragins, William London.   /s/ Stephen Collins.   Proven 19 April 1774 by William Hill; Champness Terry JP.   Rec 30 June 1798.

p.335-337   Dannett Abney to John Riley. Deed, 14 February 1798, £5 paid by Sammuel Beak have sold unto John Riley 10 acres being part of tract adj land of John Riley and William Abney on Persimon Creek. Wit George (A) Abney, Samuel X) Abney. /s/ Dannet Abney. Proven 29 June 1798 by George Abney who saw Dannatt Abney sign & deliver within instrument to Saml Beaks for purposes within mentioned; Nathl Abney JP. /s/ George (A) Abney.   Recorded 30 June 1798.

p.337-339   John Lucas Senr, yeoman, to John Lucas Junr. Deed, 25 June 1798,

$45, 20 acres being part of land laid out for James Haris in 1772, corner of sd John Lucas Junr, on new marked branch to the spring, from Spring to John Ryans road, line of John Lucas Junr. Wit Abraham Lucas, Daniel Parker. /s/ John (I) Lucas. Judge Joseph Hightower certifies relinquishment of dower by Mary Lucas wife of within John Lucas Senr; 26 June 1798. /s/ Mary (M) Lucas. Proven 30 June 1798 by Abram Lucas; Rd Tutt JP.   Rec 30 June 1798.

p.340-342   John Ryan, yeoman, to Abram Lucas, gentleman. Deed, 3 May 1798, $250, 125 acres bounding on John Lucas Senr, Samuel Crafton, waggon road from #3 to the five notched road the road being part of the line, part of 384 acres surveyed by Bennet Crafton formerly the property of Moses Kirkland known by #4 conveyed unto John Ryan by John Barwick, Thomas Warring, John Ewing Calhoun commissioners of forfeited estates; conveyed from sd Ryan to Abram Lucas 3d May.   Wit Joseph Griffin, Joseph Rondine. /s/ John Ryan. Judge Joseph Hightower certifies that Martha Ryan wife of within John Ryan relinquished dower, 6 June 1798. /s/ Martha Ryan. Proven 30 June 1798 by Joseph Griffin; Rd Tutt JP.   Rec 30 June 1798.

p.343-345   John Ryan, yeoman, to Joseph Griffin, planter. Deed, 16 February 1798, $128, 100 acres on Horns Creek bounding land laid out to Moses Kirkland, Samuel Robertson, Harman Gallman, originally granted unto John White 7 May 1774, since conveyed from sd White to Solomon Lucas 1778, since conveyed by Lucas to William Maples 24 January 1785, and from Maples to John Ryan 2 July 1788. Wit Abram Lucas, John Lucas Junr. /s/ John Ryan. Judge Joseph Hightower certifies relinquishment of dower by Martha Ryan wife of within named John Ryan, 26 June 1798. /s/ Martha Ryan. Proven 30 June 1798 by Abram Lucas; Richard Tutt.   Rec 30 June 1798.

p.345-347   Dannett Abney to son Samuel Abney. Deed, 20 December 1797, $150, 150 acres upon Persimmon lick Creek of Little Saluda River originally granted unto sd Dannett Abney, adjoining lands of Joseph Griffin, George Abney, Walter Abney, Glade lick Creek. Wit Joel Abney, Esau Brooks. /s/ Dannett Abney. Proven 5 January 1798 by Joel Abney; Nathl Abney JP.   Rec 13 June 1798.

p.347-350   John Ryan to James Walker, gentleman. Deed, 25 June 1798, $310, 155.5 acres bounding on land of John Lucas Junr, James Cobb, Joseph Griffin, crossing Newmarket road, Spring branch, Rutledges land, originally granted unto James Barrington 1774, since conveyed from Jas Barrington to John Ryan 7 & 8 March 1775, now conveyed from sd Ryan to James Walker. Wit Abram Lucas, Joseph Griffin. /s/ John Ryan. Judge Joseph Hightower certifies relinquishment of dower by Martha Ryan wife of John Ryan, 26 June 1798. /s/ Martha Ryan. Proven 30 June 1798 by Abram Lucas; Richard Tutt J P.   Recorded 30 June 1798.

[The next three instruments were microfilmed out of order. See page 95.]
p.300   Jesse Forest deposeth he saw Richard Lewis and Mary Lewis sign within deed, deponant with Adkin Conley, Solomon Nobles subscribed their names as witnesses thereto; Wm Robertson JP. Recorded 12 May 1798.

p.300-301   John Bolger to John Coleman. Bond, 4 April 1798. John Bolger sold to John Coleman 261 acres, sd John Bolger binds himself in sum £50 to be paid to sd John Coleman; in case wife of sd Bolger at his decease should claim her dower in sd land. Wit Chesley Davis, Susannah Davis. /s/ John Bolger. Proven 14 April

1798 by Chesley Davis; Nathl Abney. Rec 19 May 1798.

p.301   John Bolger to John Coleman.   Deed, £150 sterling, two tracts containing 261 acres, late property of Mathew Will[torn] decd, being laid off to his widow as part of dower, who is now wife of John Bolger, one tract of 61 acres situate upon great

p.350-352   Joseph Tucker to Jeremiah Strother.   Deed, 2 January 1798, £45 sterling, part of a tract on Cyper, Bird & Cuffytown Creeks, survey dated 20 March 1775 granted 1787 to sd Joseph Tucker for 282 acres, lies by road from John [blot] Lyon[?]'s store and by Abner McMillions to Cyper Creek. Wit Shadk Stokes, Evans Stokes, George H Perrin. /s/ Joseph Tucker. Proven 2 July 1798 by George H Perrin; Jas Harrison JP.   Rec 2 July 1798.

p.353-356   Reuben Lisenbee to John Mainer.   Deed, 28 August 1797, £70 sterling, 600 acres being parts of two tracts formerly granted to Thomas Dozer, first granted 1 Sept 1788 by Thos Pinckney; second part granted 7 Jan 1793 by William Moultrie; adjoining land of Joshua Deen, Thomas Scott, John Green, Starling Center, Abram Railey, Alex Boling Stark, lying on Big Creek. Wit Theophilus Eddins, James Eddins. /s/ Reuben Lisenbee. Judge Arthur Simkins certifies relinquishment of dower by Susannah Lisenbee wife of within named Reuben Lisenbee, 11 September 1797. /s/ Susannah (x) Lisenbee.   Proven 30 June 1798 by James Eddins; John Blocker J P. Recorded 2 July 1798.

p.356-358   Andrew Oden, planter, to Thomas H Howel, planter.   Deed, 13 January 1798, £40 sterling; 100 acres on branches of Loyds Creek being part of 300 acres granted unto Hezekiah Oden decd who willed 100 acres to sd Andrew Oden, plat by Wm Coursey 11 Jan 1798; wit William Coursey, Moses Jackson. /s/ Andrew Oden. Judge Joseph Hightower certifies that Elizabeth Oden wife of Andrew Oden relinquished dower, 2 July 1798; /s/ Elizabeth (x) Oden.   Proven 2 July 1798 by Moses Jackson; Henry Key J P.   Recorded 2 July 1798.

p.359-361   William Tennent, sheriff, to John Spann.   Deed, 2 April 1798, by virtue of writ issued at suit of William Parker against Robert Stark, sheriff sold to John Spann, highest bidder, at Cambridge, for $101, 460 acres now occupied by William Bell, bounding on Moses Kirkland, Michael Watson, Daniel Hartley. Wit S May, Tolo Levingston. /s/ Wm Tennent Sheff EC. Proven 19 April 1798 by Tolover Levingston; Jno Trotter JP.   Rec 2 July 1798.

p.361-363   Hugh Middleton to John Holliday.   Deed, 27 January 1795, £50 sterling, 50 acres north side of branch of Cuffetown Creek leading from Priseys old field to Capt Bacons land where he now lives being the same branch belonging to a tract run out for Lewis Powell[Porvill?]; also 50 acres south side afsd branch being part of 500 acres granted to Abram Martin 1772. Wit Daniel Barksdale, Jos Barksdale. /s/ Hugh Middleton, /s/ Lucy Middleton. Proven 21 February 1795 by Capt Daniel Barksdale; Hugh Middleton JP.   Recorded 2 July 1798.

p.363-367   Roger Smith of Charleston to Daniel Baugh.   Deed, 1 October 1797, £102 sterling, 220¼ acres on Beaverdam Creek, part of 300 acres originally granted to Charles Pinckney Esqr in 1774 adjoining old bounty of McGiltons, by [blank]

Smiths land, on John Frasers land. Wit John Kelley, William (x) Arrenton. /s/ Roger Smith. Justice George Reed certifies that Mary Smith wife of Roger Smith relinquished dower, 10 April 1798. /s/ Mary Smith. Plat shows Beaverdam Creek, McGiltons land, John Oliphants land. Pursuant to request of Col James Mayson Esqr, laid out unto Nathaniel Ford 295¼ acres out of a tract of 3000 acres originally granted 9 November 1774 to Charles Pinckney Esqr & purchased by Roger Smith Esqr now the proprietor thereof lying in Edgefield County on Beaverdam Creek and branches thereof bound SW on old Bounty of McGilton, and on John Oliphant; Surveyed 10 August 1791, Jas Robert Mayson D S. Receipt for £102 from Daniel Baugh; wit John Kelley, William (x) Arrington. /s/ Roger Smith. Proven 27 April 1798 by William Arrington; John Blocker JP. Rec 3 July 1798.

p.367-369   Joseph Dawson and wife Elizabeth to Richard Lewis. Deed, 3 October 1797, £65 sterling, 225 acres on Mountain Branch of Turky Cr of Savannah River, being part of granted unto Peter Mangoult Esqr by Hon Wm Bull 14 May 1771 and from sd Mangoult conveyed unto Wm Watson and by sd Watson unto Joseph Dawson. Wit Das Williams, Hezekiah (x) Nobles, Solomon (x) Nobles. /s/ Joseph Dawson. Proven 2 July 1798 by Davis Williams; Richard Tutt. Rec 2 July 1798.

p.369-371   Zadok, George, Joshua and Dempsey Bussey with their wives Ann, Frankey, and Lucy Bussey to Frederick Caps. Deed, 20 March 1798, $100, 44 acres, part of 200 acres originally granted to James Russell and transferred to Geo Bussey Senr deceased, joining Stephens Creek and Gunnels Creek. Wit Mathew Caps, Moses (x) Rily. /s/ Zadok Bussey, /s/ George Bussey, /s/ Joshua Bussey, /s/ Dempsey Bussey. Proven 22 March 1798 by Matthew Caps; Hugh Middleton JP. Rec 2 July 1798.

p.371-373   Jesse Rountree to David Barnett. Bill of Sail, 20 February 1797, £60 SC money, Negro wench about 16 yrs old named Sue and her child Miller 6 months old. Wit Elizabeth (x) Boothe. /s/ Jesse Rountree. Proven 14 August 1797 by Elizabeth Booth; Chas Old JP. Recorded 2 July 1798.

p.373-376   John Elam to John Buckhalter. Deed, 22 July 1797, $500, 200 acres on Beaverdam Cr of Savannah River, granted by Hon Wm Bull unto Nathan Johnson 8 July 1774, conveyed from sd Nathan Johnson to sd John Elam 10 September 1789 and examined by Richard Tutt. Wit William Longmire, John McPatrick, John Lyon. /s/ John Elam. Judge Arthur Simkins certifies relinquishment of dower by Mary Elam wife of John Elam; 20 Sept 1797. /s/ Mary Elam. Proven 9 July 1797 by William Longmire; Henry Key J P. Recorded 2 July 1798.

p.376-378   Dionysius Oliver to Thomas Jones. Deed, 17 March 1797, $342.86, 140 acres part of 272 acres granted to John Mason in 1772 on Beaverdam Creek bounding on land held by Jesse Scrugs, Charles Jones, William Terry & others. Wit Eugene Brenan, Burges White. /s/ Dionysius Oliver. Proven 2 July 1798 by Eugene Brenan; Rd Tutt JP. Recorded 2d July 1798.

p.378-379   Robert Melton to Saml Hill. Bill of Sale, 27 March 1798, $400, Negro woman Sarah. Wit Jonas Holmes. C H Coursey. /s/ Robert Melton. Proven 27 March 1798 by Jonas Holmes; Henry Key J P. Rec 2d July 1798.

p.379-380   Robert Melton to Hughes Moss. Bill of Sale, 27 March 1798, $600,

Negro woman Betty, Negro boy London. Wit William Thurmond, C H Coursey. /s/ Robert Melton. Proven 27 March 1798 by Wm Thurmond; Henry Key JP. Rec 2d July 1798.

p.380-383   William Minter to William Terry, planter. Deed, 30 June 1798, $400, 200 acres Beaverdam Cr of Turky Cr of Stephens Cr of Savannah River, granted unto Ward Taylor by Gov Chas Montague at Charleston 12 Dec 1768, by sd Ward Taylor conveyed 1774 unto Joseph Minter decd, and by will of sd Jos Minter dated 13 June 1788 bequeathed unto his son John Minter, and by decease of sd John Minter same 200 acres descended unto his son & heir William Minter; sd 200 acres now bounding on land of John Mayson, Good, sd Terry. Wit John Terry, Abraham Hill. /s/ William Minter. Proven 2 July 1798 by Abram Hill; John Blocker J P.   Rec 2 July 1798.

p.383-386   Nathan Talley and wife Nancy to William Terry, planter. Deed, 2 May 1798, $200, 200 acres on Scrugges Branch of Beaverdam Cr of Turkey Creek of Savannah River, being part of 250 acres granted unto Joshua Lockwood and by Lockwood transfered unto sd Nathan Tally, adjoining land held for Goods orphans, Thurmonds land, and sd Terry, plat certifyed by William Coursey 27 December 1793. Wit Robert Boyd, Abraham Hill. /s/ Nathan Talley, /s/ Nancy (x) Talley. Judge Joseph Hightower certifies relinquishment of dower by Nancy Talley, 2 July 1798. /s/ Nancy (x) Talley. Proven 2 July 1798 by Abraham Hill; John Blocker JP. Recorded 2 July 1798.

p.386-389   Demcy Bussey to Zadock Bussey. Deed, 6 June 1798, $50, 50 acres on Stephens Cr bounded by land of John Martin, part of tract originally granted to Robert Russel. Wit George Bussey, Abraham Yeats. /s/ Demcey Bussey. Proven 2 July 1798 by George Bussey; Henry Key J P.   Recorded 2 July 1798.

p.389-391   John Huffman to Thomas Oden. Deed, 13 January 1798, $200, 50 acres on Stephens Cr bounded by lands of Mr Logan, George Bussey, Elisha Palmore, Mr Brazeel, being part of a tract originally granted to Thos Key. Wit Zadok Bussey, Geo Bussey. /s/ John Huffman. Proven 12 March 1798 by Geo Bussey; John Blocker J P. Recorded 2 July 1798.

p.391-393   James Lyon, planter, to Dempsey Bussey, planter. Bill of Sale, 4 February 1798, $300, Negro girl Suckey. Wit John Lyon, Mary (x) Coursey, William Coursey. /s/ James Lyon.   Proven 30 June 1798 by John Lyon; Henry Key J P. Recorded 2 July 1798.

p.393-395   Olleyman Dodgen, planter, to William Ward, planter. Deed, 23 May 1798, $100, 100 acres on Bayles Branch of Saluda River, bounded by S Mays, John Abney, William Wilson, part of 680 acres originally granted to Joel Pardue and conveyed to Olley Man Dodgen 1794. Wit W Anderson, David Liles. /s/ Olley Man Dodgen. Proven 3 July 1798 by Wm Anderson Esqr; Rd Tutt JP. Rec 3 July 1798.

p.395-397   William Vance, Saint Mathews Parish, SC, to Samuel Mays. Release, 24 May 1798, $200, 400 acres on both sides of Halfway Swamp Creek bounded on lands of William Hill, Samuel Mays, William Deen at time of survey, originally granted to William Flood 1771 and conveyed by sd Wm Flood to Moses Vance father of sd William Vance. Wit William Hill, Paul Abney. /s/ Wm Vance. Proven 15 June 1798 by William Hill; W Anderson JCE. Recorded 3 July 1798.

p.397-399   Abney Mays, planter, to William Hill, planter.   Release, 17 January 1798, $100, 204 acres being part of a tract of 314 acres originally granted unto sd Abney Mays on 2 March 1789, on Pen Branch of Halfway Swamp of Saluda River, bounded by land of William Hill. Wit Olley Man Dodgen, William Holloway, Austen Eskridge. /s/ Abner Mays. Proven 15 June 1798 by Austen Eskridge; W Anderson JCE. Rec 3 July 1798.

p.399-401   Jane Cunningham, executrix of David Cunningham decd of Abbeville County, to Abney Mays.   Deed, 13 January 1798, 206 acres in Edgefield on Halfway Swamp Creek of Saluda River, bounded on William Hill, Reuben Holloway, sd Abney Mays, originally granted to Martha Eakins 67 Feb 1786, conveyed by Martha Eakin to David Cunningham, sold by David Cunningham in his life to Abney Mays. Wit Dannett Hill, Nathaniel Samuels. /s/ Jane (J) Cunningham. Proven 13 January 1798 by Dannett Hill; Julius Nichols J P.   Recorded 3 July 1798.

p.401-403   Abney Mays, planter, to Samuel Mays, planter. Deed, 10 January 1798, $100, 110 acres on Halfway Swamp of Saluda River, adj Saml Mays, part of 314 acres originally granted to sd Abney Mays 2 March 1789. Wit Olley Man Dodgen, William Holloway, Austin Eskridge. /s/ Abney Mays. Proven 15 June 1798 by Austen Eskridge; W Anderson JCE.   Recorded 3 July 1798.

p.403-405   William Hill, planter, to Abney Mays. Release, 17 January 1798, $100, 950 acres, part of 2000 acres originally granted to sd Wm Hill 3 Dec 1792 on Halfway Swamp of Saluda River, adj Wm Hills land, Abney Mays, Alexander Boling Stark, John Troops. Wit Olley Man Dodgen, William Holloway, Austen Eskridge. /s/ Wm Hill. Proven 15 June 1798 by Austen Eskridge; W Anderson JCE.   Rec 3 July 1798.

p.405-407   Martha Pardue, widow & executrix of Joel Pardue decd, to John Sadler.   Deed, 27 November 1797, pursuant to a bond given by sd deceased to James Oharrow for £300 sterling payable by sd deceased, make lawful title to 150 acres on Big Creek of Little Saluda River, release unto John Sadler assignee of sd James Oharrow, sd 150 acres being part of a tract granted to sd Joel Pardue by Gov Wm Moultrie. Wit Michl McKie, Nicholas Maynard, Jesse Reagin. /s/ Martha (x) Pardue. Proven 2 March 1798 by Nicholas Maynard; Nathl Abney JP. Recorded 3 July 1798.

p.407-409   Samuel Mays to William Hill.   Deed, 31 May 1798, $105, 210 acres on Halfway Swamp of Saluda adj sd Samuel Mays, Abney Mays, Wm Hill; originally granted to Wm Flood 1791; conveyed by sd Wm Flood to Moses Vance and by Wm Vance son and heir to Moses Vance to sd Samuel Mays. Wit Stanmore Butler, William Mays. /s/ S Mays. Proven 15 June 1798 by Wm Mays; W Anderson JCE.   Rec 3 July 1798.

p.409-411   David Liles, planter, to Olley Man Dodgen, planter. Deed, 21 March 1798, $300, 90 acres on Halfway Swamp of Saluda River adj [blank] Holliway, Philemon Bozman, Abney Mays, being part of 370 acres originally granted to Abney Mays 5 June 1786 and conveyed to David Liles 1787. Wit Isaac (x) Sadler, Willm (x) Ward. /s/ David Liles. Judge William Anderson certifies relinquishment of dower by Deborah Liles wife of David Liles, 23 May 1798. /s/ Deborah Liles. Proven 23 May 1798 by William Ward; W Anderson JCE. Rec 3 July 1798.

p.412-414   Joshua Deen to William Hill.   Deed, 12 February 1798, $500 to be

102

paid on or before 25 December next, Negro wench named Frank about 50 years of age, and livestock(description here omitted), household furniture, farm equipment. Wit S Mays, A Eskridge. /s/ Joshua (--) Deen. Proven 3 July 1798 by Samuel Mays; Rd Tutt JP. Recorded 3 July 1798.

p.414-416   Roger Smith to John Frazier Junr. Deed, 31 October 1797, £26, 68 acres part of two tracts of 3000 acres originally granted to Charles Pinckney Esqr 1774 on Beaverdam Creek adj land of Daniel Baugh, [blank] Smith, Oliphant. Wit John Kelley, Wm (x) Arrenton. /s/ Roger Smith. Justice George Reid certifies that Mary Smith wife of Roger Smith voluntarily released her interest in sd land. /s/ Mary Smith. Proven 27 April 1798 by William Arrenton; John Blocker JP. Rec 3 July 1798.

p.416-418   Joshua Lockwood to Nathan Talley. Deed, Charleston District, 10 April 1798, Lockwood of Charleston District, $250, 250 acres on Scrugs Branch of Beaverdam of Turky Creek of Stephens Creek of Savannah River bounded on land formerly surveyed for David, George & Jesse Scruggs, Chapman Taylor and Joseph Minter, granted unto sd Joshua Lockwood by Lt Gov Wm Bull at Charleston 16 Sept 1774, certified 1774 by Jno Bremer D Sur Genl. Wit Joshua Lockwood Jr, Daniel Baugh. /s/ Joshua Lockwood, /s/ Mary Lockwood. Proven 3 July 1798 by Daniel Baugh; Rd Tutt. Recorded 3 July 1798.

p.418-420   Joshua Lockwood to William Terry. Deed, Charleston District, 10 April 1798, $50, 50 acres on Chaps Branch of Beaverdam of Turkey Creek of Stephens Creek waters of Savannah River bounded on Joseph Minter, John Mason, Chapman Taylor, granted unto sd Joshua Lockwood by Lt Gov Wm Bull 1774 at Charleston. Wit Joshua Lockwood Junr, Daniel Baugh. /s/ Joshua Lockwood, /s/ Mary Lockwood. Proven 3 July 1798 by Daniel Baugh; Rd Tutt. Rec 3 July 1798.

p.420-422   Executors of Aaron Loocock, late of Charleston, deceased, to William Butler Esqr. Deed, 12 May 1798, by will 14 April 1791 required executors William Clarkson and Nathaniel Russell to sell estate, $600, 1000 acres originally granted to Jas[Jos?] Parsons 18 May 1773 on Little Saluda River. Wit G Reid, James McKeller. /s/ Willm Clarkson, /s/ Nathl Russell. Proven 12 May 1798 by George Reid Esqr; Peter Francan JP. Rec 3 July 1798.

p.422-425   Olley Man Dodgen to David Liles. Deed, 16 March 1798, $300, 262 acres on Big Creek of Saluda river bounded on land of estate of William Wilson, Samuel Mays, William Ward, Gideon Christon, being part of two tracts originally granted to John Cheney 1786 and conveyed to Willm Deen and conveyed by Wm Deen to sd Olley Man Dodgen; the other granted to Joel Pardue 1793, conveyed by sd Pardue to sd Olley Man Dodgen. Wit William Hill, S Mays. /s/ Olley Man Dodgen. Judge William Anderson certifies relinquishment of dower by Sarah Dodgen wife of Olley Man Dodgen. /s/ Sarah (x) Dodgen. Proven 3 July 1798 by Samuel Mays; Rd Tutt. Recorded 3 July 1798.

p.425-427   Rhydon Grigsby, planter, to Jonathan Moore, planter. Release, 29 June 1798, £160 sterling, 520 acres on Richland creek of Little Saluda River bounded by Jacob Smith, Robert Allen, Michael Deloach. Wit Thos Butler, Jno Grigsby, S Mays. /s/ Rhydon Grigsby. Proven 14 September(sic) 1798 by Samuel Mays; Rd Tutt JP. Recorded 4 July 1798.

p.427-429   Sheriff Jeremiah Hatcher to Richard Tutt. Sheriff's Titles, 1 October 1796, at suit of Richd Johnson Jr against John Williams, directed Sheriff to sell to highest bidder two tracts; land struck off to Richard Tutt for £17.15 he being highest & last bidder. Land on Turkey Creek of Savannah River, 258 acres bounded by James Barrontine, John Roberts. Wit S Butler, S Mays. /s/ J Hatcher Shff EC. Proven 7 July 1798 by Sampson Butler; John Blocker JP. Rec 7 July 1798.

p.429-431   Sheriff Jeremiah Hatcher to Richard Tutt. Sheriff's Titles, 6 May 1797, suit of Samuel Willison agt Charles Banks & Abraham Richardson, sheriff sold to highest bidder, Richard Tutt, for $52, on Good Spring Branch of Big Horse Creek of Savannah River 1000 acres granted to John Holson by Gov Wm Moultrie 1793, adj Maj John Hampton, George Gregory, Charles Banks. Wit S Butler, S Mays. /s/ J Hatcher Shff EC. Proven 7 July 1798 by Sampson Butler; John Blocker JP. Rec 7 July 1798.

p.432   Sheriff Jeremiah Hatcher to M C Leavenworth. Receipt. Horse Creek 17 Feby 1798 Received of Melines C Leavenworth $245 in part of $395 which he has agreed to pay for Cesar a Negro boy sold under an execution of Ephraim Ferrel vs Thomas Lamar by me. March 15, 1798, recd of Melines C Leavenworth $150 in full for within mentioned Negro Cesar. /s/ J Hatcher, Shff EC. Proven 7 July 1798 by Sampson Butler; Rd Tutt JP. Rec 7 July 1798.

p.432-435   Philip Lamar to Melines C Leavenworth. Deed, 24 February 1798, $500, 5320 acres on Town Creek bounded by the Beaverdam and lines of Thomas Lamar, Widow Zinn, R Lamar, James Jones, Joseph Nix, Isaac Parker. Witness Leroy Pardue, David Wetmore. /s/ Philip Lamar. Proven 24 February 1798 by David Wetmore; Joseph Hightower JEC. Rec 7 July 1798.

p.435-438   Samuel Marsh to Thomas Walpoole. Deed, 10 April 1797. By indenture made 18 Feb 1797 Theodore Stark conveyed to Samuel Marsh 160 acres on branches of Horse Creek, John Grays line, old road from Augusta to Island ford, lines of Derosters, Thomas, Daniel Rogers, Mitchels. Now for £75 Samuel Marsh sells to Thomas Walpoole 125 acres of above premises known as Fair Hill tract. Wit Hinchey Mitchell, John Addison. /s/ Saml Marsh. Judge Arthur Simkins certifies relinquishment of dower by Elizabeth Marsh wife of Samuel Marsh, 13 March 1798. /s/ Elizabeth Marsh. Proven 4 August 1798 by Hinchey Mitchell; Rd Tutt JP. Recorded 4 August 1798.

p.438-440   Richard Johnson Junr, planter, to Moody Burt. Deed, 12 March 1798, $100, 378 acres on Turky Creek at Halls corner, lines of Garrett, sd Moody Burt, Augusta road; originally granted to sd Richard Johnson by Gov Chas Pinckney 1792. Wit Eugene Brenan, William Burt. /s/ Richard Johnson. Proven 4 August 1798 by William Burt; Rd Tutt J P. Rec 4 August 1798.

p.440-443   Jourdain Brooks and wife Mary to William Terry. Deed, 28 May 1798, $200, 200 acres on Beaverdam Creek of Turky Creek of Savannah river, being part of 946 acres granted to William Coursey by Gov Wm Moultrie at Charleston 7 Aug 1786, transfered by sd Coursey unto Jourdain Brooks, bounded by Nathan Talley, Goodes orphans; plat by William Coursey DS. Wit Daniel Baugh, Lucy Baugh. /s/ Jourdain Brooks, /s/ Mary (x) Brooks. Judge Arthur Simkins certifies relinquishment of dower by Mary wife of Jourdain Brooks, 5 July 1798. /s/ Mary (x) Brooks. Proven 3 July 1798 by Daniel Baugh; Rd Tutt JP. Rec 4 August 1798.

p.444-447   Mackerness Minter and wife Delilah and Peter Morgan and wife Anne-meriah to John Elam. Deed, 28 June 1798, $300, 350 acres on Beaverdam of Turky Creek of Savannah River, bounding lands granted to one Bell, to Obediah Killcrease & granted unto William Minter deceased by Gov Chas Montague at Charleston 1772 and by will of Wm Minter deceased bequeathed to his daughters Milley Minter deceased in her minority, sd land descended to Mackerness Minter and Annemeriah Minter wife to Peter Morgan the only heirs to sd deceased. Wit William Brooks, John (x) Witt. /s/ Mack Minter, /s/ Delila (x) Minter, /s/ Peter (x) Morgan, /s/ Annemeriah Morgan. Judge Arthur Simkins certifies relinquishment of dower by Delila Minter wife of Mackerness Minter, 5 July 1798. /s/ Delila (x) Minter. Judge Arthur Simkins certi-fies relinquishment of dower by Annemeriah Morgan wife of Peter Morgan, 5 July 1798. /s/ Annemeriah Morgan. Proven 13 July 1798 by William Brooks; Henry Key JP. Recorded 4 August 1798.

p.448-450   Joel Lipscomb to Abraham Crews of Newberry County SC. Deed, 3 Au-gust 1797, $300, land originally granted to Martin Ott, 100 acres on Ninety Six Creek bounded by land of Thomas Od[cut off], conveyed unto Joel Lipscomb by Isaac Crowther. Wit Walter Anderson, Thomas Edwards. /s/ Joel Lipscomb. Judge William Anderson certifies relinquishment of dower by Betsey Lipscomb wife of Joel Lipscomb, 3 August 1797. /s/ Betsey Lipscomb. Proven by Thomas Edwards, 3 August 1797; Wm Anderson. Rec 6 August 1798.

p.450-451   Frances Jones to granddaughter Polley Burton. Deed of Gift, 6 February 1798, for good will and affection, Negro woman Peg together with her increase, given before marriage to Polley Smith who since married William Burton. Wit Frances Jones Junr, Maston Smith. /s/ Frances Jones. Proven 23 June 1798 by Maston Smith; Wm Robertson JP. Rec 6 August 1798.

p.451-453   Hiram McDaniel of Columbia County, Georgia, planter, to Pleasant Thurmond, planter. Deed, 10 August 1798, £70, 100 acres on Cuffeetown Creek adj lands of William Carson, Richard Tutt Senr, William Bobbett, William Evans. Wit William Jones, Hermon Cosper, Thomas Carson. /s/ Hiram (x) McDaniel. Proven 11 August 1798 by William Jones; Jas Harrison JP.   Rec 13 August 1798.

p.453-454   Isaac Hayne of Charleston District near Jackson Borough to Col Samuel Mays. Power Atty, 8 May 1798, to sell three tracts of land, two lying on Saluda river in Abbeville County containing 500 acres each, the other on Reedy River Laurence County containing 250 acres. Wit Luke Smith. /s/ Isc Hayne. Proven Newberry County, 31 July 1798 by Luke Smith; Daniel Parkins J P. Rec 16 Aug 1798.

p.455-456   William Edwd Hayne to Samuel Mays. Power Atty, 21 April 1798; by will of Isaac Hayne of St Bartholomews Parish, Charleston District, decd, land devised to Wm Ed Hayne; appoints Col Samuel Mays to sell sd land. Wit Wm Nibbs, Ab Dozier. /s/ Wm Ed Hayne. Proven Abbeville County, 23 July 1798, by Abraham Dozier; Jno Trotter J P.   Rec 16 August 1798.

p.456-458   Charles Jones Colcock to Samuel Mays. Bill of Sale, 20 July 1798, £160 sterling, two Negro men named Glasgow and Frank. Wit Patk McDowall. /s/ Charles J Colcock.   Proven, Abbeville County, 29 August 1798, by Patrick McDowall; Jno Trotter J P.   Rec 12 Sept 1798.

p.458-459   Benjamin Manning, lately of Edgecombe County, North Carolinina, to
Thomas Hancock.   Bill of Sale, 3 March 1798, $700, two Negro women, Nell about 20
years old, and Suck about 24 years old with her small child named Jacob with future
issue of the females. Wit G Leslie. /s/ Benjamin Manning. Proven 13 June 1798 by
George Leslie; Chas Olds JP.   Rec 12 Sept 1798.

p.459-462   Matthew Devore to Edmund Watson. Deed, 12 June 1798, £28 sterling,
90 acres on Little Dry Creek bounded by land of Willis Whatley, John Pursley, Frances Coleman, Jno T Lowe, Reuben Cooper, Buckhalters Creek. Wit George Delaughter,
Charles Bussey, William Watson. /s/ Matthew (M) Devour. Proven 12 September 1798
by William Watson; Richard Tutt JP.   Rec 12 Sept 1798.

p.462-463   John Morris to Nathan Parker. Deed, 22 March 1798, $40 all land
in original grant 108 acres granted unto sd John Morris 1 Sept 1796 on Jones branch
of Crooked run of Turky Creek of Savannah river adj land of Ward Taylor, James
Coursey, William Pritchet. Wit Daniel Bird, Jas Blocker. /s/ John Morris. Proven 1
Sept 1798 by James Blocker; John Blocker J P.   Rec 1 Sept 1798.

p.464-465   Benjamin Tutt to Clement Cargill. Bill of Sale, 20 June 1798,
$1200 SC money, Negroes Charles, Patt, Charity, Matt, Lott, Isaac and their
increase. Wit Barnard Caffery, John Lewis, Saml (x) Jeter. /s/ Benj Tutt. Proven
14 Sept 1798 by Samuel Jeter; Richard Tutt JP.   Rec 14 Sept 1798.

p.465-468   Minor Killcrease, son and heir of John Killcrease decd, planter,
to Christopher Glanton, planter. Deed, 29 August 1798, $100, 105 acres in fork
between Stephens & Turkey Creeks, adj line of Robert Mitchel, -- Thomas, Shadrack
Homes, Robt Killcrease. Wit Morris Calliham, John Killcrease. /s/ Minor (x) Killcrease. Proven 31 August 1798 by Morris Calliham; Henry Key J P. Rec 14 Sept 1798.

p.468-469   James Tutt of Abbeville County to Clement Cargill. Bill of Sale,
16 March 1797, $692.52, three Negro men Frank, Cuff, Joe. Wit Samuel Lewis, Joshua
(x) Dean, Dionysius Oliver. /s/ Jas Tutt. Proven 17 March 1797 by Joshua (x)
Dean; S Mays J P.   Rec 14 Sept 1798.

p.469-471   Rebekah Hogan to Bathsheba Holt and her heirs Rebekah and William
Wilson, Elizabeth and Bailey Holt. Bill of Sale, 8 March 1798, £150 sterling, one
Negro woman Mary and her increase, furniture and household goods. Wit Benjamin
Ricks, James Sullivan, Robert Wilson. /s/ Rebekah (x) Hogan. Proven 15 Sept 1798
by Benjamin Ricks; Richard Tutt J P.   Rec 15 Sept 1798.

p.471-473   Elizabeth Holmes, widow, to grandson Mathew Brooks, infant. Deed
of Gift, 23 July 1798, for good will & affection, all land I purchased from Robert
Brooks 37 acres on Beaverdam of Turkey Creek of Savannah river, being part of 1000
acres granted unto Edward Vann, by sd Vann transferred unto Wm Coursey; above piece
of land from Wm Coursey unto Robert Brooks, bounded on lands granted unto Obediah
Killcrease, Fedk Holmes. Wit William Coursey, John Lyon. /s/ Elizabeth (+) Holmes.
Proven 22 Septr 1798 by William Coursey; Rd Tutt JP.   Rec 22d Sept 1798.

p.474-476   Joseph Newton to James Eddins. Deed, 11 April 1798, £100 sterling,
296 acres fork of Little Stephens Creek, being part of 3 tracts; first part granted

to Garrett Buckelew; second part granted to Samuel Lewis; third part granted to Silvanus Stephens; all parts joined and surveyed by William Coursey D S, adj land of Benjamin Eddins, George Buckelew, Mary Beal, John Mainer, John McCreeless, Wm Deen, William Crabtree. Wit Benjamin (x) Eddins, Joseph Eddins. /s/ Joseph Newton. Proven 10 Sept 1798 by Benjamin Eddins; Wm Daniel JP.   Rec 24 Sep 1798.

p.476-477   Lucy Prince to Saml Scott. Dower. Judge Joseph Hightower certifies that Lucy Prince the wife of within named Edward Prince privately examined did declare she freely released unto Samuel Scott all her right of dower. 18 Aug 1798. /s/ Lucy Prince.   Rec 25 Sept 1798.

p.477-479   Martha Forman to her children James & Mary. Deed Gift, 2 June 1798, two Negro boys, Jesse to James, Jerry to Mary, to inherit same when they come of lawful age; if I Martha Forman shall decease I give unto my two children a Negro wench named Mellow and a Negro girl named Liz, and their increase to be equally divided between them, with all the rest of my goods; and in case of lawful issue then the said James and Mary shall share equal dividend in the property last mentioned. Wit William Hill, Fedk Hill, Ann Hill. /s/ Martha (x) Forman. Proven 25 Sept 1798 by William Hill; Rd Tutt JP.   Rec 25 Sept 1798.

p.479-480   Britain Brassell to His Children. Deed of Gift, 14 September 1798, love & affection: to son William land whereon I now reside with my crop & tools; my son Isom blacksmith tools & colt name of Deller; daughters Polley & Barshaba two creatures known by name of Pullen and Sall and household furniture, to my daughters Elizabeth & Sarah the cattle, hoggs and geese with their increase. Wit John Wells, John Rogers. /s/ Britain Brassell. Proven 27 Sept 1798 by John Rogers; Richard Tutt J P.   Rec 27 Sept 1798.

p.480-481   Mary Johnson to Thomas Glasscock. Dower, 22 May 1798; Judge Joseph Hightower certifies relinquishment of dower by Mary Johnson wife of Richard Johnson Junr. /s/ Mary (x) Johnson.   Rec 29 Sept 1798.

p.481-483   Thomas Glasscock of Richmond County, Georgia, to Jesse Rountree. Deed, 19 June 1798, $100, 315 acres on Savannah river, being part of land formerly owned by Chickasaw Indians, confiscated by South Carolina & sold by Commissioners for that purpose appointed, #7 & 8 in plat of sd lands. Wit Benj Hightower, Job Glover. /s/ Thomas Glasscock. Judge Joseph Hightower certifies the relinquishment of dower by Mary Glasscock wife of Thomas Glasscock, 19 June 1798. /s/ Mary Glasscock. Proven 19 June 1798 by Job Glover; Joseph Hightower JCE. Rec 29 Sept 1798.

p.483-485   John Glover to Jesse Rountree. Bill of Sale, 22 September 1798, $5000, 16 Negro slaves: Ben, Jeffry, Isaac, Phillis, Dol, Chloe, Isabel, Jacob, Harry, Martin, Ned, Creasey, Lucy, Dinah, Patt, Aggy and future increase of the females. Wit Mary Meyers, Elizabeth Mealer. /s/ John Glover. Proven 22 Sept 1798 by Elizabeth Mealer; Joseph Hightower JCE. Rec 29 Sept 1798.

p.485-486   James Campbell of Orangeburg District to Abraham Herndon. Deed, 13 October 1796, £30 sterling, 1000 acres on head branches of Little Horse Creek & Chaves Creek lying both sides of waggon road from Augusta to Columbia, joining land called the old Walls. Wit John G Cooke, James May. /s/ James Campbell. Proven 13

August 1798 by John G Cook; Chas Old JP.   Rec 30 Sept 1798.

p.486-490   Samuel Mays, Sheriff, to Philip Lamar. Deed, 12 November 1796;
Andrew Pickens & Company obtained judgment against Thomas Lamar for £230.11.5; Shff
to sell Thomas Lamar's 500 acres lying between Savannah River & William Campbell,
adjoining sd Lamar, Ben Beaven. Sheriff sold for £40 sterling to Philip Lamar. Wit
Joseph Beckley, Lilleston Pardue. /s/ S Mays SEC. Proven 7 January 1797 by
Lilleston Pardue; Richard Tutt JP. Rec 7 January 1797.

p.490-492   Jeremiah Hatcher, Sheriff, to Samuel Williams. Sheriff Titles, 1
October 1796; at suit of Eugene Brenan & Company against John Williams, Sheriff to
sell to highest bidder the plantation of John Williams; sold for £21.6, highest and
last bid, 334 acres on Turky & Rocky Creeks, adj Buffington's corner. Wit Eugene
Brenan, Wm Burt. /s/ J Hatcher Shff. Proven 6 October 1798 by Eugene Brenan; John
Blocker JP. Rec 6 October 1798.

p.493-495   Edmund Whatley & wife Phillis to Timothy Cooper. Deed, 8 October
1798, 20 shillings sterling, 90 acres bounded by lands of Joshua Marcus, Daniel
Marcus, Ann Summerall, John Martin, and by sd Timothy Cooper. Wit Rd Tutt, Jeremiah
Roberts. /s/ Edmund Whatley, /s/ Phillis Whatley. Judge Arthur Simkins certifies
relinquishment of dower by Phillis Whatley wife of Edmund, 8 Oct 1798; /s/ Phillis
(+) Whatley. Proven 8 Oct 1798 by Jeremiah Roberts; Rd Tutt JP. Rec 8 Oct 1798.

p.495-498   Dempsey Beckham to Joshua Marcus. Deed, 5 May 1798, £50 sterling,
75 acres bounding on John Martin, Demsy Adams, Sherod Whatley, Thomas Palmer, Horns
Creek, originally granted to Thomas Beckham 15 May 1771. Wit Thomas Palmer, Daniel
Flandigame. /s/ Dempsey Beckham. Judge Arthur Simkins certifies release of dower
by Elizabeth Beckham wife of Dempsey Beckham, 8 Oct 1798. /s/ Elizabeth (x) Beckham. Proven 8 Oct 1798 by Thomas Palmer; Rd Tutt JP. Rec 8 Oct 1798.

p.498-500   Daniel Marcus to Henry Waldrum. Deed, 6 October 1798, $300, 164
acres adjoining Timothy Cooper, John Martin, Morgain, Edmund Martins estate. Wit
Thomas Westby, Jeremiah Roberts. /s/ Daniel Marcus. Judge Arthur Simkins certifies
relinquishment of dower by Mary Marcus wife of Daniel Marcus, 8 Oct 1798. /s/ Mary
(x) Marcus. Proven 8 Oct 1798 by Jeremiah Roberts; Rd Tutt JP. Rec 8 Oct 1798.

p.500-502   William Hill to William Mays. Deed, 31 May 1798, £50 sterling,
460 acres on Halfway Swamp and Big Creek of Saluda river, bounding on William Hills
land, Joel Pardues land, William Taylors land, being part of grant of 2000 granted
to sd William Hill 3 Dec 1792. Wit S Mays, Stanmore Butler. /s/ William Hill.
Proven 15 June 1798 by S Mays; W Anderson JCE.   Rec 8 October 1798.

p.502-504   John Watkins to youngest daughter Sarah Watkins. Deed of Gift, 1
September 1798, love & affection, feather bed & furniture, two cows, tableware. Wit
George (x) Watkins, Solomon (x) Collum. /s/ John Watkins. Proven 13 Sept 1798 by
George Watkins; Elkanah Sawyer JP. Rec 8 Oct 1798.

p.504-506   John Salter & Darkes Salter to their brothers James Ward & John
Ward. Bill of Sale, 10 June 1798, property executed by a judgment obtained by Alexander Wilson of our father Abdan Ward, sold at public sail and purchased by his

daughter now wife to John Salter; to James a cow & increase, bed & furniture, &c; to brother John cow & increase, bed, sow & increase, bay horse. Wit James Allen, Robert Allen. Proven 5 Oct 1798 by Robt Allen; Russell Wilson JP. Rec 8 Oct 1798.

p.506-508   John Garrett & Mary Rivers exr & exx of will of Robert Garrett decd to George Sutherlin. Deed, 6 April 1796, 73¾ acres being part of 167¼ acres sold to Alexander Oden on Stephens Creek adj Catlett Garrett, Jones Rivers, Alexander Oden, and sd George Sutherlin. Wit Peter Farar, John C Garrett. /s/ John Garrett Exr, /s/ Mary (M) Rivers Exx. Proven 7 April 1796 by John C Garrett; Samuel Mays JP. Recorded 8 Oct 1798.

p.508-511   William Conner of Abbeville County to William Stalworth. Deed, 2 September 1797, £110 sterling, 433 acres on Cuffeetown and Ninety Six creeks, bounding on lands of Wm Hagood, John Holladay, Wm Holladay, Pendergrass and Johnson, Ann Conner, sd land originally granted to William Davis 29 April 1768. Wit Nathan Lipscomb, William Lipscomb Junr, William Huggins. /s/ William Conner, /s/ Mary Conner. Judge William Anderson certifies relinquishment of dower by Mary Conner wife of Wm Conner, 13 Sept 1797. /s/ Mary Conner. Proven 2 October 1797 by Nathan Lipscomb; C J Colcock JP. Rec 8 Oct 1798.

p.511-512   Rachel Rambo to her Children. Deed of Gift, 22 June 1798, love & good will towards children James Rambo, Laurence Rambo, Polley Rambo, Sarah and Rachel Rambo, all my estate, also the part coming to me at my Mothers death agreeable to my Fathers James Adams will to be equally divided among them. Wit Littleberry Adams, Sarah (x) Adams. /s/ Rachel (x) Rambo. Proven 8 October 1798 by Little Berry Adams; Rd Tutt JP. Rec 8 Oct 1798.

p.512-513   Mary McDonald to Jacob Hibbler. Renunciation of Dower, Judge Arthur Simkins certifies that Mary McDonald wife of William McDonald freely renounced her right of dower & freely signed the release, 8 October 1798. /s/ Mary (x) McDonald. Rec 8 Oct 1798.

p.513-519   James Williams to William Odum. L&R, 23 September 1791/24 September 1791, £100 SC money, 400 acres on Ephraims branch of Stephens Creek bounded by land of sd James Williams, Alexander Bowlling Stark, Azariah Lewis, John Harkins, originally granted unto James Williams 1790 by Gov Chas Pinckney. Wit James Harrison, John Smith, Mary (x) Crabtree. /s/ James (W) Williams, /s/ Ruth Williams. Proven 28 Nov 1797 by Mary Crabtree; Henry King JP. Rec 8 Oct 1798.

p.518-523   William Deen to William Odom. L&R, 20 February 1790/21 Feb 1790, £20 sterling, 146 acres Sleepy Creek of Savannah River, being part of 310 acres laid out for Wm Dean & granted 1787 by Gov Thos Pinckney. Wit Henry Noble, John (x) Adams, Charles Adams. /s/ William Dean, /s/ Nancy Dean. Proven 27 December 1790 by Charles Adams; James Spann JP. Rec 8 October 1798.

p.523-526   Thomas Davis and wife Rachel to William Tillory. Deed, 22 April 1797, £20 sterling, 58 acres Coodys Cr, part of 158 acres granted to Robert Morely Senr 1786 by Gov Wm Moultrie and sold to Willoby Tillory, adj land of Widow Coody, Henry Parkman. Wit Butler Williams, Samuel (x) Williams, Eppey Tillory. /s/ Thos Davis, /s/ Rachel (x) Davis. Proven 8 Oct 1798 by Saml Williams; Rd Tutt J P. Rec

8 October 1798.

p.526-528   William Day to Ephraim Franklin. Deed, 23 April 1798, $10, 100
acres granted 5 August 1793 on Shaws creek, bounding on Wolf Branch. Wit Benjamin
Jernagan, Daniel Day, Jacob Luker. /s/ William (x) Day. Proven [blank] May 1798 by
Benjamin Jernagan Senr; Van Swearingen JP. Rec 9 Oct 1798.

p.528-530   John Day to Ephraim Franklin. Deed, 23 April 1798, $10, 100 acres
being part of 221 acres granted 7 May 1787 on Shaws Creek. Wit Dannel (D) Day,
James Day, Silas (x) Green. /s/ John (D) Day. Proven 4 Sept 1798 by Danial Day;
Van Swearingen JP. Rec 9 Oct 1798.

p.530-533   William Howle Senr of Wilks County, Georgia, to Burrell Johnston.
Deed, 20 June 1798, $149, 90 acres granted 6 Dec 1790 by Gov Chas Pinckney adj land
of John Wright part of the same survey, Mary Rivers, Brazels heirs. Wit William
Chastain, Richard (x) Bailey, Thos Howle. /s/ William (x) Howle. Proven 9 Oct 1798
by Thomas K Howle; Rd Tutt. Rec 9 Oct 1798.

p.533   John Bailey to David Thompson. Lye Bill, 5 September 1798. John
Bailey acknowledged himself to be a lier in a false and melicious report that he
raised against David Thompson Esqr respecting saying that he saw him the said David
being in an uncomely way in broom straw with a certain Negro woman and that he the
said John Bailey raised that report with some other reports of the same nature out
of pure spite and mallace and what certain citizens has said in the aforesaid case
is just and true and also ackd that he came here before me without any conpulsion
or fear of David Thompson voiding any injury more than the law directs. Hugh
Middleton JP. /s/ John (B) Bailey. Rec 9 Oct 1798.

p.534-535   William Anderson to Isaiah Blackwell. Deed, 6 March 1797, £75,
500 acres granted to Paul Trapier Esqr [blank] Nov 1772 on Stephens Creek bounded
by Paul Trapiers land when surveyed. Wit William Prichard, John Anderson. /s/ W
Anderson. Proven, 24 May 11797 by William Prichard; Henry Key JP. Rec 9 Oct 1798.

p.536-538   Elizabeth King to Geo Bussey. Bill of Sale, 9 October 1798, $20,
Negro wench named Bel and a cow. Wit Burrel (x) Johnson, Thos H Howle. /s/ Elizabeth King. Proven 9 Oct 1798 by Burrel Johnson; Rd Tutt JP. Rec 9 Oct 1798.

p.538-539   Elizabeth King to William King. Deed, 8 October 1798, $50, 50
acres being part of land now held by John King and bounded by land of Mary Rivers.
Wit Burrell (x) Johnson, Thos H Howle, George Bussey. /s/ Elizabeth (x) King. Af-
firmed 9 Oct 1798 by Burrell Johnson; Richard Tutt, JP. Rec 9 Oct 1798.

p.539   Willis Johnson to Celah Davis. Deed, 10 acres on west side of
Stephens Creek, being part of a tract originally granted to Henry Key Esq [pages
missing]

No number. [name cut off] to James King. Elizabeth King for $[cut off] one Negro
girl Jean and ho[rse?]. Wit Burrell (x) Johnson, Thos H Howle. /s/ Elizabeth (x)
King. Proven by Thos H Howle [cut off]
End of Book 15

Other books by Carol Wells:

Abstracts of Giles County, Tennessee: County Court Minutes, 1813-1816 and Circuit Court Minutes, 1810-1816

CD: Tennessee, Volume 1

Davidson County, Tennessee County Court Minutes, Volume 1, 1783-1792

Davidson County, Tennessee County Court Minutes, Volume 2, 1792-1799

Davidson County, Tennessee County Court Minutes, Volume 3, 1799-1803

Dickson County, Tennessee County and Circuit Court Minutes, 1816-1828 and Witness Docket

Edgefield County, South Carolina Probate Records, Boxes One through Three Packages 1-106

Edgefield County, South Carolina Probate Records, Boxes Four through Six Packages 107-218

Edgefield County, South Carolina: Deed Books 13, 14 and 15

Edgefield County, South Carolina: Deed Books 16, 17 and 18

Edgefield County, South Carolina: Deed Books 19, 20, 21 and 22

Edgefield County, South Carolina: Deed Books 23, 24, 25 and 26

Edgefield County, South Carolina: Deed Books 27, 28 and 29

Edgefield County, South Carolina: Deed Books 30 and 31

Edgefield County, South Carolina: Deed Books 32 and 33

Edgefield County, South Carolina: Deed Books 34 and 35

Edgefield County, South Carolina: Deed Books 36, 37 and 38

Edgefield County, South Carolina: Deed Books 39 and 40

Edgefield County, South Carolina: Deed Book 41

Genealogical Abstracts of Edgefield, South Carolina Equity Court Records

Natchez Postscripts, 1781-1798

Rhea County, Tennessee Tax Lists, 1832-1834, and County Court Minutes Volume D: 1829-1834

Robertson County, Tennessee Court Minutes, 1796-1807

Sumner County, Tennessee Court Minutes, 1787-1805 and 1808-1810

Williamson County, Tennessee County Court Minutes, July 1812-October 1815

Williamson County, Tennessee County Court Minutes, May 1806-April 1812

Made in the USA
Coppell, TX
19 October 2021